ECHAD 2:

SOUTH AFRICAN JEWISH VOICES

general editors ——

ROBERT & **KALECHOFSKY**
ROBERTA

Echad 2: South African Jewish Voices
Copyright © 1982 by Micah Publications
255 Humphrey Street, Marblehead, Massachusetts 01945,
U.S.A.

Library of Congress Catalogue Card Number: 81-83903
ISBN: 0-916288-10-2

Printed by McNaughton & Gunn, Ann Arbor, Michigan 48106

Cover Design: Miriam Milamed
Production: Robert and Roberta Kalechofsky
Technical Assistance: Robert Kalechofsky

This volume was made possible through the support of
The Massachusetts Council on The Arts and Humanities

MICAH PUBLICATIONS
255 Humphrey Street
Marblehead, Massachusetts
01945

Acknowledgements:
For permission to publish or reproduce the material in this
anthology, acknowledgement is made to the following:
Lionel Abrahams, "The Moment," "Invisible Worm,"
"Knowledge," published in The Celibacy of Felix Greenspan,
Bateleur Press, Johannesburg, 1977.
Jillian Becker, excerpts from The Keep, Chatto and Windus,
London, 1967; "The Stench," Quarry: New South African Writing,
ed. by L. Abrahams and Walter Saunders, pub. by Ad. Donker,
South Africa; "Another Final Battle on The Stage of History,"
from Terrorism: An International Journal, vol 5, no. 1-2,
Russak and Co., Inc., 1981.

Denis Diamond, "A Name in Africa," "Flower Garden,"
"Letter To The Ruler of the Zulus."
Shirley Eskapa, "Between The Sheets," Purple Renoster;
"White and Injured," The Cornhill, 1972.
Nadine Gordimer, "A Hunting Accident," A Soldier's Embrace,
Viking Press, 1980.
Dan Jacobson, "Beggar My Neighbor," South African Writing
Today, ed. by N. Gordimer and L. Abrahams, Penguin Books,
1967.
Joan Jacoby, "Diary of A Polesitter," The Bloody Horse;
poems, "Homecoming," Poetry South;"Here is Nowhere."
Bernard Levinson, poems, "Dear Anne," "Charles," "Kineret,"
"Massada," "For Fran," "In Your Darkness," From Break-
fast to Madness, Ravan Press, Johannesburg, 1974. "Tokai,"
". . .and He Chose A Mule," "The Night Motke Behr Danced."
Rose Moss, "The Shopping Trip," The Antioch Review, Spring/
Summer, 1972; "Light Dark."
Riva Rubin, "Sisyphus," "Sequins," "Suicide Achieved,"
The Tel Aviv English Poets, Broad Sheet, no. 1, Dec., 1978-
Jan., 1979; "Process," "Ladder."
Helen Segal, "It's all/very well," "Anniversary," "To Mark
on An Anniversary," "Continental Shift," "To John Berryman,"
the footprint of a fish .
Barney Simon, "The Fourth Day of Christmas," "Monologue
for Danny," "Our War," "The Birds," Joburg, Sis!,. Bateleur
Press, Johannesburg, 1974.
Rose Zwi, excerpts from Another Year in Africa, Bateleur
Press, Johannesburg,1980.
Photograph from jacket design of Another Year in Africa,
permission to use granted by Rose Zwi.

TABLE OF CONTENTS

Section 1V: <u>Armageddon,</u> and <u>Other</u> <u>Problems</u>

Introduction

Many years back, reading a book on the Peasant's Revolt
in England in 1389, I came across a sentence in a letter of
that era, written by a lady of the upper classes, which has
remained with me. In the letter, she tells a relative not to
visit her at a certain time because she expects to be occupied with the business of midwifery. She is going to attend
the birth of a child to one of her serfs to see "yf they brynge
forthe as we doe."

No other sentence I have read has conveyed to me the
totality of estrangement that can happen to human beings--
the loss of the elemental, the biological definition of human.

We cannot take refuge in the idea that this lady, being a
citizen of the fourteenth century, was heir to superstitions
and ignorance alien to us. First, there is the fact that she
could read and write, and was therefore educated to some
degree. Secondly, in her interest in the childbearing problem she shows herself to be a woman of lively curiosity,
neither delicate nor intimidated, an "independent spirit."
Her problem is not herself. Her problem is the world she
has inherited--one in which the idea of the biological con-
nectedness of human beings has atrophied, and she can no
more see around this world or over it than we can see
around a corner. She has lost access to an elementary
piece of knowledge through sheer estrangement, not through
ignorance, for her words testify to her knowledge of the
childbearing process for some: "yf they brynge forthe as
we do." But she cannot speculate in advance of her eye-
witness experience of how serfs give birth to children:
she simply doesn't know.

Still she is willing to go and find out, and great credit
is due her for this.

Long before this lady found this dark spot of ignorance
in her understanding of the world, in fact at the Council of
Elvira in the fourth century, Christian leaders passed a

series of laws circumscribing the public and economic life of
Jews. It was the beginning of what we may call the apartheid
mentality. The most pernicious of these laws were not the
ones which sought to circumscribe Jewish life, but the laws
which forbade "Christian cleric and layman to accept Jewish
hospitality": the laws which aimed at the estrangement between
Jew and Christian.

Such laws were passed repeatedly within the following centuries, with various force, application and advocacy, and we
all know with what eventual results. Long before the Holocaust,
which took a quantum leap in the direction of estrangement between Jew and Christian, many Christians already had come to
regard Jews as being biologically different from themselves.

At the same time that these unfortunate laws were being established, the Catholic church took a position regarding another
law, which was very important. This was with respect to the
inheritance rights of serfs. For in the Middle Ages, serfs
were legally defined as "sequela," literally meaning "litter."
The analogy here to animal life will not be lost and explains
the difficulty the lady of the fourteenth century had in imagin-
ing how her serfs "brought forthe." The church in this century
determined that the children of serfs had the right to inherit.
Mind you, at this time, all that was involved mostly were
bowls and blankets and in rare cases, an ox or a goat. But
being granted the right to inherit eliminated the odious definition of their children as "litter"; for human beings inherit, and
what they inherited in this instance was their human nature.

Legend follows laws. It must have been upon pondering
this contradiction in terms between the definition of the children of serfs as "litter" and their right to inherit--a human
right--that made this lady of the fourteenth century determine
to go and see for herself "yf they brynge forthe as we doe."
I wish I had been with her when the child was born.

Legend follows laws. It is bred in the conditions in which
we compel people to live, often by law. It does not arise out
of some phantasmagoria from outer space. Human beings
make laws and breed legends, and laws whose purpose it is to
estrange human beings from one another cause a breach in
human understanding which must weaken the foundation of political and moral life.

ii

South African Jewish Voices is the second in a series of
anthologies of contemporary Jewish writing from Africa, Asia
and Latin America, from Jewish communities out of the main-
stream of European tradition, because it is the voices which
are less well known to us and which, living in nations where the
sociological, political and ideological conflicts of this century
are most intense, are voices to be listened to.

Jews came to South Africa out of the same migratory experience of the last hundred years that brought them, as well as
other Europeans, to the United States and Latin America.
Many of the writers in this book, such as Nadine Gordimer,
Dan Jacobson and Jillian Becker have written extensively about
South Africa: its political problems, its geography, its social
stratification; while others express the life of the Jewish community there, and still other writers do both. "There is no
Jewish school of South African writing," as Lionel Abrahams
has said, but there are loci of interests, and the format of
this book tries to express this. Several authors, such as
Nadine Gordimer, Lionel Abrahams and Barney Simon have
been importantly involved in the literary life of South Africa,
not only as writers but as publishers and literary editors.
Lionel Abrahams founded Bateleur Press with Patrick Cullinan
as well as Renoster Books which published the first volumes
of Oswald Mtshali, Mongane Wally Serote, Robert Royston and
Eva Royston. He co-edited with Nadine Gordimer, South
African Writing Today for Penguin Books, and with Walter
Saunders, two issues of Donker's Quarry, an annual anthology
of South African writing. Barney Simon has been very active
in South African theater, and in the United States directed two
of Athol Fugard's plays. He succeeded Nat Nakara as editor
of The Classic, an important expression of present black writing, which published Dugmore Boetie, and he collaborated
with Boetie on Familiarity is The Kingdom of The Lost. Many
of the authors in this book have been published in anthologies
in South Africa and several, like Jillian Becker who now lives
in England, write about South Africa and the countries they
presently live in; or the current international problems which
engage us all, as found in her book on terrorism, Hitler's
Children.

There are biographical notes at the back of the book for further
information about the authors. An interesting thread which con-
nects many of them--Lionel Abrahams, Nadine Gordimer, Dan
Jacobson, Jillian Becker--is that they were born in the decade
of 1923-1933 and attended the University of Witwatersrand in
Johannesburg within a few years of each other: during the decade
of the mid 1940s to the mid 1950s. What makes this biographical
connection sociologically interesting is the role the university
has played in the racial problem in South Africa, and the precise
reflection it gives of it. Witwatersrand was one of the two universities (Cape Town was the other) which admitted non-
Europeans to its teaching facilities and student organizations
in the 1940s and the 1950s. In 1959, the "Extension of University Education Act" gradually eliminated nonwhites from the
universities. Fifteen years later, there were 258 nonwhite students in attendance at Witwatersrand, and in 1964 there were
eleven.

The stories in this book not only reflect a place, but the point
of view of a privileged era of higher education in South Africa.

Omissions of some names are always inevitable and regret-
table, particularly that of Ronald Segal, whose work may not
be quoted or published in South Africa. His work, "Childhood,"
an excerpt from his autobiography, Into Exile (in South African
Writing Today) has its spiritual liaison with the works of those
authors included here.

Roberta Kalechofsky
Marblehead, Massachusetts
September, 1981

Section 1

Polesitting

from The Keep

Jillian Becker

Thus and thus were the visits to the Zoo. And then, on their
last visit, the children had witnessed a feeding which they hadn't
seen anything like before. Into the soundproof cages of the py-
thons, cobras, mambas and boa constrictors (which lived, singly
or paired, in miniature wildernesses, each with its concrete ig-
loo, its bare forked 'tree') the keepers pushed live guinea pigs.
Simon and Josephine watched one of the little creatures tearing
up and down on its very short legs, pressing against the glass as
it frantically tried to find a way out, and they saw quite distinctly
that it was weeping real tears which ran down its face and stained
its hairy cheeks. So it must have known what its fate was to be,
and realised quickly that it was trapped: and it must have known
its enemy, the black snake, though never before confronted. The
predator did not move for several seconds after its supper had
been put in the cage and began the desperate beat. It was neatly
wound beside its tree, a shining hose. It slid out at leisure, the
flat head coming from the midst of its coils, advanced over its
outer rim, and paused to flicker a while at the passing pig. At
last it went further, gave itself more play, curved its neck in an
arc, opened its jaws amazingly wide so that the fangs showed
full and clear, and placed its mouth like a portal arched with
scales in the path of its victim. The guinea pig, perhaps blinded
by tears, or perhaps eager for the end as a terror final at least,
or perhaps crazed by fear, or perhaps carried by its own im-
petus faster than realisation, ran into it, and was swallowed
whole, head first. Josephine, giddy with clammy hands, turned
away, and even the grass turned red.

1

Between The Sheets

Shirley Eskapa

I always long for winter. Transvaal summers are too hot
and last too long. I like the look as much as the feel of long
hair, and in the summer my neck sweats and glues my hair. I
am not one for the outdoor life, and although our swimming
pool looks as refreshing as a bowl of crushed ice, I never so
much as wet a toe, not even on the sunniest day.

The bite of a winter's night is precious to me. With arms
and shoulders covered I am sheltered. Soft flannel sheets which
look and feel like blotting paper draw out and absorb the day's
accumulated dying; the cradle of the pillows console, like a
caress against a breast. Inside the sheets I feel supreme
relief.

In the outward sense, I do not live alone. I have a husband
to share my bed, and to share the days, at the time I want to
tell you about, my son Justin, who was then aged three, and
inside me, growing without the least of my help, another child.
I feared the loneliness. When the child had spurned and left
the womb, I would be bereft.

My husband did not find the light disturbing, and while he
slept I read. The fragile sighs of the child did not break my
compulsive drive across the ages. I devoured books and often
could recall nothing of them. Even the presence of a separate
life breathing only my breath,could not take or break or mute
the call of my own future death. In the shallow milk of my
pallid daily conversations depth existed only in books. There
I submerged.

At about two in the morning, when the too-short winter was
coldest, sleep entered. It would take me a few moments to

2

get warm as I moved into my twined posture, (remembered
from the womb?) before sleep, my restored amniotic fluid,
would embrace me, cover all of me, would carry me to safety,
absolute safety, sublime safety.

For a moment--on that night--I was dropped from sleep
into consciousness. I thought I had kicked a book off the bed,
and then sleep drew me back in again. Once again I was dropped,
the lights flashed on. I sat up and screamed. I dug my elbow
into my husband's ribs. He sat up and screamed.

"Shhh! Shhh!" They were holding their hands to their
mouths. "Shhh! Shhh!" They were moving towards us on shoe-
less feet, the axes over their shoulders glinting lavishly in the
electric light. Their clothes were black, their foreheads and
their chins were hidden behind black balaclavas, their hands
were black. They were shadowless. They came slowly, tor-
tuously, like three moving sculptures. A charred triumph
stared from black eyes.

One halted at the foot of the bed, moved his axe fractionally
forward. The other two slowly, noiselessly, marched on, divided, came either side of the bed, stopped.

I screamed again. The axe nearest me moved slowly down-
ward to rest against my neck. (I almost wrote 'nest', the axe
had the shape of a bird on the wing.) Afterwards my neck was
slightly grazed. "Shhh! Shhh! Shut up or we'll kill you." I
held still. But wouldn't we be killed anyway?

"We want your gun, give us your gun or we'll kill you!"
They flung my pillows to the carpet where they lay like crumpled angels. There was no gun in the bedroom. They were
moving about.

"Money." The one nearest me said.

"In my bag," I could make my voice answer.

One of the others flung the bag. He snatched it. Only silver
coins. (I have never kept my money in a purse. It is scattered.

3

I abhor order.)

"But this is only silver." Shifting his axe to his left
shoulder.

"I can't take your bus fare!" (Pronounced 'fay-er.')

"Please take it. . . . ."

They were wrenching down suitcases, he turned to help.
Afterwards he came back and scooped the silver coins into his
hands.

"My wife is pregnant." My husband said again and again.
"My wife is pregnant!" Mad to say it. So what? They were
pregnant with death. . . . .What were they saying? What were
they arguing about in their black language?

Silence. Two of them advancing towards me. Time slipped
away from my mind, it was static time in a dream. I knew what
was happening only, not what might happen. . . . .Two left
hands removed blankets. The edge of the axe came nearer.
Sharpened and knife-thin. My woollen nightgown untangled as
it was raised. Very gently raised. A fleeting hand examined.
I felt the hand. A bulging hardened belly. The nightgown was
lowered. Such tenderness.

One of them axed the telephone. He had padded himself
against the cold. He swayed, like a golliwog dancing. He
slashed the 'phone straight and crooked. Quick blows. Always
vicious. When the 'phone disintegrated into tiny pieces he
turned on the tray of tea-cups.

The noise. Suddenly there was Justin blinking into the room.
I. . . .I'd forgotten his existence till he stumbled through the
door. Death was all I'd been thinking of, my death, I'd been
fearing a slow death, an arm severed, a leg, a slow butchering.
The terror, not death itself, but the long route it would take
before arriving. But Justin standing under the arch of the
axes had released me from my terror. The three of us in the
bed seemed safer.

A strange trustingness. I felt a complicity flowing through
the six of us--(uniting us?)--we were all in something together.
I was the soldier, arms raised in surrender. I was the patient
dependent on the psychiatrist. The world was shut out. At the
pitch of our life-long conditioning--fear, distrust, permanent
emergency--this trust had been born. There is something un-
wholesome in the kind of trust the psychiatrist wants. But ours
that night had an honesty, like the trust between a prostitute and
her client: a deal would be done. They're saving my life, I
felt, saving it. You trust the man you think has the choice of
your life or your death.

But the pulse of trust was strongest that hour, when it
was born.

"Would you mind leaving me with one suit? I won't be able
to go to work." My husband smiled.

We grew the capillaries of friendship that night, a secondary
friendship, like the secondary circulation they say an injured
heart has to grow. . . . .

They picked up the suitcases. My guardian, the one who
said 'fay-er' for 'fare', stopped at the door. "I'm sorry, Ma'am."

They were gone and our calm with them. The gun was in
another room. My husband leaped, ran for it. I heard its
firing, firing, his most horrible screams for help. They must
have been lying in wait for him. They must be hacking him to
death.

"Come." I dragged Justin. "They are killing Daddy. We
must go and get killed too!"

. . . .

It was we who had broken faith, lied and tricked them. They'd
believed us when we said there was no gun. And we had a second
telephone downstairs.

When they were caught it was said the punishment for armed
attack would be death. I was ill. I went to a nursing home.
I was tangled in all the cycles of hate. "Kaffirs, they'll swing
for this," I heard again and again. "Death is too good for them
. . . ." A few friends and some strangers asked what being
raped was like. . . . . Because they were Black they were
culpable. But for me, blackness darkened reality, pardoned,
and transmuted guilt into innocence. When I said I would kill
anyone, even you, if my child was starving and I couldn't get
work because of a piece of paper, they thought I was deranged,
and said so, at the trial.

They began to hate me, too.

The ten year sentence is almost over. As I said we broke
faith, we fooled them, and I wait now as I have been waiting
for ten years.

Sleep no longer nourishes or carries me. For ten years I
have dreamt that I am at a tea-party in a little thatched summer-
house at the bottom of my mother's garden, swinging upside-
down from a rope, and in my hand I have an axe, and with each
swing, with a deft flick of the wrist I randomly sever whatever
head falls within my range, like a golf-club cracking a ball.

I am addicted to sleep.

White and Injured

Shirley Eskapa

If--after a long break--you visit your home-town, there is
nothing quite so neutralising yet sheltering as staying at a five-
star hotel that was not there before you left; and when the phone
rang, didn't pick it up at once.
"Professor Gayworth?"
"Yes."
"Flora Manheim. Welcome back to South Africa."
"Why, thank you, Mrs. Manheim---"
"Please call me Flora. . . .We've been hoping you'll be
free to come to our New Year's Eve. . .You've only just ar-
rived, haven't you?"
"I'd love to," I said, noting at once--with malice though not
without chagrin--that Josephine, my wife, was not even men-
tioned--it was the kind of invitation she coveted.
I might have coveted it too--once. I'd no idea that Flora
Manheim knew of my existence, let alone that I was back again.
Naturally, I knew who the Manheims were--who in Cape Town
did not? A leading family who collected art (the only Francis
Bacon in South Africa) the way they collected successful people,
until we were all objects in the same exhibition. I suppose the
invitation from the Manheims came much too late for it to
bring any sense of exhilaration. But then ten years ago I
hadn't been a professor of cardiology at Harvard. Nor a
thirty-five-year-old-bachelor-to-be, and an unwilling tourist
on a painful, determined visit to the country Sharpeville had
flung me out of.
Still, there it was, and Flora Manheim's invitation merely
underlined the unpleasant facts.
New Year's Eve at the Manheims' was never held in the
house, but some distance from it, in spectacularly designed
rooms known as the poolhouse. I hadn't been to a South African
party for ten years, yet nothing had changed--there was the
inevitable elderly African servant, a scarlet sash over a white
uniform puffing off starch into the light of the flare with which

7

he pointed the way. He conducted me over steep rock steps,
and in a display that made brilliant use of both lighting and
range, the Manheims' Bacon, like a Coca-Cola sign, was pre-
posterously visible. The work of four or five currently famous African style sculptors jutted the pathway with no less
irresistible command. But I was most taken with an enormous
stone head of a sad Zulu woman. I had to stop and stayed with
her too long, I think, for a hoarse African voice found it necessary to direct me, "This way, master." To show I no longer
belonged, I said at once, "Not master, don't call me master.
I'm Professor Gayworth." The servant lifted his flare. "The
party's up there," he said.

Far below was the ocean. In my present melancholy it
seemed fitting that from here the seas were still, the segregated
beaches invisible--even by day, they would be obscured by cliffs
and introduce no discordant note--the pure white liberalism of
the Manheims need suffer no reproof.

Claude Manheim gave me a drink in the quick manner of
the host who likes to sidestep his own bar-men. He introduced
me to the nearest group, then slid away. I'm not a naturally
congenial guest--I have to work at it--so I stayed with the circle using that polite, and I hoped, charming smile with which
I'd so painfully innoculated myself.

"When did you get here?" someone asked.

"Five days ago."

"Too soon to tell us what you think of the place, hey--"
He turned away, and wifeless, I was free to stare without
reproach.

She was standing uncompromisingly apart, when I first saw
her. It was a lukewarm midsummer's night, excuse enough for
a blazing log fire, over which, hands clasped behind her back,
she hunched meditatively. A silky black stuff gripped her body:
all she exposed were hands and neck. She scowled into the fire.
Suddenly she stretched--sprung her neck backwards, laced her
hands high over her head as if to untwist what--bored ligatures?
It was such a deep stretch and so entire, that it was at once
intimate and public.

Her grooming wasn't all she thought it was: a split seam exposed her underarm. It was clear that she wished to be left alone,
and though I'm not by nature contrary, I felt constrained to disturb her.

"Why stand alone? It's New Year's Eve."

"So it is."

"I'm Geoffrey Gayworth."

As if bright with some kind of reprieve, she said, "You're American?"

"Right. I am. At last."

"But your accent? You must be American born--surely?"

I could see she was the sort who wanted to know who you were, what you did and why. South Africans think they're warm, I find them merely blunt. I said, "I left this place ten years ago in nineteen-sixty--remember that year? to specialize in cardiology." I wanted her to know why I'd left. "I'm working at Harvard now. You are--uh--- "

Impatiently, as if her name was worth nothing to her she said, "Nesta Wagner." And then, "You must be an American citizen to have imbibed their accent like that. Ten years? Mind you," she said in a tone which scraped my sunburn, "I've known people perfect it in as little as two."

"Right. Right again, I'm susceptible to America." I wasn't sure whether she was being rude. I said mildly, "Are you really as sharp as you seem?"

"I'm sorry," she said, meaning it. She gestured towards the dancers. "It's New Year's Eve."

"And you don't like celebrating?"

Her shrug drained her eyes, but ensured that immense grace of hers. I measured her at about thirty. I said,

"No--New Year's Eve's not my style either."

"Do you come back often?" she asked.

"Here? Hell, no! First time in ten years!"

"Well--that's unusual," she said. "So many of our friends come back each Christmas--it breaks their winters and they get sun-tanned."

"I'm not one of them--" She would not concede that I'd become a visitor, and so I could not be the mild, polite guest I'd wanted to be. "When I turned twenty-five I left. I swore I'd never come back. I married a South African girl and we didn't even come back for the wedding. Our folks flew to Boston. Now we're both back here for a divorce. Financial arrange- ments." I gestured towards the servants in their painfully white uniforms. "In the States, you see, we don't get those so easily."

"So one has heard," she said in a jarred voice. "So one
has heard." And then more to soothe than to condone she began
again, "Well, there are pleasanter things than housework. It's
not the most inspiring occupation, you know." She floundered--
"It's not difficult to see how your wife---"
I interrupted scathingly, I thought, "You've tried it then?"
She managed a laugh. Then looked at me so I'd know there was
a great deal she could say--but what would be the point? She
said only, "I see all too well what you mean--I won't have
living-in servants. I never have. Richard thinks I'm--"
I was scarcely in the mood to be interested in husbands. Still,
I asked, "Which one is your husband?"

"Over there," she said, pointing. "The good-looking one."
She caught his eye and flicked the kind of handwave that dis-
tributes approval: he was obviously not required to quite be-
long to anyone, either. I don't know much about dancing, but
even I could see he danced well. His partner's exposed navel
danced too, though out of rhythm, and the revolving coloured
lights flashed against the moisture which had collected there.
It was really quite tempting, that navel, it would close around
your finger like a sea-anenome. "You--uh--happy?" I said,
and instantly regretted my absurdity.
"I don't have a great propensity for happiness," she said
dismissively.
There are moments when only a banality will do: "Ah well--"
I said, "I suppose happiness is a myth rather than a by-product."
She said absently, "Perhaps." Just then a door opened, ex-
posing the kitchen. The door was shut immediately, as if kit-
chens, unlike navels, were private regions not fit to be seen.
Nesta laughed. "Did you see that? Did you see that?"
"The kitchen? What's so funny--"
"Not the kitchen. The dishwasher--"
"So what?"
But she went on--she hadn't heard me. "They even have a
dishwasher down here--in the poolhouse--Jesus, even I wouldn't
have believed it! What progress! Flora Manheim won't have a
vacuum cleaner because she says they roar, and all her acres
of carpet are swept by hand. A dishwasher! Oh, of course you
wouldn't understand any more; you've left--no one has a dishwasher in South Africa--a real machine. Real machines need
service--human ones are more easily replaced. You get a new

one. Honestly the Manheims must think they're enlightened."

I let her indulge. In ten years nothing had changed. Nothing.
Snug and passive in their life-proofed down, a sarcasm was still
their way of disowning a system. . . . Then an insulting little
formula sneaked out. I said: "Feel better now? May I re-
arrange your cushions?" Had I really only been back five days?

She was instantly apologetic again: "I am sorry. I really am
sorry. But there's so little here that's funny--still, it was
wrong of me--"

"Uh--come on, come on," I said, and added, probably out of
habit, "You're O. K. "

And of course she was pleased. From the moment she had
begun her apologies she distractingly held on to a lock of hair.
Her forehead was bared, and tilted delicately, perfectly; and
there in the centre was a large patch, white and injured, that
had missed the sun. This patch, though easily corrected, was
nevertheless a flaw, the only flaw in a face which was an absolute oval, aristocratically boned, pierced by kind grey eyes.
There was no satisfaction in having hurt her.

The dancers tracked by. We neither of us went for dancing,
and the sharing of an ordinary dislike somehow helped; when
dinner was announced, I took her hand without any effort at all.

Attentive to the pyramids of food, Nesta assumed an appropriate gravity. "Shall I help you?" she said in the manner
of a guest who likes to be useful at a party. "A little of everything? The Manheims are famous for their salads. " It suddenly seemed years since I helped myself at a buffet party.

I thought, nothing but a death could have brought me back
here. And then I realised that divorce was a death, a crema-
tion even; already my soul had turned to ash. For comfort I
reminded myself that I was one of the youngest associate pro-
fessors at Harvard--but what sort of empty anodyne was that,
I thought impatiently--would I never escape trivial pride of this
kind? And for all my weariness, I could not help feeling that
nothing in my life would ever be as flattering, even as exalting,
as having rubbed out South Africa by leaving it; if I repatriated
myself there'd be nothing left.

Nesta brought me an oversized oval plate. I caught a pale
flash of skin again--more stitching had failed. She said busily,
"I hope this'll do. Be with you in a moment. " She waved the
other plate. "I've got to give this to Richard."

It seemed I'd misjudged her; she probably handled her husband as gingerly as sunburn.

She returned sooner than I'd expected, and my sense of relief surprised me, for I'd not known I'd been waiting for her. She said, "Do they have Auld Lang Syne in America too?"

"New Year's Eve? Sure."

"The Manheims always play a recording of Big Ben striking midnight."

"Well--it won't be long now," I sighed, "nineteen-seventy-one."

She sighed too. "Yes," she said, "nineteen-seventy-one."

The waiters, like the resigned nannies they were, smiled with ambiguous generosity, as if even as they distributed gaudy paper hats, packets of confetti, and Don Perignon, the antics of the spoilt was something they had never got used to.

"I suppose I ought to do the right thing," Nesta said. She scraped her hair back and fitted on an orange clown's hat. The white patch in her forehead looked raw. "You're very sunburnt," I said. "Except for this bit." I traced its outline.

"Yes, I know." She didn't move away. "But you've got to wear a silly hat too."

Loss of dignity leaves me nervous. Still I put on the stupid paper helmet. Nesta leaned forward and adjusted it; she did it naturally, and with exquisite tact. I could not imagine her flirting. "You look better now," she smiled. "The green matches your eyes."

Big Ben tolled. And stirred into, not by, the hysterical surfeit of affection that rolled after, I had the feeling that these embraces were no more evanescent than the year which had ended, the year which had begun; all seemed provoked by the sense of imminent extinction scarred with constant emergency. The only permanence lay in shared alarm.

Well--I'd got rid of all this.

Just then the African women servants of the Manheim household giggled into the poolhouse. The caps of some were aslant, jaunty, familiar, as if mobilised for that annual touch, the hand-clasping which only Christmas and New Year could authorise. They stood at the edge respectfully enough, even if there was something disorderly in their approach; and their uniforms crumpled now by jollity, not work, and hinted at flesh. One of them caught sight of the sea-anenome navel that had worried me, and pealed out: "Ow, ma'am, you look smart!"

These moments without change, without Josephine my wife,
were intolerable. . . . But I hadn't kissed Nesta. I found her
and said, "You didn't kiss me!"

"Didn't I?" She took off her paper hat.

It was a nice kiss--unexpectedly open--a cobweb of promises.
I wondered whether she hadn't deliberately waited. And I thought,
for a moment, that if I came back and worked in Cape Town, I
need give up neither my children nor Josephine, and I could probably have Nesta too. And why not? After all, you can expect no
less than everything here. All Josephine asked was that I come
back, back to the kind of warmth she had failed to live without,
back to the warmth which would end those unbearable apologies
of hers. Our country had been our only quarrel. . . . Then
Nesta half-tapped, half-caressed my cheek and it was like her
kiss, like that earlier moment when she had adjusted my paper
hat; she once more nudged and made more of my stale but still
alive glands.

She said, "If you listen carefully, you'll hear them."

"Who?"

"The carol singers."

"There's cabaret too, then," I said unpleasantly.

Her voice was sharp. "Not quite. Not quite." She went on
more evenly. "It's a tradition around here. On New Year's
Eve, they're welcome."

The party blazed on. Discotheque rhythms crashed.

Then I heard a distant crooning. The song climbed slowly,
almost visibly, and in a sudden rush my depression melted. We
saw their candles spiral along in single file. Then we saw them.
They were a group of about twenty, some children--the smallest
one could not have been more than five--others almost adult;
and the choir mistress, large and comfortably middle-aged,
walked backwards over the rocky steps as she conducted--her
capacious buttocks curved in the shape of a baby bundled in a
blanket behind its mother's back, rocking like a twinned metronome. An ill-printed sign on a lantern, fashioned out of the
same bright crinkly stuff as our hats, said SISTER BROWN'S
CHOIR SINGERS. They had certainly done all they could.
All the girls were wearing white lace veils, white dresses,
white cardigans, white stockings; the young men, shirts and
trousers that were an equal blaze of white. And everything--

even the stockings--was authenticated by starch. They sang in
Cape-Coloured accents, feathered by missing teeth, their expressions leaning somewhere between devotion and anxiety,
and the overall effect of the carols came as close to being
spiritual as anything could be for me. The darkness of some
of the singers was intense enough to qualify as African; the
whiteness of others, though no less intense, would never quite
pass. . . .Had I really been back only five days? A child of
five coughed hackingly. It was quickly stifled. She stopped
singing, and it may have been nothing more than the effort of
holding back the cough which made her forehead sweat. For a
while only the roasting of tunny fish and of sheep sounded beneath the singing. Then the party-makers began to whisper.
I heard the paper of notes, and the chink of coin, as the peevish
whispers turned to talk. Boredom accumulated like debt. Dog-
gedly, the choir sang on, though at a quickened pace, now
scarcely pausing between carols, as if naively they believed
that by getting through more of their repertoire hates could be
overtopped. I saw Nesta look towards the Manheims, her hands
in readiness. Mrs. Manheim marched outside and leaned into
the ear of the choir mistress who nodded, but continued conducting. . . .I believe I saw Nesta's tears and then her eyes
closed. . . .Someone said loudly, "They just don't know when
to stop. They'd go on forever if Flora didn't stop them. It's
the same every year!" Then followed those inevitable, knowing
sniggers. . . .an old hatred lurched, and I thought sourly that
hatred was stronger than compassion. I hated these people because even if they were liberal, they could not help being white
and I was again one of them. I waited for that singing to end,
as I have waited for sleep, for the moment when I would no
longer be compelled to witness that unnatural goodness. And I
couldn't help thinking, despite myself, that their goodwill was
only a way of transcending their submissiveness. Locked in
hate, I could not even attempt to clap. Nesta's elbow, combined with her incredulous, "Clap! You must clap--can't you
even clap?" whipped my hands into action.

    She sucked in her lower lip as if it were a thumb, and her
eyes, fever-bright, prepared by anguish, struck at me.
"Weren't they marvellous? Oh, I simply must tell them," she
said, applauding still. She rushed after them.

    The Manheims wouldn't think me impolite, I decided, if I

left now; yet I found myself following her. I stopped strategic-
ally, a short distance away, where I was in earshot of both
Nesta and the party; I knew they'd talk about her. Nesta was
saying, "Oh--I thought you were all so wonderful. I wish you
could have gone on forever. You must have practised so hard."
I listened to their faithfully polite murmurings, "Ja, Missus.
Danbie, Missus. OOh ja, Missus." Nesta went on. "The
little ones have done so well--in spite of the late hour. I just
wanted to thank you." I heard the flutter of paper, and was let
down, unreasonably perhaps; I knew they needed the money.
"It was a wonderful concert. Thank you--thank you." The
child's cough erupted. Nesta made a great show of speeding
back to the party, but stopped short as if she wished to make
sunglasses out of trees; she seemed to be looking towards the
sound of the sea. The carols floated upward from the path below, the coughing continued. Then they were lost to the ear.
They talked about Nesta:
"Little Nesta ought to join Black Power.'"
"Why such extremes? She only has to look at Notting Hill
Gate--"
"She's one of our pathetic little liberals. All emotion."
"It keeps her young anyway--she's never really grown up. "
Then came ugly flaunted laughter which was intended, I sus-
pected, to bind them more tightly, rather than to crush her.
They obviously considered the likes of Nesta as something of
a joke. Yet I wondered at their laughter: white bright, flushing
from layers of darkness and dread--dread of the coming struggle they believed they had not chosen, but to which, if need be,
they would commit themselves as though there could never have
been any other alternative.
And I knew I shared nothing but dread with them.
Again, though this was the last thing I wanted to do, I disturbed her. Perhaps it was merely the luminous night which
made her seem so vulnerable and which drew me so defence-
lessly to her--or perhaps, and likelier, I needed shelter.
My sunburn stung again, though more sharply; I stifled under
my scorched skin. She must have heard me approach yet she
did not so much as sigh. It was only after I had called her
twice, in a pent and injured voice, that she flinched in my direction. She said, "I'm sorry. I didn't hear you. I must have
been miles away."

15

Without meaning to, I said, "So you're a liberal!"

"I wish I were. Oh, how I wish I were a true liberal! --not the kind you see all about you here. I'll die regretting never having gone to prison!"

It was a fine night. These high primal African nights are like no other: they make ordinary nights seem like scraps, and in America my longing for these nights has wrangled my sleep, and fretted my days, for such nights carry a peace that you can touch if you like, and more--they can be waded into if you're prepared to strip.

I said, "They say you're a pathetic little liberal. All emotion."

"Oh, that--!" She shrugged dismissively, though her scowl furiously overarched her eyebrows. "Yes, I know how they think of me." Then, "My God--that cough! I didn't know a child could cough like that."

"Yes, I didn't like it. There may be cause for some concern."

"Concern?" She laughed gutturally, unhappily. Then repeated, "Concern? But its's no concern of yours. You left. You couldn't stand it. So you turned your back--virtuously, of course--on the whole lot of us."

"Come on--come on, now. . . .I am a doctor, you know."

"Oh yes, I'd forgotten. Sorry. I am sorry." Her frown deepened. "What do you think it could be?"

"Difficult to say." I assumed my non-committal tone, the one I use whenever I need falsely to convey that symptom is not what it is.

But she quickly sliced through my technique. "It couldn't be T. B. , could it? Not T. B. ?"

She was almost certainly right; no interesting diagnostic problem here. "Always a possibility around these parts, I reckon," I said.

"We can't go after them now--they're singing at another party." Agitatedly she twisted her hair back while her upper arm cradled her face. The seam had opened wider, and that pale unguarded crescent, even in the gloom teased. . . .I said, "Your seam's split."

"Where?" she asked apathetically.

"Under your left arm."

She lowered her arm at once, to check. Irritated, and not wanting to waste any time, she said, "Who cares about a seam!

That cough!" We had been standing fairly close to each other.
Now she twisted fitfully, and caught my arm. She whispered
wildly, "She needs a doctor!" Helplessly, now openly sup-
plicatingly, "She needs a doctor!"

"Sure, she needs a doctor. That, I should have thought, is
obvious. I don't know why you make it sound so impossible.
The hospital is perfectly adequate. In any case, you could ask
your own physician to see her--"

At this she snorted her guttural laugh again. "My physician
--once I asked him to visit my maid who was seriously ill. He
wouldn't come. He said he was not a native doctor."

She had not untightened her grip on my arm. Her nails
pressed into my sunburn. That emotion of hers now seemed to
overwhelm her reason, for she said: "But you'd see that child,
wouldn't you? You could see her. Then she'd have a really
first-class personal Harvard attention, the best in the world.
Oh, that would be wonderful!"

I could not, would not, acquiesce straightforwardly. I said,
"Why not?"

"Is that a promise?" She didn't wait, but explained. "You
see, my doctor would feel put upon. . . .he'd quickly hand her
over."

Recovering, she said, "I'm sorry. But at least you don't
think it unfair of me to have asked you--I'm absolutely thrilled
that you've said yes."

I said abruptly, "You remind me of my wife."

She laughed, this time easily. "That's a familiar defect of
mine. I always remind men of their wives. We'd better get
back to the party, or people will get the wrong idea!" She
scrutinised me then, almost brazenly, I thought. "You shouldn't
have left. We need people like you."

Josephine had never put it like that. . . .I said, "You go on
in, Nesta, I'll join you later." Her misplaced belief in me
troubled like a giddy unswattable fly, and I was glad she'd been
so vulgar as to have given them money; she'd made it easy for
me to alienate myself from her.

The Manheims had scarcely noticed my presence and it was
pointless to say goodbye. I edged my way slowly past their
reproachful Zulu sculpture and turned for a last look at the
Bacon. Behind me, I was aware of the different pigments of
the cold Atlantic and warm Indian seas meeting in shameless

unlegislated passion. It was then I understood my wife and children were finally lost to me; impaled, none of us loves as much as we dare.

If there was no direct flight to the States I would go via London. In less than twenty-four hours I would be out of it, away in that other world where no one could penetrate my moral claim on me, and where, because I had the inalienable right to be foreign, I belonged.

The Stench

JILLIAN BECKER

They were boiling a horse.

That, the schoolmaster was to discover eventually, was the cause of the stink which rose from the mud-hut village half-way up an adjacent hill to his own house on the top of the higher rockier one; and also sank into the valley where the road wound, forcing the rare passing drover or rider to narrow his eyes, pinch his nostrils closed, twist his head this way and that but without escape, while his oxen plodded and swung on imperturbably, their noses too close to dust and perhaps too full of it to be irritated by anything else; but the ponies and hinnies snorted, nodded, and stamped harder in the warm powdery margins of the stony track. The occupants of the car which bumped along in the late afternoon of the second day since the stink had begun were less exposed, but could not have missed it.

The schoolmaster Schwallendorf – a bald, stout, heavy-jowled Saxon – did not make the discovery himself. He had hesitated to venture down among the huts – the presumable source of the stink – into its density and to its very nidorous epicentre. But then a directive came, tactful, amiable, but unmistakable; in the form of a request but nonetheless compulsory; from District Commissioner Bertel Maria Pik, a small Afrikaner in black serge forever troubled by facial impetigo and hay-fever, who, with respect to his hay-fever, shirked the task which should have been his immoveably. He climbed to Schwallendorf's house – four rondavels united by a central square kitchen roofed with pleated tin – by a steep, circuitous path, in an effort to get round the nastiness he had had to drive through: leaving his official blue Chevrolet in the charge of his Xhosa driver, who parked it in the bedraggled shade of eucalyptus, within sight of the store where the tribeswomen came and went.

Schwallendorf was sitting in creased white clothes on the stone step outside his back door, the cooler but hardly less smelly side of the house, and rose to greet his visitor as Pik reached the level pressing a white handkerchief to his wet, erupting face, and poking it down under the high collar of his shirt.

'Good evening, Meneer. How goes it?'

Meneer Pik had no breath to answer. He slumped into a bamboo chair on one side of the small table on which a whisky bottle stood and two glasses as though he had been expected, or been seen approaching.

'If you please,' he panted as Schwallendorf raised the bottle, and he stuffed the crumpled handkerchief into a trouser pocket, took a fresh one from his jacket, unfolded it, wound a corner over the tip of a forefinger and dabbed gingerly at his nose.

'Fiff! But what a stink, hey? You'll do me a favour Schwallendorf. If you please. I cannot go and see myself. This nose of mine. You would oblige me. Or do you know what it is?' He bubbled as he breathed. His nostrils red and damp, his eyes brimming over.

'I've asked the washgirl and the houseboy,' Schwallendorf assured him. 'But they pretend not to know. So I'll go and see what I can find. Of course. Certainly.' – As if to oblige and not obey. And they toasted each other with a raising of their glasses.

Pik fastidiously refolded his handkerchief to dry his lip with its sore spot or two. 'It's this nose of mine, you must see. It's an allergy, you must understand. A lot of people are allergic to something. But I am allergic to everything. Alles.' He swung his infected head to indicate all; and closed his eyes on the long-suffering of all; enflamed western clouds, abrasive gravel, pungent leaves of eucalyptus, a black mote of a bird in the exposure of blue.

'Shall we move into the house?' Schwallendorf suggested. 'It's not so bad with the windows shut.' And he puffed out his lips and cheeks as he waited for the answer.

'No! I cannot stay here any longer under these circumstances.'

'Oh!' The schoolmaster's lips remained open and round on the syllable, his eyes wide, but his cheeks falling flaccid again; a foolish expression, not as if he were disappointed but as though he had been rebuked.

Pik drained his glass and rose. 'I must go. I should never have come up.' He plied his handkerchief again. 'I should have gone on home and telephoned you. Even with the windows up it filled the car like a poisonous gas. I've borne as much as I can. But we'll get to the bottom of this thing. Find out what those kaffirs are up to.' (For men as much as nature plotted against Pik.) 'I can't bear it much longer,' he warned, standing there and dabbing.

It was as if Pik were waiting for Schwallendorf to confess – that he had had a hand in starting the smell, or had carelessly allowed it to erupt, or had tolerated it when he might have stopped it. Schwallendorf felt guilty for having postponed investigation – but the smell had been even more intense then than it was now.

But Pik reassured him. 'I regard,' he said, narrowing his eyes as though what he regarded might sting, 'your co-operation. I must go, I must go.' He hurried off. 'Ring me up in the morning, ja?' He started down. 'Obliged,' he called. And again after a moment, 'Obliged!'

Schwallendorf felt the ambiguity of it, and looked unhappily after Pik as he sidled away down the rocky path, handkerchief over nose; and plodded along a dry stream-bed past yellow-blossoming thorntrees which could only torment him with their sweetness.

Now the screendoor of the kitchen groaned as it was opened behind him, creaked as its tendency to bang shut was curbed, so that it rejoined its jamb without violence; from which Schwallendorf knew without turning round which of the several possible persons who might be coming out of the house this was.

He said, 'That was the D.C. He wants me to find out what's causing the stench. I can't blame him for shirking it. I'm not sure I can stomach it myself.'

'I'll go!' The peremptory announcement was made. *Ich werde gehen!*

As the man who said this with such finality came to stand beside him, Schwallendorf turned to him with the look if not the words for 'Are you sure you want to?' The words had been forbidden by that tone. But the younger man was deliberately looking away, and the schoolmaster could not see much of his face, only the firm-set line of the jaw, at the end of which a ball of muscle was thrust out by the clench of determination, and was throbbing and quivering a denial that this man was made of anything harder, less vulnerable, than other men are – and so also a plea that his resolution go unquestioned.

The schoolmaster grunted.

He believed that he understood: nasty as the stink was, it was not such a challenge, and the grit with which it was being met was less a response to the occasion than a habit of resolution and self-discipline.

'So – if you will,' the easy-going schoolmaster accepted. 'But there is no hurry. Tomorrow will do. By the morning it may have cleared a little.'

That was most probable. Which could have been the reason why the other man said, 'No, I'll go now.'

The large surface of Schwallendorf's face was flattered by the softening light.

And the other's face was also flushed. Its skin was of that sensitive thinness which quickly reddens on exposure to the sun. It was a face in which the bones showed, not gauntly but distinctly enough. Unlike Schwallendorf's, this face – and body – had no redundancy of flesh. Because of its physical hardness it was not a face which changed much with the shift of thoughts or feelings in the man. It might have been unexpressive, set to the point of impassivity, had not conflict – of the will against weaknesses – revealed itself through that quiver in the muscle. No – the hardness was itself an expression, conscious and consciously maintained; so much so – and so plainly to anyone who observed or talked to the man for more than a moment – that even the narrow nose, the cheekbones, would seem to have been wilfully achieved rather than naturally endowed: and further evidence could have been found in the hair, for although Konrad Reitzger was not yet twenty-six, his black, thick, short-cut hair was turning an iron-grey at its edges. His eyes were pale as steel, deep under black eyebrows, but there was no animosity in them. They were clear, questioning, open. Not, they would seem, the eyes of a self-obsessed introvert, but of a man who would probably look well before he judged: a man more interested in seeing a thing clearly than in expressing a quick reaction to it.

'As you prefer, Reitzger,' the older man consented – or gave formal permission to the volunteer. He added, 'Danke!'

Schwallendorf watched the rather strange young man, in conventional white shirt and grey trousers, go off round the house to make his discovery.

Schwallendorf's oldest friend, Max Feuchthaber, had sent young Reitzger to him. The letter had arrived a month ago. Barry Theobald had brought it over from the store as soon as he got back from meeting the train at Butterworth. It looked important, he said, coming all that way, and could he have the stamps for his step-son who was at the T.B. hospital in the Transvaal, yes improving thanks, but very slowly. Theobald knew that Schwallendorf had been waiting some months now to hear whether he'd be granted a pension if he went 'home' to the Bundesrepublik where in fact he had never set foot except to sail from Bremerhaven.

'Dear August –'

Disappointed, and simultaneously pleased, Schwallendorf read the letter from his friend.

'We were at school together,' he told Theobald. In Leipzig, the Gymnasium, and then the University; where he had studied Theology, and Feuchthaber had studied Physics and laughed at God, so their intimacy had begun to lessen. Then Schwallendorf had come to Africa, and they might have lost touch altogether, but their mothers too were friends: and during the war – when August himself was in the internment camp – his mother had moved to the south to live near her sister in Augsburg, and old Frau Feuchthaber had also moved to some small town near Munich where she had relations. Both were widows, both lonely, and they visited each other from time to time. So from his mother, after the war, August heard news of Max. He heard he had become Professor at Heidelberg. He wondered if Max was less lonely than he. Ten years ago his mother had died, and he had heard no more of his friend, until now.

'If you receive this, write at once so that I can give your address to a former student of mine who is coming to "investigate" Africa . . .'

Feuchthaber had used the English word, perhaps because *untersuchen* or *erforschen* could equally well mean 'explore', which is what anyone might do who was coming to Africa. Schwallendorf had wondered about this, and now he thought that Feuchthaber had cleverly caught, with that one word, something of the character of young Reitzger. He could see exactly what Feuchthaber – whose affection for Reitzger had also, *nichtsdestoweniger*, been suggested – had meant to imply when he said 'investigate'. Or was it perhaps a word that Reitzger himself had used, when telling Feuchthaber his plans? Reitzger spoke excellent English, at least as good as Schwallendorf himself.

'Investigate.' Yes. In three days this Reitzger had asked more questions about the country, its climate, its people, its past and present, its birds, beasts and plants than Schwallendorf had learnt the answers to or even thought to ask in thirty years.

Well, this appetite for information might be useful now. Reitzger was not the man to miss whatever was happening down there, and if the reasons were not obvious he'd do his dogged best to find them out. And yet, even if he persuaded some of the villagers to use their English, they were unlikely to tell him much. Not enough to satisfy Pik. He should have thought of that. He'd have to go himself, after all.

But then again, Schwallendorf had to admit, they were not likely to tell any white man more than they had to – certainly not Pik. Only last week Pik had taken away one of the men – Johnjohn, whom everyone knew was the headman's son and who'd come back from the mines a year ago to his home village. But Pik had maintained that he had no right to be here, and had 'endorsed' him out of the territory, no one knew where. The headman had asked him, Schwallendorf, to intercede – and he'd gone at once to Butterworth, but who on earth could make Pik change his mind? 'I'm sorry, Meneer Schwallendorf, the law is clear and I do my duty.' Then the headman had ridden off to Butterworth himself, as if he could succeed where a white man failed. Perhaps he hadn't even believed that Schwallendorf had done his best. For the sad thing was, they didn't trust him either. This was the tragic *Ausfall* of his whole life. Though most of them had been or were still his pupils, they no longer trusted him with their secrets. In the last five years he seemed to have lost what he'd gained so patiently and conscientiously in the twenty-five years before. Now there was an atmosphere of disgruntlement, if not rebellion: or building up of storm clouds in the minds of men – that's what they were achieving, Pik and his kind! And though it wasn't through any fault of his own – he was sure of that – it amounted to a personal failure all the same. There was no reclaiming the lost ground now. He had wanted to stay in this job for their sakes, but what good was a man to those who didn't trust him? 'Co-operation' with Pik might keep him his job for a while yet, though most of the other white Protestant teachers – and all the Roman Catholic missionaries – had been sent away. But if that co-operation meant his losing the trust of the very people he wanted the continued chance to serve, what was the use of his staying on any-way?

He sighed. A stout old man getting fuller of doubts and shorter of the spirit to deal with them. Feuchthaber had laughed at God, and yet became Professor at Heidelberg, and had many friends. While he – Hadn't he wanted to be a father to them, no matter his colour and theirs?

He was feeling particularly dejected this evening, as though something were missing that he depended on: yes, it was like nostalgia, but not for anything he could name; not for lost friends, or youth, or Germany; but for something the past had always contained until recently. Hope for something perhaps. But for what exactly, he could not grasp; though it wavered about him, inapprehensible but pervasive, like the stench – which was probably, he concluded, itself the actual cause of the unpleasant mood.

He went into his house, seeking some refuge from the pervading rotten smell.

As Reitzger descended into the stronger zones of the smell, he reminded himself that squeamishness was easy to overcome. He had wanted to make this investigation since he had woken up to the foul stench on the second morning after his arrival, but Schwallendorf had insisted no, they would wait, he would ask, there was no need. Reitzger liked answers. He wanted all the phenomena of this country to be identified and explained. The impact of Africa was strongly physical; it appealed immediately to the senses. It could hardly be expected to stimulate the imagination as old cities and man-worked landscapes did. Rather, it assailed a man: these primitives of heat, wilderness, mountain and valley and plain, of intense colours in a generally unrelenting sunlight under a ceiling of hard even blue, harsh sounds of birds shrieking and chattering and purring but not singing, the tastes of things distinctive but not subtle, and now this penetrating smell, roused mood, distracted the mind with irritation and offence, if one didn't keep hold. It could distort one's view – in the atmosphere of sunset and stench the whole landscape might seem warmed to the point of decay: gangrene of the bush; the sulphur-yellow of fever-trees. But his eyesight was extraordinarily good. He saw, as red rocks crumpled in the deepening – at last relenting – light, each ridge defined; and grasses burning out individually.

He reached the valley, where the stink seemed less intense: but as he climbed up again towards the village it thickened. And when the path brought him to a level where he turned off to walk among the huts he was enveloped and filled with it, he could have choked on it, but refused to of course.

Women long skirted and bare breasted continued to pound with pestles into deep wooden mortars – but they watched him pass, and the babies on their rocking backs gazed at him. Men dressed in togas of blue cotton with matching turbans, and girls in little more than beads, appeared from all sides, and as they passed they turned their eyes towards him, but none of them stopped or spoke to him. They surely knew why he had come. There was curiosity and perhaps amusement in their glances, but not fear. The pounding went on, the walkers passed him, this one with a tin of water on her head, that one with a bundle of sticks across his shoulders. And Reitzger said nothing to them. He did not even nod at them. His nose directed him.

He came out beyond the last of the huts into a stony space. There was a fire in a square shallow pit; and over it, balanced on logs, a huge tank with a scaffolding erected on one side providing a ladder and a platform. One man was pushing branches down into the pit. Another stood on the platform and was using a branch to stir the contents of the tank. A woollen scarf was wound round his nose and mouth. He was smoked and steamed, but persisted. The job must be very important to keep a man at it in such discomfort. Women approached him, one hand pressed to mouth and nostrils, and he would let go of his huge spatula to lift the tins from their heads and empty the water into the tank. The smoke came round and billowed over Reitzger. He did not move away but waited for it to be shifted again by an otherwise undetectable current of air. His eyes watered and stung. The slow procession of water-bearers continued to advance towards the platform, and the attendant up there to empty the tins and stir. His presence did not apparently perturb them. Whatever it was they were doing was calmly proceeded with, as with any normal occupation. He could look on to his heart's content, no one minded in the least. But the smell was abnormal, terrible. And in the red light, in the stench, in the smoke, the silent business seemed lurid and sinister.

Reitzger stood watching, and prepared himself for what he might see when he climbed the ladder. Prepared himself, that is, for the worst, that experience, which had exceeded imagination, could warn him of: a scene which came back to him vividly from his first day at the University of Heidelberg. In a large hall of the Medical Faculty, a rectangular pool, wide and long enough to be a swimming-pool, but full of mustard yellow water. He had gone to the edge and peered down into it, expecting what? – fish? – lilies and reeds? – and found it was full of floating human corpses; with swollen green-white flesh, streaming hair, bulging eyelids. He had felt his gorge rise, but stood still and ordered it down, closed his eyes, drooped his shoulders; and though sweat had broken out on his forehead he had been able to walk steadily down a busy passage among bustling white coats, and vomited when he reached the lavatory. So his shame had not been public, but in any case severe. He was aspiring – had intended since childhood – to become a surgeon! Before the war he had dissected animals without a qualm. What had reduced him to this then? The cold eye of the dissector, the detached mind of the science-student had surely not been changed by hunger or fear. Fear had been overcome, by grit, which was the product of willpower and intelligence. So why should not an augmented courage, which had helped him face the near possibility of his own death and the actual deaths of others who if not exactly friends were by then in any case familiar, help him to look calmly at a tankful of cadavers? What was this – was it pity, or was it revulsion? Neither was called for. And as for why – though a question one did ask – a man cannot take a scalpel to himself!

One had not changed one's course then, or at least not for some time,

and not for that cause; and one would not now, when one was quite prepared.

He climbed the ladder of rough split eucalyptus logs, tatty with peeling
bark, to stand beside the cook who paused in his stirring but did not look
at him. The reeking steam made his eyes sting, and at first he could see
nothing through the billows of vapour and the scum and the bulges of
heaving water at the boil. Then it swam up, the horse. Stiff legs, enormous
hooves, open bulging eyes, streaming mane and tail, split skin, the bowels
floating out. A scene by Hieronymus Bosch, he thought. And he stood
steady, and steadily looked down, breathing in the sickening stench without nausea or even disgust.

He climbed down unhurriedly, and went back among the huts. 'Pardon,'
he said to one of the busy villagers, and stepped in front of him to make
him stand still.

'Boss?'

'Is Walter here? Walter? Is he still here? I want to speak to him.'

The man stared at him stupidly.

'Walter,' Reitzger repeated, louder but not impatiently.

The man tipped back his head as he understood, and then he pointed.
Round there and straight on, his hand told the stranger.

Reitzger went the way he was shown, and soon saw the person he was
seeking, standing in front of a hut. It was as if he had been standing there
waiting for Reitzger to appear, for he promptly raised one hand and
smiled in greeting.

'Mr Reitzger!' he called, pleasantly, familiarly. 'Welcome, my friend!'

Reitzger had found Walter for the first time three days earlier.

Two cranes, huge awkward birds with gold crowns; grey, white bellied,
with tails of butter and mauve, soared up and slumped upon the top of a
tree in full blossom of scarlet, but with no leaves. The tree grew beside a
river – of water, not a dry bed. Still water, in a valley at noon. On the
other side a cornfield, wrecked by its harvest; pale bent sticks in stony
furrows of the red earth. And in the middle of the field, in the sun, on a
high chestnut horse, a hefty black man in a yellow shirt, smooth polished
riding-boots with silver buckles, a crop in his hand.

Reitzger had crossed a bridge made of heaped stones. Then over the
hard red earth through the devastation of the sticks. And called out,
'Good morning!'

The man raised a hand in salute, then lowered it to the pommel of his saddle and leaned forward graciously to enquire.

'Yes sir. Can I be of some assistance to you?'

Reitzger asked for directions.

'It happens,' the equestrian replied, 'that I am proceeding there myself immediately. It is unfortunate that I cannot procure another horse for you to accompany me.'

How far was it? Could one not walk?

'It is not too far. In nine - ten hours you could be at your destination. But you would conclude your journey in a state of exhaustion, even if you did not lose your way.'

They considered the problem, which both placed at a distance from themselves where the valley flowed away into the sky. One of the cranes rose, circled widely, returned to its mate. It took time.

Reitzger turned back to look up at the man again.

'My name,' he said, 'is – Konrad.'

'Conradie?'

'Not Conradie. Just Konrad. It is my first name. The other is hard to pronounce.'

Reitzger had been told by two or three women – one of them his mother – that he lacked not only 'charm', but, more seriously, 'tact'. He was intending to achieve tact now, but as he spoke became uneasily aware that he was falling short of it again.

The man said, in the same clear, strong but quiet tone as before, and without straightening again with any bridling movement, 'I have been through High School, and I have matriculated. I was in the war as a medical assistant. I can read and write three languages. In particular my spelling of English is exemplary.'

Exemplary. Reitzger gave in.

'Reitzger,' he said. 'Konrad Reitzger.'

'Mr Reitzger.' The man pronounced it impeccably. And went on, 'You are German then. Which means that once you were officially my enemy.' This time the two men in the middle of the red and plundered field made their considerations while looking at each other's eyes: the one straightened now on his height, looking down; the other on stiff legs planted apart in the red dust, looking up. Waiting. The valley held the heat in stillness. But then the horseman smiled, widely, showing his white teeth. 'But not necessarily my enemy now. What would your opinion be on that question?'

'Not necessarily,' Reitzger agreed, who was however in no hurry to

reassure or befriend, and saved his emphasis for what he must insist on –
his own determination. He would not plead. He would not make strenuous
efforts to convince. He was the last man to smile foolish smiles and stutter
in efforts to create goodwill.

'So,' the other went on, content enough with this answer, 'you can call
me Walter. Yes. That is my English name. My Xhosa name clicks, and
white men have difficulty with clicks. You, Mr Reitzger – ' again he repeated it just as he had heard it, with the guttural German 'r' – 'would not
be able to pronounce it.'

Touché!

Reitzger moved his eyes from the dark ones of the mounted man to the
tail of the horse which was flicking at horse-flies on its haunches. The
same idea was growing in both of them. But neither was in a hurry to tell
it. They looked away to the birds, one of which raised its wings in a restless half-rise, then flopping and wing-rowing scrambled again for a claw-
clutch.

Reitzger's awkwardness, his shyness, was concealed – or divulged – by
stiffness. 'Walter,' he said, looking at the cranes, 'could let me ride on his
horse –'

Walter did not move or speak.

'– behind him, on the haunches.' He put a hand on the wide flanks of
the animal. Another man might have slapped it.

'You mean,' Walter corrected him, 'if it would not make me uncomfortable, would I consider such an arrangement?'

'I could pay –'

But Walter raised his voice to stop him. 'With pleasure. And if you
were to offer me recompense, Mr Reitzger, I should definitely refuse.'

And he smartly removed foot from stirrup on Reitzger's side, and held
the leg forward and one arm rigidly down, so that Reitzger could use
stirrup and arm to swing himself up, to sit astride the horse close to the
broad yellow back of its master.

'Forward Ukuthula!' Walter commanded, and tapped the hefty shoulder
with his crop. Ukuthula curved his neck and paced through the field,
stamping down the sticks, the bent and the straight, and some still with
papery leaves, which stood in his way, crackling and faintly rustling, and
starting up small spurts of the soft red dust. Over the bridge, past the
tree with its reflection, scarlet and scarlet, and the four cranes, two high
in the heat and two low in the cool brown water.

Konrad Reitzger did not like to entrust himself to another person. Equally he would not like others to entrust themselves to him. Not because he shirked responsibility but because, on the contrary, he believed that everyone should accept full responsibility for his own actions. Men should meet on terms of equality. Respect yourself and respect others – unless they should prove themselves unworthy.

As, in his opinion, his father had. Who had demanded the respect of his children as a duty, denying their right to judge what he was or what he did. 'A weak man, a moral coward, afraid of authority, inclined to be servile, kowtowing to his bosses,' was the conviction he had confided to Professor Feuchthaber, one of those rare people whom Reitzger found it possible not only to respect but even to like. 'I know the type well,' Feuchthaber had said. And yet, while Konrad had no doubt that these qualities belonged to his father, he was not convinced that having said that he had said all there was to say about the old man. As a boy he had been puzzled by him – why was he so grand and grave with the family at dinner, and so different, loud and laughing, winking and whispering, when there were visitors? What was it about him that made the younger children hang their heads and answer in whispers when he spoke to them, and made Konrad, though he would stand straight, and look into his father's eyes, and speak up, feel his face grow hot as if he had something to be ashamed of, or was lying when he wasn't?

Kurt Reitzger was a thick man, not fat but solid, who sat and stood and walked in a rigid manner, with the straight back of an old Prussian officer – though he came of a Bavarian burgher family none of whom had ever been in any regular army. He had worked for a chemical company, one of the biggest in the world. His position was secure but not eminent. When he found out that Bernhard Kuhn, the son of his chief and classmate of his own eldest son, often invited Konrad to the palatial Kuhn house on the other side of the river near the Schloss, he summoned Konrad into his study ('in that pompous way he had,' Konrad recalled), to inform him of his approval of such a 'respectable association' and hoped it would 'blossom' into a 'close and lasting friendship'.

For years Konrad had squirmed for his father's sentimentality and vulgarity; though he only put the names to these things when he was quite grown-up. In the evenings after dinner they all had to sit together for an hour 'to show that we are a proper loving family'. If there were guests, his father would tell his Joke. It didn't matter to him if he'd told it to the same guests a dozen times before, it must be told again because it proved him an amusing fellow. It was about a stutterer walking inadvertently into a cow-pat, and exclaiming *Sch- sch- schon reingetreten!* When this joke stopped being one of the great adult mysteries because he came to understand it, Konrad wondered why his father bothered to tell it, and why the visitors pretended to find it funny.

On Sundays they had all to go to Mass together. When he was fifteen he had asked his father, 'How can you be a scientist and believe in God?' To which he received a long, solemn and unconvincing reply. The expression of disbelief or even contempt on his son's face roused his father eventually to red-faced anger. And it may have been out of a desire for revenge that a few days later he refused Konrad's request for a set of scalpels of his own. Konrad had been staying late after school in the laboratory to investigate the quadrate bone of the snipe, and write a paper on it under the supervision and encouragement of his new but very old biology teacher, who had been called back from retirement now that the war was absorbing the young men. Konrad wanted to carry on at home after the school had to be locked up. He wanted to finish his paper in time to enter it for a national competition, and now his father was too mean to help him. '*Scheiss!*' he hissed, as he left his father's study. He was called back at once. 'What did you say?' the old man demanded, his eyes bulging. 'I said, *schon reingetreten*,' Konrad said, stiff with defiance. The old man stared helplessly, his mouth opening and shutting silently, and Konrad marched out of the room.

Perhaps old Reitzger was afraid of losing his son's respect. He took him once to Ludwigshafen, to the laboratories of the Company. There was a fat woman there, some kind of secretary. His father called her Lili and patted her bottom. She had metallic yellow hair wound up in plaits, and wore a dirndl. She giggled when the old man whispered to her. He looked stupidly pleased with himself, but became serious, pompous as ever, as he showed Konrad how to filter chemicals and how to mix them by shaking them in a test-tube. Still the boy looked unimpressed. 'Ask me anything you want explained,' he said. But it was obvious that he didn't really know the answers to the boy's questions. He filtered some more chemicals, and shook them in the test-tube. Konrad's face remained wooden, and they drove home in silence.

Konrad won a prize for his paper – an ornate certificate which he soon lost, and more importantly an exemption from service as an anti-aircraft gunner which would otherwise have been compulsory when he turned sixteen. He was allowed to stay at school until he was seventeen. In that year he began to investigate genetics, breeding generations of *Drosophila melanogaster*. Then, in the last year of the war, he had to go into the army.

'Now be careful you don't catch syphilis,' was all his father could think of to say in his jocund bar-room manner the day Konrad left for his training.

The regiment was sent by train into the Battle of the Bulge. 'I may die soon,' Konrad thought, 'and I hardly know anything.' What was there, he wondered, that he could learn at this late hour? Perhaps he could learn to drive a locomotive. He went to ask the driver to give him lessons, and drove himself into battle.

He was wounded, not severely, but hospitalised at Mannheim. His father came to see him.

'You just get better, my boy, and when all this is over you won't have to worry. With the contacts I've got you'll get a good start up the right ladder. That I can promise you. You know you can rely on me,' he said. 'When peace comes –,' he kept saying. '*Kommt der Friede. Hab' keine Angst* – don't worry!'

And very soon after Konrad was sent back to the front, the peace did come. He was captured in a town called – he appreciated – Misery.

The prison camp was an open field enclosed with barbed wire, without shelter of any kind. A perpetual drizzle and the piss of thousands of men turned it to slush. The prisoners, wet and hungry and itching, sat or lay in the mud and scraped at it with their hands in the hope of reaching firmer ground. The young pink Americans watched suspiciously from the wooden towers at the corners of the field from behind their machine guns. Sometimes a prisoner, soaked and mind-wandering, would get up and try to run through the mud towards the fence, and the fingers of a frightened Pinkface would fly to his trigger, the gun would rattle and bullets spray the running, the digging, the sleeping, a whole line of be-wildered men. Once one of the guards shot his counterpart in the diagonally opposite tower. But despite wild and frequent rumours few of the prisoners believed that their extermination was intended. Each was given a bar of chocolate – his only rations – per day. Konrad Reitzger wondered if his bowels had lost their capacity to function, but after three weeks, an hour's labour, and a contribution of blood to the communal bog, he shat a rock.

In the fourth week – it was early March – some officer conceived the idea that it would be better to intercept and reason with those men who lost their nerve and squelched towards the fences than to shoot them down, especially as this method of dealing with them had proved so hazardous for the guards themselves. They needed an interpreter, and enquiry soon brought them to Reitzger, who thereafter spent his days sitting high on the back of a jeep, being driven round and round the mudfield, spotting, shouting at, explaining how things stood to those who'd had enough of mud and chocolate and lice and rain and thought they might prefer bullets. His padded uniform was so torn that all over it the padding hung out in little clotted mudballs, reminding him of a costume hung with bells that he had seen on Papageno when his mother had taken him to the opera in Salzburg on his tenth birthday.

The jeep was an improvement on the mud – to which however he returned to sleep. And it wasn't long before his English took him to the green pastures of a bed, regular meals, clean clothes, water and soap at the American base, for he was handed over to a priest who needed an interpreter who was also Catholic and educated. Reitzger hid his atheism and his contempt. 'The Mess was worth a Mass,' he was to explain to those who would agree, like Feuchthaber.

His usefulness delayed his return to civilian life, but one did not starve as long as one stayed with the American army. Home in Heidelberg that winter of forty-five to forty-six he found out how scarce everything was. Or would have been, even for him, had not the American High Command set up its headquarters there. And of course the intelligent man would survive if survival was possible. And not only survive, but survive well. And the real test of intelligence (Konrad Reitzger said) was life itself.

He became a waiter at the American Club. One took one's tips and commission in cigarettes. A 'bar' of them was a bar of gold. Clumsy money, but it bought food, clothes and even books.

The Americans themselves organised a lending library for civilians. As 'Now the war for the minds begins,' the padre had been fond of saying who had been Reitzger's patron, and to whom he had therefore restrained himself from answering with his own opinion – 'Nazism – Catholicism – one irrational faith or another – is a poor choice if any at all.' And when he searched the library he found nothing there either – mostly the conqueror's naive and misplaced faith in Steinbeck and O'Neill. The first time he went in there a woman kept trying to catch his eye and smirk at him. On a later visit she said, 'Don't you remember me? I remember *you*. My name's Lili – I used to work at – ah, now you remember! And tell me, how is your father these days? He used to be very amusing your father, very good company!' Lili's hair was shorter and darker, and no longer plaited and wound. She was thinner and usually dressed in a red suit; and her lips and nails were red. She told him she was engaged to an American called Al. When he told her that he was working as a waiter at the Club she became cooler. Yet she couldn't have earned as much in a month as he did in a single night.

The Club was smoky and noisy with a piano and singing and frivolity, and full of women with square beaded shoulders and hair in sausages on top of their heads. At four in the morning Konrad would go home to sleep. At eight he would go to the apartment of two stout old ladies, the central exchange and chief agents of the Black Market.

Little pearl earrings pressed into their lobes. One wore a tangled wig like beige coir; the other's white hair was pinned in a tight knot with big black hairpins. The skin of their necks looked like grey used chamois. They smelt as musty as their apartment. The wigged one had been married, and the broad gold ring pressed into her flesh. The other had a big watch chained to her belt. Their feet were squeezed into schoolgirl shoes, on each a cushion of flesh between the curve of leather and the strap. Their many high dark rooms were crowded with enormous articles of polished furniture, and silent motionless clocks, antimacassars, a multitude of ornaments – bucolic china children with faces like buttocks, orange dogs with blunt muzzles and blank round eyes. Rugs worn to the jute. Canvases of cracked oil paint in pompous frames. Crowds of portrait-photos on an upright piano. The Goethe, the Schiller, the aspidistra. Torn velvet curtains with fringed valances. The windows nailed shut. The chandeliers in calico bags, grey and lumpy and bulbous as wasp-nests. One waited and waited, so often and so long, in the dining-room or a drawing-room or a music-room or a bedroom or even in the kitchen, that one became familiar with the objects and the atmosphere. In each room someone waited. And the two old ladies came and went between them, arranging the deals. Buyers and sellers never saw each other. No doubt the old ladies took the biggest profit, but nobody did badly who had patience.

Socks, twelve pairs of, whisky, pens, watches, wool-tweed a bale of, one overcoat. How many bars for the overcoat? Wait. A cut-glass vase on a painted cloth in the middle of the oval table had grey dust in the bottom. Things taken no notice of, no longer admired or used. As though the ladies were only tenanting lives which their former selves had built and owned.

Sixty bars for the overcoat? Very well, I'll take it.

The cold air of the street was welcome then. A thick white light. Agitated grey river, grey light-stained river. Harsh rattle and sparks of the trams. Hungry intent faces, mufflers across mouths as if people were deliberately gagging themselves. Once, a man standing on a bridge, his bare red-raw hands held out in front of him like a sleep-walker: a cap so low over his eyes he could surely not see, and its flaps tied down over his ears, and a muffler across his mouth – I have seen no evil, heard no evil, spoken no evil, but what have I *done?* A cloud on others' spirits as on the mountains compressing the town. Pigeons, grey flocks of. Sorrows, other people's. For oneself there was a new warm overcoat, and one knew where one could go and buy Russell on Einstein in the original English.

And then there was still one bar of cigarettes left over.

'Ach, Konrad! Is that you?' the old man would call from his study, putting on surprise, when he'd been watching from the window, craving what he would not ask for – 'You've brought cigarettes for me? That is very lucky!'

Konrad would reach round the door, drop the bar of ten packets on the desk without glancing at his father and retreat without a word.

'I must pay you back!' – the old man hurrying out into the hall and following him to the foot of the stairs, brandishing a few useless Reichsmarks, pretending that these cigarettes were some sort of extra ration that his son was somehow regularly awarded by the new authorities. As if he were deaf, the son would go on up, to his room at the top of the house, with his new book.

There had always been English books at home, belonging to his mother, who had gone to school for a time in Sussex. He and his sister and two brothers had been brought up to speak English by a nursery-governess named Miss Baldwin, who claimed relationship with the Prime Minister of Great Britain. She had never learned to speak German well, but had gone home in nineteen thirty-nine very reluctantly, having become so fond of the children and their mother.

Konrad's mother was stern and practical, but witty and intelligent. She was much younger than his father and, the adult Konrad realised, scornful of him. At this time she used her cleverness at cards which she played twice a week, with ladies who came in from the country. Their debts were paid in eggs, chickens, ducks, potatoes, which stocked the otherwise empty larder of the Reitzger house in Handschuhsheim, though occasionally Frau Reitzger had to part with pieces of her family silver. Her books were mostly novels, some poetry. Her son had no use for them any more. Nobody had. And they were less likely to recover value one day than the silver was.

The old man, home all day now with nothing to do but complain, had always enjoyed food and wine. He had kept a good cellar before the war, and had tried to teach Konrad about wines. And the boy had been interested enough, but found that his father could make any subject boring. Now he was boring them all with his complaints. His children not only refused to sit and listen in the hour after dinner, but Konrad, always the

most recalcitrant of them, wouldn't even come to the dinner table. When
he was in the house at all he kept to his own room. And 'the Lord knew
where he got to the rest of the time,' old Reitzger groused to any of his
other children who might be provoked into answering.

But he did know where Konrad got to.

Visitors, of whom there were few enough, but at least the farmers'
wives – 'not unrespectable women' he would have it known – who came
to play skat with his wife, would be told: 'My son is working for the
Americans, you know. Yes, I arranged – that is to say, I encouraged him
to offer his assistance to the officers –'

To his son he said: 'A waiter! With your education. With that science
prize you won. Surely you can get yourself a better job than that. Have
you spoken to the right person at the right level?'

The son would mount the stairs away from the voice, shut the door on
it. His room contained nothing but a bed, a table, a chair and a bookcase.
There had been a wardrobe which he'd moved out on to the landing.
Bare floor. No heater: though he would leave his door open at night to
let in the warmer air rising from the rooms below. Konrad thought of
himself as an ascetic scholar, cleanly occupied with science, the opposite
of his father who was weak, soft, ineffectual, a sensualist. He could imagine
how his father would behave in the Club with all those women: the coarse
jokes, the bottom-slapping. Of course his mother must despise such a
man.

– About whom, however, there was something elusive. What had he
now to be so proud about? He still strutted, he still tried to dictate – the
useless, snobbish ignorant old ninny! Konrad dismissed him from his
thoughts to concentrate on algebra.

The time for real study came at last. – But on the very first day, the
shock of the bodies in the tank. Of course he had not allowed that to
deflect him from his intention of studying Medicine. Not, at least, until
he was sure, and reassured by all his teachers, that his talent was really for
Mathematics and theoretical Physics after all.

'Mathematics!' old Reitzger had protested, peevish because he had not
been consulted, and barely informed. 'What is the use of Mathematics?
It never earned a living at the best of times!'

But he wasted his breath, and he knew it.

The two men on the horse swayed through the valley.

'What do you call those big birds?'

'That bird? In my language? We call him i-Hem. It is the noise he makes. It is good that he is here – he brings the rain.'

Soon Reitzger wanted to change the position of his dangling legs, shift the weight of his shoulder-hung bag from left hip to right, but instead sought distraction. He asked, 'Are you a chief?'

'No sir. But I am a chief's son.'

'Will you be Chief when your father dies?'

'My father has many sons. My personally becoming Chief is a matter only of possibility.'

'Do you want to be Chief?'

'I would be glad to have the opportunity to govern my people. Or rather, let me say, to help them in the government of themselves. You understand, that is a different thing from being Chief of a people under the government of foreigners?'

The foreigner asked, in his direct way, 'For the sake of power? Or because you wish the good of your people?'

'That,' Walter granted, 'is an important question. It is a necessary question that a man must ask himself. And I can answer it. I say, because I wish the good of my people.'

'I've heard that the Government talks of letting this land of yours become self-governing.'

' "Self-governing"? Now please, I ask you for your opinion sir, as a man of the world. What sort of freedom will we get? All the big country – it will be their Republic. They say that soon – five years, ten – it will be their Republic. No more English Kings and Queens over the water. They will divide it. Yes sir. We must live in the parts they call our "homelands". But they will be our guardians, because they say we are like children and not yet civilized enough to look after ourselves. Paternalism, Mr Reitzger. I have just been to see a white father. He told me he knows better than I do what is good for my son. He does not mean good for my son, of course. My son Johnjohn is a big man already among my people, although he is only young like you, Mr Reitzger. The white fathers fear Johnjohn because my people listen to him and believe what he says. So they send him far from his land of the Transkei, far away among strangers.'

'What does Johnjohn say?'

'He says, this division of the land of which the white fathers speak, it will not at all be equal. They are very few and have very much land. Very good land, where the rain falls. We are very many and will have little. Look, Mr Reitzger. Look all about. Look down there, at those big holes in the earth.'

They had come out between the narrowing hills, on to a winding road along a ridge. The land dropped away on either side, dry rocky hill after hill to both horizons, where the red of earth met the blue of sky. An ox as thin as if constructed of sticks grazed the margin of the road. There seemed to be no other grass in the land, in all the billowing dark plush of dust.

Walter pointed with his crop, a wide-armed gesture.

'Dongas, that is all we are rich in, sir. Look at our cattle. Are your cattle in Europe like that, sir? They say it is our bad farming which makes the dongas. Look there on that hill – that is where the government agricultural expert showed us how to plough. Last September month. Where did the seed go? What will be the harvest? You can see the furrows but you cannot see the crop. The man said, do it this way and when the rain comes your crop will not be washed away. The soil will not be washed away. But where was the rain, sir? Where was the rain?'

'Yes, I see.'

They proceeded for a while in silence, through the barren but beautiful land. Only the deepening light enriching the red hills.

'Not even,' Reitzger enquired, 'the hope of freedom then?'

'No hope? How can you say that? How can a people live without hope of freedom?'

'How then?'

'Men can live without hope for themselves if they can have hope for their children. We hope for good land, and we hope for freedom. Perhaps we must have freedom before we have good land.'

'How will you get it?'

'Ah Mr Reitzger sir, we have much to learn. Now we will rest for a short time.'

They dismounted in the shade. The African stood looking over his plains. The European sat against a thin tree trunk, his knees bent, an ache in his thighs.

'If your friend Mr Schwallendorf,' Walter said, 'had been my teacher when I was a boy, I would have asked him to teach me German. Do you know why? Because if any man has anything to teach you that you do not know you should try to learn it from him. Europeans have very much they can teach us Africans. What they know makes them very strong. Very powerful. So we must learn from them.'

'I think so too, that one must learn whatever one can,' the European said.

A pair of small black birds dipped and went. What were they called?
Beans dangled on the trees. What sort of tree was it? Pink-spotted seeds
lay scattered in the shade. Were they edible? The sun bloomed as a poppy.
The earth-holes brimmed with shadows. They mounted again and proceeded. Reitzger dozed and woke, to find that his head was pillowed on
the warm wet yellow back of the big African. He felt too sleepy to lift his
head. He had dozed like this on the back of his grandfather, who had
carried the infant Konrad up and down in the shade of his garden when
the boy had had his terrible headaches, which the doctors had said he
might grow out of, and which he had in fact seldom suffered from in the
last ten years or so. Again he shut his eyes, and again he woke. Red of
earth and red of sky were infusing each other until their meeting-line
could no longer be distinguished. Slept again, woke again. The sun was
on a level with his own bent head. An orange disc sunk into, and cutting,
as the horse jerked up and down, like a round saw, through the red earth.
And slept again.

'Mr Reitzger, we are here.' The man's voice resonated through his back.

The horse had stopped.

Dark hills. Big bulging stars and splinters of stars, the alien configura-
tions. Orange window-lights from a house on a hill, the shapes of huts
dancing in firelight on one another.

He climbed stiffly down.

From among the stars Walter bent down and held out his hand.

'It was my pleasure, Mr Reitzger,' he said.

'It is good you have come to visit me.'

They were sitting facing each other, on flat-topped stones.

'I came,' Reitzger corrected, 'to find out what is causing the smell.'

'I hope you are well sir.'

'I am well. I have been living further from the smell than you. I am
surprised it has not made you sick.'

'I found it very bad at first, but now I am used to it. And it is diminishing, I think?'

'I came to find out.'

'Ah,' Walter said, not 'why', but perhaps Reitzger thought he had, or
meant to. So he answered, 'It is always interesting to know what is the
cause of something.'

'And you have completed your investigations? You know what is the
cause?'

'Yes. I know that the cause is the boiling of a horse.'
'The curiosity is satisfied sir?'
'It would be interesting also to know *why* the horse is being boiled.'
'Ah.'

Walter's eyes were bloodshot. So were the others, of the men and women and children who came and went near the stranger, looking at him but not stopping. It seemed that everybody's business took him along this route past Walter's hut.

'You will drink some beer with me, Mr Reitzger?'

Reitzger bent his face to the stuff in the tin; tipped it until it showed yellowish white, and smelt it. Not too bad. Nothing like the smell from the horse-cauldron. He glanced at Walter, who was watching him, and as he looked up Walter said, 'I drink to the coming of the rains.'

'The rains,' Reitzger agreed, and tasted the stuff. Gritty, flaky, sour.

'Do you like the taste of our beer, Mr Reitzger? It is different from yours, is it not?'

'It is completely different!'

'Do you like it?'

'No.'

Walter laughed. Perhaps he enjoyed the man's candour. Or perhaps he intended to tease him. 'Some white men are afraid to drink it. They are afraid that we brew it with harmful or disgusting ingredients.'

'And do you?'

'No sir!'

'Where is your horse?'

'My horse? *Ukuthula?* Mr Reitzger!'

'Where is he?'

'My horse? You think I would kill my horse? I will tell you how much I have paid for my horse. Six cows, Mr Reitzger. It is more than some men give for their wives. *U-ku-thu-la.* It means Peace, Mr Reitzger. What is that in your language?'

'*Der Friede.* But why are you boiling the horse?'

'*Derfriede.* That horse,' Walter said, 'died. One, two weeks ago, he died.'

'Two weeks ago? Where was he found?'

'He died here, near here, on the grass beside the road, where he was eating.'

'Why?'

Walter shrugged. 'He was old.'

'He died a natural death?'

'Yes, sir.'

'And then?'

'And then what, Mr Reitzger? What is "and then" for a horse after he has died?'

'What did they do with him? They weren't boiling him the day you brought me here. It started up the next night, the smell. Had he just been left lying about?'

'No sir, Mr Reitzger. He was du-ly *buried*.'

'Buried.'

'Yes sir. Buried in the earth. And now I am going to ask you a question if you will permit.'

'Go ahead.'

'You say it is only out of interest that you have come to see what is the cause of the smell?'

'That is so.'

'I see.'

'You and your friend received a visitor this afternoon, I believe.'

'A man came. I did not meet him.'

'You did not have the pleasure of meeting the Commissioner of the District? The Grootbaas? Meneer B. M. Pik, *Esquire*?'

'No.'

'But your friend has told you what an important gentleman is this Grootbaas?'

'No.'

'Ah. So you are making these enquiries entirely on your own behalf.'

'Yes. I have come only because I wanted to come. But Mr Schwallendorf has also been disturbed by the smell. He would also like to know about it.'

'We have no wish to disturb Meneer Schwallendorf. On the contrary sir. He has been our friend for many years. We have much respect for Meneer Schwallendorf. And poor Meneer Pik – he has such a weak nose! He would like to know about us here in the village. He asks us questions, questions, questions, all the time. But he does not believe what we tell him. He believes only what he can understand. And what does Meneer Pik understand? He understands that kaffirs are liars. He knows we are dumb kaffirs and liars. He knows. But you are a visitor, Mr Reitzger.' (Was there a slight mockery now in the way he said the name?) 'You may come, you may ask. I will tell you about the horse. And please – you will inform Meneer the Teacher. He will be very pleased to know why we are boiling the horse. We say to each other, we must listen to what the Teacher tells us. He is a white man who knows many things we do not. He knows how we must plough our fields. He tells us and we do not listen, and when the rain comes it will wash away our crops. We are dumb kaffirs, so we must listen. He tells us about hygiene. He tells us how we must boil to kill the goggas that jump a sickness from one to another. So maybe this horse did not die from just being old. Maybe he had a bad sickness. We must dig up this horse and boil him. That is what we say to each other. I am giving you this information, Mr Reitzger, and if you will tell Meneer the Teacher he will be very pleased.'

And the 'dumb kaffir' reached for his beer. The matriculant whose spelling of English was exemplary, and who believed one must learn from the white man, learn from any man whatever he could teach! He drank deep, but kept his eyes on his confused visitor, and when he lowered the pot, he laughed. The laughter spread. Reitzger looked about at the villagers, who had stopped at last and were all showing their teeth. As Walter laughed his eyes narrowed and almost disappeared, but now and then as he opened his mouth for a loud guffaw, his eyes opened too, very wide, to take in the sight of his serious visitor, and then shut deep in their folds again as his shoulders shook and his hands thumped his knees. He stopped at last. The others too.

Reitzger did not mind the mockery as much as the disappointment – in the explanation, but also more importantly in Walter himself.

'It's sheer nonsense,' Schwallendorf spluttered. 'They can't have gathered from me that they must dig up dead animals and boil them for reasons of hygiene! If it's some dreadful medicine they're brewing, I only hope they pour it on the lands and not down their own throats. Well, Pik will have to make what he can of it. He's suspicious enough to invent some fantastic reason for anything.'

All the windows had been shut against the smell. But the house was unbearably stuffy. So Schwallendorf opened the two leaves of the dining-room door, leaving the screen closed against the insects which flashed out of the darkness into the light and left bits of their wings and bodies stuck to the wire. A glow on the hill opposite and below marked the village, the source of the air's sepsis, and the persistent doubt.

'They and I,' Schwallendorf mourned. 'We built the first school-house together, with our own hands. I worked with them, I didn't just give the orders. We made it out of galvanised iron. Just a great shed, yes?

You should have heard it when the rain came down. Like being inside a drum! We used to try and sing above the noise.'

Schwallendorf swallowed his whisky and looked down glumly upon the red glow on the other hill, his cheeks hanging heavy as if from the habit of disappointment.

Reitzger wanted to ask him about Walter. But he did not want to be questioned about him. So he did not even mention his name.

'But there must be a reason,' he insisted. It bothered him more than it did Schwallendorf, who was soon asking him, as he had on the previous nights, about what it was like 'at home' nowadays. But he seldom listened to what Reitzger told him. Instead he would interrupt to explain how it used to be, as though it had not only been better then, but right. He didn't ask about the war, not Reitzger's war, though he did mention that his father had been killed, as Feuchthaber's had too, in France in nineteen-seventeen.

But tonight, as he drank more, he began to describe the past differently. A childhood cold, obscure, in a greyness of weather and closed houses, snow and rain; shame of body, guilt of sin; autocratic, devout parents; joylessness. And then he had come here – to a four-roomed house on a hill and a piece of ground in the valley where his school was yet to be built: but to a country which seemed new from the Creator's hand, sounding out, scented, shot-from-the-dye! And tall people, in bright blue cloth, riding over the hills. He had succeeded in making friends with them. Why had they become his enemies? Why had his achievements rotted away?

'From Ezekiel – do you know – ?' His hand shook as he poured more whisky. ' "Wearing clothes of blue, captains and rulers, all of them desirable young men, horsemen riding upon horses." '

'Goodnight, Herr Schwallendorf!' Konrad said.

'Goodnight, Max!'

Another sentimental old fool, the young man thought. Feuchthaber had certainly sent him to this man only because of where he was, not what he was. Feuchthaber could not have remembered, perhaps, just what his friend was really like. Or had he lost respect for him – Reitzger – since he'd had to leave the University after the currency reform, and take up journalism? No! Feuchthaber knew that he had every intention of going back and taking up the struggle again, with relativity, and the quantum. It was hard to be young, and to know what potential you had in you, while no one else knew it and you had to be patient, and prove it.

And yet he could not think of a reason for the boiling of the horse.

He left Schwallendorf, who was still drinking; and as he lay in the dark in his rondavel he could hear the old boy bumping about, still muttering to himself. '. . . *alle junge, liebliche Gesellen, Reisige, so auf Rossen ritten.*'

Reitzger felt the sort of throbbing which used to come before a headache, but he fell asleep, and dreamt of his father.

Kurt Reitzger had had some of his wealth restored to him when his shares in the company, which had been wound up after the war, became valuable again as new companies were made from remnants of the old. But the gloom which had settled on him did not leave him. It had started when his chief, Friedrich Kuhn, had been tried for war-crimes at Nürnberg. Old Reitzger seemed to have been disturbed both by the fear that he too might be called to answer for having worked in the department that first made and patented the Zyklon-B crystals for the gassings in the extermination camps, and a strange humiliation that he was not considered important enough. Or so his son had interpreted him.

The old man died one night in his sleep. In the morning, in the darkened room, by candlelight, the son reviewed the father, whose skin was beige now and blobbed with blue. Konrad had waited to feel what emotions would come to be instantly quenched – remorse, regret, guilt, or painful realisation of his own mortality: but all that came was a thought, in English (a language the old man had never spoken well): 'Old Gorgonzola – there he lies!'

Now, in his dream not his memory, his father was being lifted out of the bed by his mother and Feuchthaber. They heaved him off and away in his crumpled white nightshirt. Then Konrad himself, against his own will, protesting but compelled, climbed into the bed, laid his head on the pillows and was covered with the eiderdown. The stench filled his nose, his whole head, which swelled as if to split; and it went down his throat into his lungs to choke him.

He woke suddenly, fully and perfectly understanding what the boiling of the horse was for.

Exactly what it had achieved – that was what it was for. It made a stench, and the stench kept Pik away, because Pik suffered from an oversensitive nose. So someone or something was there which Pik must not find. Something which, however, Schwallendorf might come looking for on Pik's orders. So the secret must be of a kind which Schwallendorf would probably not betray to Pik. And the secret of who or what this was which Pik must not discover in the village was clear to Reitzger beyond all doubt.

In the morning, before Schwallendorf was up or the table laid for breakfast in the largest rondavel, Reitzger went out through the front door, not letting the screen-door bang behind him. It was past six o'clock, but as he went down into the valley he could hear the cocks of the village still crowing as lustily as if it were dawn. The cool air was spoilt by the smell, which had not lessened much if at all. And as on the evening before, it was worse in the village itself.

The bare-breasted women were stirring pots over fires. Again they watched him pass. There were a few men about, dressed only in loin-cloths and blankets worn as shawls. Some of them followed him at a distance as he made for Walter's hut. In front of it there was a young woman feeding a fire with sticks.

'Is Walter awake yet?' he asked her.

The girl looked up at him and then returned her attention to the fire. The men who had followed him drew nearer.

'You want me, Mr Reitzger?' Walter came out, dressed in trousers only.

'Yes.'

'You have something you want to ask me, or tell me?'

'Both to ask and to tell.'

'You still wish to know why the horse is being boiled?'

'No. I know why. That is what I have to tell you.'

Walter said nothing. Everyone was still.

'At least,' Reitzger went on, 'that is part of what I have to tell you. I must also say that I shall not tell anyone else, not even Meneer Schwallendorf.'

Still Walter said nothing. The girl watched the fire. But the other men, young and old, edged forward, and more appeared between the huts on either side.

Reitzger raised his voice so that all might hear him. 'Now I shall ask my question. Walter, which of these young men is your son, Johnjohn, who has been endorsed out of the Transkei?'

Nobody laughed at him this time.

'I believe,' Walter said, 'that your curiosity may be satisfied without the answer to that question, Mr Reitzger.'

His curiosity, yes. And his need to solve this problem. But the great problem which the solution revealed, Walter's problem, Johnjohn's problem, the problem of all these people and millions more, that was not within his power to solve even in theory. Men like Pik made such problems, out of beliefs which Reitzger scorned: beliefs he was all too familiar with: beliefs which stank much worse than a dead beast.

'In the end,' he said loudly but sadly, looking round at the men, 'you'll have to fight.'

'We know that, Mr Reitzger,' Walter said. 'When we met, you and I, sir, I told you we had been enemies once. The truth is, sir, that we were enemies still, we are enemies now, and we will be enemies for a long time. Sir.'

'You and I? Why? I am not your enemy. I am the enemy of Pik and what you call the white fathers.'

'You are white. I am black. That is enough reason, Mr Reitzger.'

'What nonsense!' Reitzger said, the way Miss Baldwin used to say it. But that way was not strong enough. '*Stinking* nonsense,' he shouted. 'The sort of nonsense Pik believes.' He turned round, glaring at the faces round him. 'You'll rot your noses with stinking ideas like that. You – you'll be another Pik, Walter, another Pik, that's all.'

He walked away. The men parted to let him through. He walked on to the edge of the village, then he tried to run, stumbling among rocks and tufts, slipping on stones, down and up again, to reach the other survivor of the spreading, rising, inescapable stench, in the ark on the top of the hill.

Diary of a Polesitter

JOAN JACOBY

Alright, laugh. Who cares about a lot of farm kêrels? That's what they are — farm kêrels. Let them laugh it doesn't bug me. But wait till I get the bread then we'll see who's laughing. Some firm — a soap outfit — is giving a money prize, a big one, for the advert. All I've got to do is break the last cat's record. And I have to say this firm's soap's what kept me up here, or helped to. All that bread just for sitting up a pole. Just sitting around. That's what I do most of the time anyway. Work's for cart horses. Like some ou said — don't remember who — there are cart horses and race horses. People he meant. Types. So that's why I'm here. To break the record and make some bucks. And I'm writing this diary too. It'll be printed when I break the record and I'll be famous, and rich too.

Well I better write this diary proper. Put down everything that happens every day. Ja well, Monday.

MONDAY: Had breakfast. Got Mike's cafe to send it up. Took their time. Thought they'd forgotten me. Pulled it all up in a basket on a rope. Porridge and eggs and bacon and all that jazz. It was cold. Sis. When I told them they said why didn't I cook it myself. Me cook? Not a chance. There was quite a crowd when they sent it up but they got tired of making like they were so clever and laughing and went away. Man it's lekker up here really. You can see everything and all what people are doing. There were some ous digging up the road. For pipes. I like watching people working. Makes me feel kind of great them working and sweating in the sun and me just watching. Like I'm a king. The sun was hot as hell. I was sweating too. Took my shirt off.

12 O'CLOCK: Had lunch. Bread and cheese and tinned fish. Did it

myself. With tomato sauce. I can see Joe's Bar from here. It's just on the corner of Market Square. Got hold of some pampoen — a black — to get me some beer but he didn't catch on. I saw Piet Pretorius later. He got me a beer. Lekker. Too many flies up here. And mosquitoes. Got bites. Hell man it itches like crazy.

TUESDAY: Same breakfast but no eggs and bacon. Same lunch only it was bully beef this time. With tomato sauce. Wish the flies would bugger off. Got sunburnt yesterday. Shouldn't have taken off my shirt. Had to stay in the tent till the sun went down. Tent's hot too.

WEDNESDAY: There was a blerry awful storm last night. Nearly blew the tent down. Man it was cold in the rain. Got blerry wet trying to fix it up. Wished I had something hot to eat and hot coffee. Have to light the paraffin stove. Good job there's a pot. Piet gave it to me. He's my pal. Didn't think I'd ever use it but I suppose I'll have to now. Open a tin of stew or something. No cooking. I won't cook. No chance. Coffee isn't cooking.

THURSDAY: More rain. There's a hole in the tent. Stuffed it up with newspaper but it's no good. Have to fix it with plastic if I can get somebody to bring me some.

FRIDAY: Got a cold, Stayed in the sleeping bag all day except to eat some stew. Read comics. Thirty-two days and fourteen hours. Hell man that's a long time. That's what that ou in England did and I've got to beat it. No record no bucks. There's a chap that stayed up in a barrel for thirty-three years. Up the pole. It was in Syria or somewhere like that. Wonder what he did all the time. Must've been nutty. But that was hundreds of years ago, so it doesn't count.

SATURDAY: Had to wash my shirt. On account of tomato sauce. Something to do anyway. Getting fed up. Cold worse. There's a fish and chip shop somewhere. Can smell the fish frying. Making me hungry. It must be somewhere across the street. Hungry all the time. Some buddies came to see me after work. Their work not mine. I don't. They were high but it wasn't beer. Got one of them to buy me some fish and chips. It was lekker man.

SUNDAY: Heard church bells. Wouldn't even mind going to church. Had to clean up the place on account of pigeons crapped all over it. Piet came with some other ous. Asked if I wanted to take a trip. Said I didn't know. Have to think about it. Don't know if it's allowed. Don't want to blow the whole thing.

MONDAY: Constipated like hell. Sitting around all the time. Got to move about they say. Tried to do a few exercises. No good. Have to take some stuff. Tonight. No — morning's better. The carts come at night. Read comics.

TUESDAY: Read comics. Must get someone to find me some more.

WEDNESDAY: Made a calendar. I mean for every day. Did sums. Not good at sums but I worked it out. Fourteen hours not counting the ones when I'm asleep — that's twenty-eight half hours which have thirty minutes each, that's eight hundred and forty minutes which is 50 400 seconds. I cross off the seconds and then the minutes and then the half hours and then the hours. Makes it seem shorter that way. At least I think it does.

THURSDAY: Piet said he could fix me up with a cap, if I wanted it. They all had it — all the ous. Makes you feel great he said. I said alright I'd try it. Hell man it's long. Thirty-two days and fourteen hours. Never had a trip before. I've got to do something or I'll have to pack up. Then I'll lose all that bread. Hell no.

FRIDAY: Had it. A trip. Piet came with a pal I never seen before. Gave it to me. Said I'd . . . better not have . . . too much . . . on a piece of blotting paper he gave me . . . This is a trip . . . Funny. Things are getting . . . big . . . then small . . . and big again . . .

Had to stop. Couldn't write then. Just lay on my back . . . nearly all day. Didn't want to move. Ja man it was wonderful. The trees were hang of a bright green . . . beautiful . . . and big leaves close up . . . I could see the wood. All the marks in the wood. Rings. The colours man . . . wonderful. Greatest thing. Still wonderful now but not so much. Tried to touch the wood . . . it was so close but my hand . . . well it wasn't my hand . . . I mean like it was someone else's hand. I had a bit of a skrik . . . I didn't like that . . . my skin feels rough like a brush . . . The sky was so blue with big clouds coming right here . . . nearly in my face . . . close . . . I can see fish . . . a big crab . . . hell man it's so close and big I have to open my eyes . . . awful . . . There was a lot of noise. Thought it was a plane . . . was a bee. I could hear flies walking. Still a bit high . . . have to stop.

SATURDAY: Lousy. Bloody lousy. Fuckin' lousy. Why doesn't Piet come. Some ous down there going into the bar. Hey! bring me a beer man . . . they don't hear. Won't hear. Thick. Nothing to do. Feel funny.

SUNDAY: Feel better but not much. Thirty-two Volkswagens went past. I counted them. And forty-five chimneys and fifty-two street lights I counted. Now I'm doing motorbikes . . . Why doesn't Piet come? Some ou came to see me. Don't know who he was. Just came up the ladder. Talked a lot of crap. About God and heaven mostly. I didn't listen much. I was thinking about how to get hold of Piet and his pal about a cap.

He went away but he left a couple of books. I went for them. Thought they might be something sexy or even a whodunnit. No chance. One's a Bible and the other's about making things. With wood. Or mostly. Some sort of do-it-yourself I suppose. Crap. Hy is mal. How can I make things up here with no tools and no wood or anything?

MONDAY: Piet came last night. I asked him about his pal — that ou that gave us the cap. Piet said they got him. Put him inside for selling drugs. Now they've all caught a skrik so I won't be able to have a trip. Piet brought some beer and cheese. Said he'd get me some more comics. We drank the beer. Had the cheese. Felt sick.

TUESDAY: Feel better. Got up to boil water for coffee and found bloody ants crawling all over the food and everything. Give me the yirries. Ants. Up here! Well you wouldn't think they'd know — about the food and all that. I mean, can they smell it? Do ants smell? I mean can they? Took a long time getting them off and cleaning everything up. Sat down and tried to think how to keep the ants off the food. Remembered someone saying you put a basin of water and pile it up with bricks. In the water. Then you put the food on top of the bricks which I haven't got. Piled up tins of jam and soup and put a tray on top and then the bread and marge and sugar and things like that. Slim. Now I can't wash because it's my wash basin. Have to take everything off to wash and put it back after. No dice. No washing. For now anyway. Made coffee. Drank it. Had bread and marge. Would've opened a tin of sardines but it was too much of a graft. When I went outside the tent there was a long line of ants running along the edge of the platform. Just going to stamp on them when I saw something bloody interesting. Some of them were pushing pieces of bread — big crumbs not pieces really, big for ants that is. Quite heavy they must've been — bigger than them. It was so bloody marvellous I had to squat down and watch them, but I killed them after. Man I can't have them getting into all my stuff. Yirra. Fancy them crawling all the way up the pole like that. Helluva clever. To know I mean.

WEDNESDAY: Woke up early. Not even properly light. Lay and listened to birds. Funny thing. Never noticed before but some were calling and some answering. Different sounds — lots of them. Thought all birds sounded the same. Except ducks of course and turkeys. But they're different. Listened for a long time, till it got light. Lots of birds up here. In the trees. Watched some making nests. You wouldn't think birds could be so clever, man. I mean birds can't think can they? And still they know how to make nests. These ous were all making the same nest — I mean they were working on one big one with lots of holes in underneath so they can get out and in. Doors. Wish I had a telescope or some verkykers. Little yellow birds with black on their heads.

I was still watching them when that chap came again — the one that brought the books. He asked me did I like birds and I said I hadn't thought about them before but I liked watching them building nests. He gave me a long spiel about birds and how every kind makes a different sort of nest and wasn't nature wonderful. And then he told me the names of lots of birds and what they looked like and the kind of nests they made. He knew a lot. Man it was quite interesting. Never thought I could listen to that sort of thing. He said if I wanted to see more birds I must feed them. You know, put bread out and fruit and things like that and water for them to bath in. The best is to have a bird table he said. I said what's that and he said just like this thing I've got — a platform on a pole — only much smaller of course. Said I could easily make it myself. I said how and he said did I look at the books he brought. I said, well, no. I felt kind of ashamed but he wasn't cross about it. Just said I would find it in the one about making things. When I asked how he thought I could make anything if I didn't hàve any wood he promised he'd bring me some. I told him what's the good anyway I haven't any tools but he said he'd bring tools too. So I said alright I'd look at the book. Then he smiled and went away. Wouldn't mind talking to him again.

SATURDAY: Had no time to write my diary. Been too busy making things. Had a look at this book. Man it's full of instructions for making all kinds of things. And it's quite easy because they tell you everything and there are drawings to show you how. I made a bird table. With wood Lucas brought me. That's his name, this ou that brought the books. He brought tools too like he said and nails and screws and glue even. I said it must have cost quite a packet and I'd better pay for some but he said not to worry it was a present. The wood he got for nothing anyway — thick pieces of plank — from a packing case. He said there's a scrapyard where you can get all sorts of things if you look — for only a few cents too and some things they let you have for free.

Lucas helped me to start. Then he went away but he said he'd come in a couple of days to see how I was getting on. The bird table didn't take long really. Except I hit my thumb with the hammer and it was helluva sore. I couldn't do anything for a while until it got better. Man I was mad because I was getting on fine. Anyway it's not bad now and I finished the job yesterday. It's a bit rough and sommer crooked but the birds aren't going to mind. It's even got a piece going round the edge for stopping crumbs and things falling off.

SUNDAY: Piet came today. He asked if there was anything he could bring me and I said yes some bird seed. He looked at me like I'd gone crazy or something. Said perhaps he'd better get a doctor because maybe it was too much sun. I said no just get the bird seed. And some bone meal. Some birds like bone meal — like bokmakieries. I showed him my bird table. He didn't know what it was for till I told him about it and this Lucas ou and what he told me. Piet said he'd bring the bird seed tomorrow. For now I'm using crumbs of bread and bits of what's left over from my food. Fruit too. He came again, Lucas did. He brought a bird book too with pictures. And more wood. He was very pleased with my bird table. Said I must put a dish of water too, as birds like to wash in it. I put it out and we sat very quiet for a bit and watched. Then they came. All kinds of birds. Man it was lovely watching them splashing and shaking their wings and feathers. Then we put some fruit on the table and even little pieces of meat. For the shrikes he said. Shrikes like meat. He showed me some of the pictures of birds in the book and he said I'd soon learn about them and their names too.

MONDAY: Making a table. For me not the birds. Just small — there's no room for anything big — to eat on and read and write. It'll be better than on my knees. I want to make a box for my tools when I get some more wood. I never thought I could like work ever but I'm liking doing this. Like anything.

TUESDAY: Piet brought the bird seed and some bone meal. He still says I'm nuts. He stood and scratched his head when he saw the wood and nails and things lying all over the place. Then he went. Said it might be catching. I said what and he said work. He didn't want to get mal too. That's what he said.

WEDNESDAY: The time goes so quick now I even forgot to cross out the days and hours and minutes on my calendar. Yirra! Lucas came again. I told him I didn't think it would be hard to beat that ou's record now. I could stay up here for a long time. Then I'll get that bread. He asked me what I was going to do with it when I get it and I said I'd give it a jawl — make like a good time and all that jazz. I'd get pissed to start with. He looked a bit sad. Said it wasn't going to last long like that and I could do something more useful with it. He said I'd better do some thinking about it. I said O.K. but first I'd get pissed. Then he said he had to go and he wouldn't see me for a while. But he said he'd come back and he was sure I'd have things to show him and tell him.

THURSDAY: Finished table. Worked all day on it yesterday and this morning too. Was getting on O.K. till I kicked over the glue. Was nearly finished but I couldn't move it on account of one leg got stuck to the floor of platform. With glue. Had to cut off some so it was shorter than the others. Didn't want to make a new leg so I cut some off the others too. Now they're all the same but the table's too low. Have to cut the legs shorter of my camp stool to fit under except the seat's torn anyway. Suppose I'll have to make a new stool. But now I've got that piece of leg stuck up on the platform. Looks blerry silly there doing nothing. Tried to get it off but it won't come loose. Have to watch it or I'll fall over it. Fell over it.

FRIDAY: Busy. Made a new stool — low to fit the table. Took all yesterday afternoon. Got to plane it some more but it looks sommer lekker. It was much easier than the table. Just a flat piece of plank across and two flat sides instead of legs.

SATURDAY: Too many pigeons up here. They chase away the birds. And dirty. Crap in the water. Have to keep putting in clean water. This book says how to feed the birds with bird seed in a bottle so they can't get too much. You put the seeds in the bottle — one like for jam and you turn it upside down on the bird tray in a dish. You have to put your hand over the hole first while you turn it over or all the seed'll fall out. I tried. Nearly lost all the bird seed. Then you let just a little out and when they've finished that you let out some more. Clever, hey? I saw some birds fly under the platform. They stayed there and more came so I lay down and put my head over the edge to look. They flew away then. They'd been making a nest out of mud. Man it looked so tricky. They were swallows I found out in my bird book. It says swallows always like to make their nests in corners like on the verandah and under gutterings specially. And thatch too. I hope they come back and finish it.

SUNDAY: Piet came this afternoon with some of the kêrels. They were full of beer. They brought some more with them and we all drank some. Then they started laughing and having a punch-up and they tried to moer me but Piet told them to bloody cut it out. When they saw the things I've been making they were verbaas. Then they noticed that piece of wood — the stuck up leg from the table — and they asked what it was for. I didn't want to tell them what I did so I tried to think quick of something and I said it was a piece of a seat I was starting to make. They thought it was funny. Rolled about on the floor laughing and said it must be bloody comfy and why didn't I sit on it now and show them. Pissed out of their heads. I was glad when they went. Piet said he'd come again without the gang.

MONDAY:Had a big storm last night. Hell there was plenty thunder and lightning too. I got a skrik like anything. Did my nut. Lots of rain — buckets. When the noise stopped I heard like somebody crying outside. Took my torch and went to see. There was a little black kleintjie all by himself under this tree near the platform. I shouted to him what's the matter but he wouldn't answer. Then I told him to climb up the ladder — I pointed with my torch to show him. Shame. Poor little bugger was soaked standing there in the rain. Couldn't get him to move at first but I went on talking nice to him and then he came up.

I asked him what he was doing out there all alone but he didn't answer. Didn't understand I could see. I couldn't understand him either. So I had to make signs — point to things. Made him take off all his clothes so I could dry them. Didn't have much on — just a shirt and pants and no shoes even. He was so cold he was shaking all over so I wrapped him up in a blanket. Made some hot soup out of a tin and he drank it up. Must've got lost. I let him sleep on the floor in the tent in the blanket. He was only tired, hey. Out like a light. I went off too but I woke up again because of so much noise from the thunder. The whole tent was flapping because there was lots of wind too. Got up to see if it was alright. Had to look outside with my torch and it lit up on something black and shiny out by that tree. Had another look. It was somebody with an umbrella and I saw it was my friend Lucas standing there in the rain. I called him. I wanted him to come up. He came up but he said he wasn't going to stay. He only wanted to see if I was alright. Then he said goodnight and went down the ladder again.

I couldn't go to sleep for a long time afterwards. Just lay there on my back and thought about him and some of the things he said. I must have fallen asleep because the next thing I woke up and the sun was shining. That swart kleintjie was lying there looking at me. Kind of a lekker kid.

I got up and cooked some porridge — oats. Instant. I don't dig that stuff much but it was easy to make and quick and its warm. Fills you up. And coffee. That was lekker. Then I went outside and there was a hang of a bloody marvellous bird sitting on top of my stuck table leg. I kept blerry quiet. I was afraid it would fly away if I moved but it stayed there for quite a few minutes. Then I had to move I was so stiff from being bent over all the time. My legs were helluva sore and my back. It flew off then. I found out later in my book it was called a crested barbet. There's a picture of it and it looked just like that.

The kleintjie went off when his clothes were dry. Hope he's alright. He said something in his taal. I don't know what it was but I suppose it was goodbye and thanks. I gave him my stool. He kept touching it. Seemed to like it so I let him have it. He smiled so big he showed all his teeth. When he went I got thinking about my friend again. Lucas I mean. And I thought I must do something for him to show him like I want to thank him. Because if he hadn't come up and brought me those books and wood and everything I wouldn't've had something to do and I don't know if I'd have been able to stick it out.

So I thought I'd make him a bird table — a hanging bird table you can put in a tree or just hang it on a piece sticking out from a pole. It's so cats can't get on. And pigeons. They don't like something moving.

TUESDAY: Worked on the bird table — the one for Lucas. Worked on it solid so's I can get it finished quick in case he comes soon. It didn't take long. Think I'll make another one for me too. I'm sure he's going to like this.

That soap firm sent an ou to see me. The outfit that's giving this prize money. Said he wanted to see if I was still up here but I suppose it was just an excuse to come. They wanted to be sure I was going to say all those things about their soap. Like it kept the mosquitoes off and the flies and all that crap. And how I couldn't've stayed up if it wasn't for their soap. But I said it didn't keep off the flies and mosquitoes. I just sommer couldn't say it because it isn't true, man. There was a bit of a row and I thought I'd really done it in this time. Then I said if they'd put something in the soap like the stuff in the fly spray I could say it did keep them off. He said they couldn't do that now because it was too late — the soap was already made. So I said well just spray some on the soap and give me some — some soap. Then I could say it did keep off the insects and things. And they could put it in the next lot of soap they were making. So he said he'd tell them to and I said alright I'll say it.

Because then it would be true. It would help anyway.

Yirra! When I think I bloody nearly lost it after sticking it all this time. Funny though. It hasn't seemed all that bad. I've kind of quite enjoyed it really specially now I've got plenty things to do. Seems I could stay here for ever now. Well not really for ever. Anyway I can beat that record now. Easily. Even perhaps that ou in Syria that stayed up for thirty-three years in a barrel. But not me — not in a barrel I mean. No dice. Anyway what good's all that bread going to be to an ou in a barrel?

MONOLOGUE FOR DANNY

BARNEY SIMON

CAPE TOWN is fantastic! Whew, it's so open—all that sky, man, and those rocks and those mountains and that sea—you can get it cold and hot, the wind too—that South-Easter can burn! But you know what a scene is, man, it's like the seasons. Spring is beautiful, summer's fantastic, autumn's getting heavy and winter's just dead—the people find each other and it's like forever, then Jill goes to London and someone hikes up to Joburg and then things fall apart and that's what I mean by winter and dying. Even the clubs die, man—Spurs, Crazy Horse, 69 ...

We had this commune—87 Kloof Road, just over the old clothes shop, seven guys and four chicks. Three of us were working, but it was just share and share alike, man—even the chicks—and no hassles, you know what I mean, just share and share alike... And those chicks could cook, man! This one cat, Desi, he could cook too, man, he used to dive for this bloody crayfish, bring it home in his old army kit-bag and stick it in the pot still kicking and then he used to make this sauce with lemon juice and that—shit, man, I'm bloody salivating.

But like I said, man, you know how it happens; Jill's old man gives her this ticket for London—I suppose to get her out of the scene—and then, you know, this other chick, Caroline, says she's hiking up to Joburg to see her off, and Desi goes with for the hell of it—and shit, that's three cooks gone, the fourth chick can only boil eggs. And then one of the bastards grinds a groove across my brand new Bowie the day I get it and they tell me not to get heavy and then Davey says it's okay to wear his jeans if I'll only wash them sometime—and then one day, the bath is filthy, man, ball-hairs the lot, and not a bloody rattle in the Vim can. Then we get this message from Desi that the grass is green, and heads are high and there's Angels riding choppers in the streets up north. So I suss it's time to measure truth or fiction and why not hike up and see for myself, and whew ... man, it's all truth, man, all truth—paradise after Bloemfontein.

You ever been there? This cat drops me off in the suburbs, and shit, I'm like a lost soul—even glad to see the fuzz. I say I'm hiking to Joburg and I'm lost and can they tell me the way and they take me to the station and they take everything apart, man, my whole scene was ironed and folded—it's my load of new resolutions—and they throw it around looking for grass and tell me to pick it up and give me all that heavy shit about me and mine and grass and acid and communist plots and like they say, etcetera. Then they kick me out and even the blacks of Bloem won't rap kindly with a cat like me.

Anyhow, therefore, so forth, etcetera—etcetera, there's a word that sounds like death, no oxygen, man, no energy, just a weapon. Anyhow, like I was saying before I began to get semantic—this is the scene, man—Hillbrow: Africa 2001. All these lights, man, and all this noise, all these floating heads! I crashed with this old navy buddy of mine, a kind of semi-cool cat, no grass, no acid, regular graft as a scenery pusher in a theatre, but clean, man, really clean—fold-out bed, sheets, blankets, pillow-case, the lot.

Anyhow, he went to work, and I hit the 'Brow—so turned on by every goddam thing I nearly set the place on fire, man—'strue's God—thirty seconds and I'm dodging Angels. Ten minutes, and I'm sharing an egg-burger at Fontana with a guy as high as Alice, on—'strue's God—heroin! So I suss, so he tells me, and so I believe, you know, the eyes, the scratch, the whole scene. Anyway, he hooks up with me and won't let me go, says I'm his boet, his china, his all-time mate and he gets me walking up and down Highpoint square singing Honky Tonk Woman—my Jagger speciality. And then it strikes me there's a cat parading behind us with Bloemfontein eyes, which leads me to think about fuzz, and the fact that they come khaki-coloured and plain, and maybe he's one of the latter, so I cut free from my boet and china, only to be accosted by a chick in a purple kurta, yellow hair, and a silver dot in the middle of her forehead, asking me if I'm in the mood for music, acid etcetera—which accounts for my first thirty minutes in the 'Brow!

Turns out she comes from Boksburg, Brakpan, Nigel, Springs; used to be an usherette, saleslady, hair-shampooer, manicurist, go-go dancer, Rand Show demonstrator, singer, East Rand Princess, and is studying to be a travel agent for the free trips that go with the job. She takes me to her pad where we share tabs with another cat and chick, whereafter she demonstrates fourteen positions, to which I add six more...

Next evening grazed off a gay at Fontana, double hot-dog, coffee and baklava for dessert—he thought he was onto a good thing, until I started rapping with the Angels outside. This one cat with big biceps asks me if I want to make a delivery, so I say, Why not, and he lifts me onto the back of his 750/4, and suddenly there's forty fucken hearts going, man—Hondas, Triumphs, BMW's—and the whole fucken 'Brow's flattening against walls and clutching poles, and skidding, and screaming and ducking and shouting and apologizing, and we burn down Twist Street there by the park, and—'strue's God—where do we end up? At a Night-Chem! And there's this chick, forty or something, with an orange bee-hive on her head, and she hands over a package and that's our delivery, to the Southern Suburbs. 'Strue's God, man! these guys are as straight as my Auntie Julia's nose, no kidding! We ride in formation making enough thunder to get the whole Southern Suburbs crawling under their beds. The cat with the arms is the king, so we ride in the middle—he shows left and the column to the left goes left, he shows right and the column to the right goes right, like bullets, they're on their way—voop-yaaaah—voop-yaaaah—and six blocks later they're with us again. All this noise, man, all these lights, all this shine, all this leather, so close, man, like through a telephoto lens. Then—and I'm holding on tight—the rap begins. Am I one of these hippies?—Who, me? No I just wear my hair like an Angel! Am I one of these kaffir-boeties? Who, me? No, I'm from the Cape, man, I don't even know a kaffir's colour! Am I one of these acid-heads?—Who, me? Neeaaa! Only weeds I smoke are Texans! Am I one of these intellectual battlers? Man, I'm starting graft tomorrow.

And I tried, man I really did. Got a job in a coffee bar. Lost it. Got a job in a record bar—never took it—whew! my social life kept getting in the way. Let's face it man, Time was not part of creation. The Lord's intentions were sweet, man—he gave us this beautiful tripping sun and all this colour and all this light, and he helps us to get tired so we can dig the dark. What's this twenty-four hour shit—this nine-to-five crap? We're fucking his scene with our shitty guillotines—he meant sweet things, man, good times, for all!

But talking time; it came to pass that times with my buddy got heavy. The sheets turned yellow and were never changed. I lost my key—it wasn't replaced. And when I swopped his three Peter, Paul and Marys for the brand-new Led Zeppellin, thinking I would thereby win his eternal friendship and devotion, I found that I did not. So I joined the space-age gang in Braamfontein: meaning the 'ultimates', what the Philistines call 'hobos'.

Got me a blanket, got me a mattress, and shacked up on the third floor of condemned College Mansions, with a fine view toward the Civic Centre. Lived by candle-light, which is what it's all about, washed at the station, pissed against the plane trees; rapped till dawn with the boys. We shared our sardines, our apricot jam and our Calcutta Cane like brothers, until my three shirts and my takkies somehow skipped the scene.

Went back to the 'Brow after four days, and—I don't know, man: everybody's so fucken straight. And staring. At me. Like I'm special freak set up for the tourists, or something. No, man: stood at Highpoint, leaning against that shoe-shop window and just stared straight back—at those fuck-proof chicks with their long, long legs that ride right up into their arses. At their guys in their clean checked shirts. At their old ladies with their new, true-blue hair. At their daddies in their skin-tight paunches. At the black whores, and the white whores, and the men whores, and the lady whores; at those Houghton chicks in their patched denims that cost them twenty rand, at those little black kids that con the shit out of us all; at the cripples, and the drunks, and the hairies, and the gays—all staring at me.

And then this cat, that one on heroin, is standing in front of me there, and staring at me like the rest of them; and I said Hi, but he didn't remember me, and he asked me for five cents, and I said I'm sorry, and he said Don't be sorry, just give me five cents, it's easier on the heart, man; and I said I know, but I haven't got five cents, and I moved away. But he came after me and he started shouting, he grabbed my shirt, and I said Cool it, and he said Where's five fucking cents, man and I said I don't know, don't ask me, ask one of them don't ask me. And he started shouting: WHERE'S THE SCENE MAN, WHERE'S THE GUYS WHERE'S THE CHICKS WHERE'S THE MUSIC WHERE'S THE SCENE WHERE'S THE CATS WHERE'S THE MUSIC WHERE'S THE SCENE WHERE'S IT WHERE'S IT? And I said I don't know, don't ask me, ask one of them, don't ask me.

THE FOURTH DAY
OF CHRISTMAS

BARNEY SIMON

THEY CAME on Tuesday, December the 28th, which was a
nice day. I mean with a nice Christmas past and New Year to
come. I argued with Granny that night, I remember, about
putting the Cape Dutch sideboard against the door too, but
she argued back. Cookie, she said, which is not my born
name but one I grew into and can't grow out of bald as I am
and forty years old—anyway, Cookie she said once we were
talking about laws when there were some and Cookie she
said there were some really worthwhile ones, like whites not
sleeping with blacks, meaning me of course and Martha, and
Granny I said, fine, call me Cookie and I'll sleep with black
girls, call me Robert and I'll sleep alone—which of course
shushed her because she knows she'll die calling me Cookie.
Anyway, Cookie she said, put the sideboard by the door by all
means, but you've got to get it out of the way in the morning.
Don't think you can slip out through a window to work like
other days. Lily and me can manage the table and chairs and
the desk, but not the sideboard, and I'm damned if I'm going
to ask everyone who calls to climb in through the window,
not to speak of my own comings and goings. So I said all
right Granny, don't worry, I'll help you in the morning. But
WAKE me at quarter-to-seven. WAKE ME! Don't say it's
quarter-to and go away!

All right! she said, I can't stand you in this type of mood. I
know exactly what's going on. You're thinking how you hate
them and you'd like to kick them in the whatnots. Very nice

indeed for all concerned. That's all I'm short of in my time of life. To lose you. By my way of thinking, a dead grandson is no grandson. So if you do anything stupid I'll kill you!

Anyway, as I already said, all this happened on a nice enough Tuesday. This discussion between Granny and me, and of course, their coming. I calculated that they would come then, although Granny said they'd be too full of holiday spirits, because the Hendersons and Prodzinskys had recently been visited. To my way of thinking we were next.

Personally, Granny said, I think we're wasting our time lugging that sideboard around. We should just take normal precautions. The dining-room table and chairs and perhaps the desk.

D'you remember, I said, that time when the Rosens put Annabelle's Hope Chest and the bed behind the dining-room furniture behind the door and they gave up God knows why and went for the Venters instead? Granny shrugged and we began lugging the sideboard together, she pushing, me dragging. We jammed a chair-back under the door-handle, and two more against the panelling and pushed the dining-room table against that and then Lily my teeny niece's writing-desk and then with much huff and puff the big black old sideboard. Oooof Granny said, that was enough hard labour for a week—I'm popping straight into a nice hot bath and then off to bed!

Nonsense Granny, I said, d'you remember what happened to Mrs. Kennedy's cut-glass collection, and Mrs. du Toit's Renoir print? Take precautions—

O.K., O.K., Granny interrupted with a sigh, take precautions while you may! If you were my age ...

Come now Granny, I said, what about your heirloom sheets?

Oh yes, she said, them I'll flatten between newspapers and slip under the lounge carpet!

And your drop ear-rings?

Oh them, she said, we'll pop into the lounge chandelier!

And your glasses?

Straight from my nose to the lounge settee! She scuttled across the room to put them there, and before I could say or do anything, the centre cushion was up and my dirty underpants exposed.

Sis! Granny cried, are these yours Cookie?

Don't be silly, I said, who's been visiting you lately?

You pick them up, Granny said, you're a boy.

I took them between thumb and forefinger. Maybe they left them last time they came.

Pop them in the dust-bin, she said, laying her glasses flat on the settee base and covering them with a big soft cushion.

You pick them up, Granny said, laying her glasses flat on the settee base and covering them with a big soft cushion.

Is that so wise? I said.

Well, they stink to hell!

The glasses I mean.

Oh, she said, safe as a house! And our watches, she said snatching mine from my wrist, they go straight behind the panelling in the kitchen!

Soon all was hidden, all was calm, Lily asleep for hours gone, Granny in her bath and me in my bed, anxious about her without her glasses.

The bath-water drained, and soon she was padding around in the passage bare-foot. You'll see, she lisped without her teeth, they won't come tonight.

Better keep your teeth in, in case they do, or whoops that big one will be off with them!

You've got a point, she said, and pitter-pattered back to the bathroom. And that was that. There was a gentle swissss swissss as she gave Lily the potty and then in no time her bed was creaking and she was calling sleep tight Cookie and then snoring. For a long, long time Granny's snoring was the only sound in the night, except for a sigh across the dark passage from Lily's little bed ...

And then I heard the lorry stop at the top of our street. Some doors slammed and a dozen or so feet came down the pavement. They paused somewhere near the Prodzinskys I reckoned, and then they moved on. I nipped out of bed and crawled across to peep out of the window. Sure enough they were there. The boys. Five of them. All sizes, all dressed in dark clothes and nearly at our front gate. One was holding a chopper, another, a monster of a man, was carrying a pick, and two small ones together were holding what looked like a log. The fifth one, very thin, very tall, very pale, was giving orders. Actually I got angry. I thought of shouting something at them or dropping some hot sunflower-seed oil on them, but I respected Granny's wish and restrained myself. I crawled back to bed and I waited. Not a sound. Not a word. Not from outside, not from Granny or Lily. Then footsteps (now then, I knew) up our path, and a terrible splitting crash. I shot across to the window again. The two small men were using their log as a battering-ram. Across the road I saw du Toit peeping out of his bedroom window. He must've noticed me, because he gave me a quick thumbs-up-for-courage sign. I ducked down again as the other two started, alternating with the chopper and the pick. I slithered back to bed.

Cookie, I heard Granny squeak from her bed, thank you very much! There goes my Cape Dutch sideboard.

Ssssh—I hissed, but before I'd finished, she came flying through my door, her nightie all over the show, and splosh she was in my bed. You don't mind if I do, Cookie she said, cuddling close, I find it strangely comforting.

I must say that I did too, although Granny's bones are inclined to hurt. We heard something give and a crunch and a creak as the furniture heaved below.

That sideboard's a marvel, I whispered, I can see them giving up!

Granny giggled nervously, ending in a whistle.

Where are your teeth? I nagged in the dark.

Ooops, she giggled, sitting up, must've left them under the pillow!

Well hurry up, I pushed her out, and get dressed! Don't look for trouble in your nightie! She skedaddled back to her room. My pyjama pants don't have a cord, and I thought of getting properly dressed too, to be agile in case of need. But I thought oh what the hell and went on lying with the chopping and the picking wilder and the creaking and the heaving getting louder and louder down below. It was obvious that the door was all but gone and only the furniture lay between them and us. God protect Granny's Cape Dutch sideboard I thought, and suddenly she was back in my bed, fully dressed. Honestly Granny, I said, what about when they come up here?

They'll just have to excuse us, won't they?

Haven't you got any sense of pride?

No, she said, none.

They started a sort of heave-ho chant down below and then the chopping and picking noises began again. Goodbye sideboard, Granny sighed.

Ah well, I comforted, it really could have worked.

There were pushing, dragging noises downstairs, then distinct sounds of footsteps and a man's voice, breathless and angry.

That's that, I said, come on now Granny, we'd better slip downstairs and see what we can salvage by chicanery.

Not on your life! Granny said, I'm staying put!

To entice them?

Actually, Granny said, you've got a point. Anyway, we'd better keep them busy. My heirloom sheets are bulkier than I thought. You can see them under the carpet.

Right then! I said, leaping out of bed and grabbing my falling pyjamas with an oops.

We went down the stairs together, me clutching my pyjama pants in a tight knot at the front, Granny with her hair in a long grey pony-tail. Oh, she whispered, I was so sure that they wouldn't come—it was such a nice holiday season.

The giant was waiting at the foot of the stairs. Are you crazy! he cried nasally, you nearly killed us with that load! Granny nudged me before I could answer. The rest of them were still picking their way through the debris. I could barely recognise the sideboard. Mahogany, Granny muttered, genuine Old Cape Dutch mahogany.

I thought it was stinkwood, I whispered.

That's what I said! she glared at me.

Well chaps, I said gaily, you came just a bit too soon! We haven't replaced a quarter of what you took last time!

They were lining up behind their leader.

Enough! He barked, standing tall and thin, what have you got to declare?

Declare! Granny exclaimed, Thank you very much, just pick up all those pieces and the family fortune's in your hands!

Jewellery? The leader pressed, his eyes two tiny pale slits. Granny gave a bitter laugh. We all moved into the lounge together.

Got any more glasses? the giant whispered to us. He was the one.

What? Granny said.

Glasses, he repeated, spectacles. I broke your last pair. Excellent. Never found another to replace them.

Neither did I! Granny snorted.

GOOD! the leader cried, TO YOUR POSTS MEN!

They marched briskly out of the lounge, only the leader and the giant staying behind. The giant to guard us. I heard the lorry, revving wildly, come down the street and stop at our front door.

IN POSI-SHUUUUUN? the leader cried.

Awaiting orders! Three voices sounded briskly from other parts of the house. The giant sat down on the centre cushion of the settee. Only Granny and I seemed to hear her spectacles crunch beneath him. Swine, she hissed through clenched teeth. I smothered a giggle.

C-O-O-O-O-MENCE! The leader roared. He pulled out a small black book and began calling and ticking.

Fruits deciduous?	Two apples one pear!
Fruits citrus?	One orange one naartjie!
Fruits tropical?	Half a paw-paw one pineapple!
Vegetable leaf?	One lettuce!
No spinach?	No spinach.

He's mad about it, Granny whispered, ha!

No cabbage?	No cabbage.
Vegetable root?	Six potatoes!
Towels?	Four dish!
	Three bath!
	Four hand!
Cushions?	Four feather one inflatable!
Pictures?	Family, snaps no commercial value!

Say N.C.V.

N.C.V.?

N.C.V.! No commercial
  value!

Mattresses? — Two adult, one cot—N.C.V.

Reasons? — Protruding springs.

In all cases? — All cases.

Chairs? — One

One? — Remainder destroyed in entry!

Pens? — One quill one ball!

Cameras? — One ink.

Ink? — Squirts ink.

No photographic
  action? — No photographic action.

Place under toys. — As ordered!

Cutlery? — Fifteen fish knives!

There was a metallic clatter from the kitchen.

Seven forks!

Five desert-spoons—no six!

And two soup!

Lily never touches the stuff, I explained.

Who's in the kitchen? the leader demanded irately, ignoring me.

The youngster, the giant said, climbing to his feet.

Put him with the loaders on lorry duty and take over kitchen!

As ordered! The giant hurried out of the lounge.

RIGHT! Called the leader pacing up and down over Granny's heirloom sheets, LINEN!

Granny giggled compulsively and I joined her.

What's the matter with you? The leader watched us suspiciously. Granny covered her mouth cleverly as if nursing a toothache, and I pinched my thigh.

Linen! he repeated. — Two table-cloths!

Six adult sheets, N.C.V.!

Reasons? — Threadbare!

Granny's giggle went wild, I pinched my thigh harder.

Two cot! N.C.V.!

Reasons? — Wet. Child still between.

Good for Lily, I whispered to Granny.

She nodded, grinning, and I gave her the potty too!

Then we heard the big boy banging around the panelling in the kitchen. Granny and I looked at each other desperately. The watches, I whispered.

Granny licked her lips. Gentlemen! she cried, raising her arms, Music?

They all stopped what they were doing, and wandered back to the lounge to stare at her. God help Granny, I thought, if she drags my record out—and my player! The piano had gone in the last barricade. As if reading my thoughts, she winked reassuringly at me and started whirling around the room humming the Blue Danube and her pony tail lashing out. But by the time she reached the second chorus, that big fat bear had yawned and wandered back to the kitchen, and before she could reach the third, without prompting, he shouted, Two wrist watches! And that was that. Granny sat down on the settee. Everyone clapped politely and dispersed. Then the leader, without any kind of warning, sauntered up to the chandelier, reached up and shook it, and the two drop ear-rings fell to the floor. Granny choked back a sob. She looked very tiny, very old. I sat down beside her and cuddled her close.

The leader went on shouting orders — foodstuffs—canned—raw—furniture—tables—destroyed in entry—beds—carpets—N.C.V.—threadbare—settee—N.C.V.— reason—collapsing—globes—seven—and so it went on and on, their voices echoing more and more as our house hollowed and our belongings piled up outside. I rocked Granny gently. Through our curtainless windows I watched our neighbours' houses and their heads popping up and down behind their window-sills.

Dentures! The leader shouted, and Granny removed hers wearily. The giant was back from the kitchen and waiting, and he snatched them from her hand and popped them right into his mouth. If only you knew how ridiculous you look, Granny lisped haughtily. He just winked.

At last the leader paused. He paced up and down while the others finished loading into the lorry. Suddenly he stopped pacing and stared at us with his thin pale eyes. O.K., Granny whispered brokenly, please that's enough. What more do you want?

Sex, he said.

Sex, she repeated wearily, with whom, Cookie or me?

I held onto my pyjama pants.

You, he said.

But I'm seventy-eight years old she said, which is as good as eighty which is thirty years beyond my vivacious womanhood. She stopped herself with a sigh. If I do, she said mechanically, will you not look further for my heirloom sheets?

Your what? he asked.

Never mind. Cookie, she said, turn around please. This is a sore sight for a grandson's eyes. She pulled down her bloomers and began to raise her skirt. I turned to the window. Soon I heard the leader rocking and panting and gasping over her. I stood at the window watching those little heads at every other window and the moon skimming and skipping wild in the clouds. The lorry was loaded and the boys began to call. I didn't turn around. I heard Granny give a little cry and then a moment later I watched the leader go down the path, spitting and zipping up his fly. The lorry revved, jerked and pulled away up the street. Some neighbours' lights went on.

Cookie, Granny said, you were marvellous.

I wandered out of the room, through our empty house. I tried to close a leaking tap but only hurt my hand. The back door was gone. Outside I could hear the lorry revving again as it turned into the highway. And then Granny called. I went back to the lounge and sat on the settee beside her. I held her to me.

We sat for a long time in the dark bare room, until the sky began to tint with light. I stood and rolled back the ragged carpet and lifted up her heirloom sheets, I held them over one arm (my pyjamas with the hand) and helped her up with the other. Slowly we walked from the lounge, leaning on each other. Granny rested her head on my shoulder. Solid stinkwood, she whispered as we began to mount the stairs.

A HUNTING ACCIDENT

Nadine Gordimer

She met her photographer at the Kilimanjaro in Dar. To the new Missionaries—FAO and UNESCO representatives, Africa-desk journalists, arts and crafts teachers, Scandinavian documentary film-makers, Fanonist-Dumontist economist sons and daughters of dead or departed settler families—this means the hotel, not the mountain, and the monosyllable stands for Dar es Salaam. She was dossing down on the floor in the children's bedroom of a woman professor at the university so she had to wait for an invitation to his room. She saw at once that the photographer was not shy but (she hadn't heard of him) was probably somebody, and not on the look-out for women. It was the old story; she was accustomed to being taken notice of in a certain way. He sat with his pipe and old-fashioned oilcloth tobacco pouch in the bar, easy to find, and put aside his notebooks less to talk than to listen to her with deep attention; but it was not in that way. He quickly became her immediate purpose: she didn't show much guile and that was instinctively wise, because he saw that she had abandoned the tactics that must serve a pretty girl so well, and she saw that he would not be able to resist honesty. When she had finished telling him something in her excited, indignant manner, he would think a long time, smiling at her, his lips pressed together, small-boned brown face fine-lined with the growing intensity of his expression, gazing green eyes darting side-glances away, as if he were laughing delightedly, privately, within, before he answered with his 'Why?' 'Would you?' 'I wonder.' He would not have the heart to reject her.

How exciting it was, to be received on such terms! In the sealed and carpeted hotel room he opened windows that were never meant to be opened and the heat-solid night into which she stretched her arm was even more airless. They agreed that velvet, foam-padded chairs and thick mattresses were Northern luxuries —Southern penances, and she talked of smooth tiles bare to soles, high walls punched free to the sea breeze by lattice. He stroked her sweaty hair away from her cheeks, and it was she who suggested they have a long shower together, he submitting to the old, sweet rites of sensuality with good grace.

It was she who brought him to Ratau's house in another African country. She tried out in her ear how other people might comment: She took him along with her from Tanzania. She thought how she might say to Ratau: Clive Nellen was in Dar, he so much wanted to photograph this country after I'd talked such a lot about it. Both were partly true. She had told him of the country she had been born in, daughter of the colonial Minister of Education, and her standing invitation to come back and stay with the youngest son of her father's old friend, the Paramount Chief. She had told him of the terracotta and bottle-green town built of red earth with hedges of Euphorbia, where the house was, and of the great tree near the house where the tribal court still met each day to decide disputes between citizens. He had come so far, it was a pity not to go farther—perhaps he had been intending to visit that country anyway; he did not discuss plans much. She brought her suitcase and duffle bag of books to his room and slept a last night with him in the hotel before they took an early plane together. They were met at the other end by one of Ratau's big cars with one of his cousins to drive them the hundred-and-twenty kilometres to the Chief's town. She watched her photographer's eyes flicking adjustment to the passing scrub and thought how when they were in bed (Ratau would at once understand they should be given a room together) she would be able to say to him: 'Didn't I tell you; that endless plain with a single hill peaked up here and there casting its single blue shadow—it's exactly the imaginary country old maps call "Land of Prester John" or "Kafferland".'

But they got to bed very late and, five or six people, some rather drunk, like noisy innocent children calling to one another from camp bed to sleeping bag, all slept at last before the fire in the living-room: Ratau had one of his house-parties. Friends from his university days in England and America, people he invited to stay when he was in various countries at various times, tended to turn up, and there were always also numerous members of the extended family of his father's three wives with a permanent claim on hospitality, taking it for granted that they would serve the household in some way while they were there. Ratau with his cajoling African laugh and his ruthless Cambridge accent had told everyone he was getting them all up to go on a hunting trip in the morning; at half-past six he was prodding at sleepers with his ready-laced boots and holding by the limp hand the little waxen-blonde Swedish potter from the crafts school in the village whom he had taken to the room he, as host, reserved to himself for the night. One of the distant relatives was behind him with a huge tin tray of coffee mugs and rusks. There was something stronger, Ratau called, for those who felt they had to keep out the morning cold. An old kitchen table stocked with brandy and gin and cane spirit stood permanently among the painted barrels of elephant ear and canvas chairs on the huge verandah that hooded the house. The guns were laid out there, too; he was giving orders to relatives summoned to act as bearers, breaking breeches, putting barrels to his left eye. 'Christie—tell me, your friend, what'sisname? He'll be one of the guns?' And she laughed, a shade disloyally, because Ratau was so attractive, so unselfconsciously male in his natural assumption of what she had been taught, at her progressive school, was the conditioned male role of killer. 'Shoot with his camera,' she said.

'Great. He'll see me get my eland today.'

'Ra-tau! Strictly prohibited! Didn't you tell me eland's pro-tected?'

'A chief's allowed one a year. My brother's turn last time, now I'm going to bag mine.' He lowered his voice, to tease or flirt: *I'll give you the skin to warm you in London.* She murmured, *Mean it?*

Always mean what I say, Christie.

The Swedish blonde was not around to hear. When Christine went out onto the gravel drive where a truck had come shaking up under the shouts of some relatives already mounted, she saw her, sitting on a white-washed boulder, yawn like a cat: she was cradling a reluctant toddler with the holy-family reverence Swedish girls display for black children. The photographer was moving about in his unnoticed way among people, his paraphernalia round his neck and bulging the pockets of his usual bush jacket and thin man's large shorts. He gave a hand with lowering the (broken) tail-gate of the truck so that people could climb in but he was not part of the shouting, squealing, laughing and innuendo that made these people who had got to know each other only the previous night feel they were such good friends. He smiled at her as he had before they were lovers; the breasts and thighs and backsides, knees, feet and arms comradely crowded together on the truck seemed to deny the reality of the physical presence he had lent her in a hotel room in Dar. He was certainly married; a passionate boy-and-girl love affair that was the basis of his privacy and whose transformation into domestic peace was the basis of his sympathetic detachment—she would take a bet on it, although she'd never asked him. She hoped, with the edge of defensiveness of one who is at fault, he wasn't sulking because she had said they'd go to the court under the tree and up to the Great Place where the chiefs were buried, this morning. She'd let herself and him be carried off on this hunting party; he might be thinking it was not the kind of thing he would enjoy, but was going along because it was the kind of thing *she* would enjoy—and she couldn't say, explain, excuse anything, lean a seducer's message against his breathing side in the press of the truck, because she was in the cab up front with Ratau driving and a young black woman, Yolisa, while he was in the open truck behind. She turned her head once and could just see him between jolts that brought others into her vision: little Ulla, the Swede, an old relative-retainer in an ancient balaclava, the huge, laughing engineer husband of Yolisa, a great round, neckless head like a Benin bronze bobbing on a vast chest —all with guns poking up between them. No of course her photographer wasn't sulking; he must be at least thirty-eight, not a young man of her own age who talked liberation and expected his girls to do whatever he decided.

Ratau drove with reckless authority through the quiet morning fires of his father's and forefathers' town and forded a river of goats on the road leading out of it. At several points in the open country a figure patched together from whatever the poor in rural areas can assemble against winter cold—scarecrow jackets, split

74

patent shoes, a red knitted cap, a sack serving as a cape, a plaid blanket—rose from a culvert or appeared where cattle had tramped down the grass round a thorn tree. A man came towards the truck as to a rendezvous, hand raised in patient, trusted respect; Ratau landed in an applause of dust, shouting from the window to his bearers on the back, calling to the man on the road, who was, indeed, there by arrangement to report on the movement of game for the information of the hunt. Ratau turned and struck out accordingly across the plain to mopane forest, through mopane forest and out into the open again. In the freedom of driving without a road to follow—a progress as suddenly full of haphazard energy as a speedboat in rough water—the skill and comment and laughter of Ratau, the looming and lurching of gold-red trees, the din of the vehicle's clattering, grinding, chuntering metal bones, the people on the back of the truck seemed not to exist for the three in the cab. Once there was a thump on the roof and Ratau, roaring with laughter, slowed down a bit, but the timing with which he changed back and forth from lower to higher gear and the sureness with which he swung his way through wilderness inspired confidence that in his hands there was no danger to anyone, he would carry everyone through with him, even supposing there actually were to be a load of poor devils somewhere up behind.

In this din and euphoria a gun-shot was hardly more than a pop. It was the ragged scream borne away on the edge of the truck's noise and the battering of fists on the cab roof that made the three in the cab recognize the explosion. Yolisa gave a woman's answering cry to any cry, she clutched Christine's thigh. The truck came to a wild stop, Ratau's smooth black arm extended a hard, efficient barrier to prevent the women pitching to the windscreen. At some second's edge in the collision of seen, heard, felt, Christine saw a large object fall past the truck. She twisted her head to the rear window, feeling her neck snap against its stem; it was Yolisa's husband—: not there between the others. His big body flung aside. She imprisoned the black girl's clenched fists in her own; terror sucked her veins flat, she saw herself, them all, standing round this girl's husband, blood running its way, running, running to its ebb and no one with the skill or means to stop it. The helpless struggle of dreams held her in the truck; within that stasis she held fast to the girl to keep death off from her.

And then there was laughter. Shouts: of laughter. The door on the driver's side hung open where Ratau had jumped out. The big engineer was at the window on the passenger's side, signalling his wife to lower it, huffing and puffing, rubbing his right ear, being dusted down by others like a child who has taken a tumble. Christine and the young woman beside her whom she had met twenty-four hours before flung themselves together in a trembling embrace. Like lovers with a moment they cannot share, they hesitated before getting down from the cab. The husband put his arm round his wife as a man does at a party and grinned: 'Don't worry, you're not a widow yet.' She moved her shoulders and looked irritated. Ratau was teasing him, expertly therapeutic against shock. 'Good lord, man, the very sound of a shot and you think you're in the next world.' 'Well, I'm not so sure I'm here now— my ear's burning like hell.' 'Not a scratch to be seen, I assure you. You jumped out of your skin, that's all.' The sun, newly risen ruddy, thrust the gaiety of firelight through bronze, carmine, copper, brown and brass cinders of the dry mopane leaves and the static of goldened dust thrown up around them. The sleep that holds all forests was broken in upon by celebrating voices and unicorn bursts of laughter went bounding away into the solitude. Somebody got down a case of beer from the truck; it was cold as champagne. The cans were passed from mouth to mouth, cala-bash fashion. The gun-bearers in their blue overalls with bare black feet close together against the cold sandy earth, giggled with pleasure. They spoke no English and the little Swedish blonde was taking the opportunity to try and communicate through the few phrases of their language she had already learnt. This one and that gave versions of how the engineer had jumped, toppled, capered, dived from the truck. He slapped at his ear. 'I tell you, quite deaf on that side now. I felt the bullet sear the skin.' Someone crept up and shouted in the ear and he cried out; Ratau stood with com-mandingly outstretched arm, finger jabbing at him, conducting the general laughter.

She went up almost awkwardly to the photographer; he really

did act as if he were incredibly staid! It would give other people the wrong impression of the kind of man she chose. 'You were next to him, weren't you?'

He was lighting the pipe and continued to make small popping noises for a moment or two, those extraordinarily beautiful eyes that had excited her in Dar deeply translucent in three-quarter profile with their expression ellipsed as, at a certain angle, is the design that makes the pupil of a sea-glass marble. He smiled a little at her, round the pipe-stem. 'The bullet went between us—top of my head and his ear.'

Yes—the man she had brought to the party was the smallest and slightest there, when it came to build he didn't look much. 'Good God. What was it like?'

'Loud. He's lucky to be alive. If it'd been an inch to the left, it would have gone over the top of my head, if it'd been an inch to the right, it would've been in his brain.' This was in a low conversational voice no one else would have heard. All he said for the company in general was—more or less to Ratau—as the truck was manned again, 'Perhaps it would be a good idea if everyone checked the guns are unloaded.' Sensible but somehow the kind of dampening suggestion that would come from someone who didn't have quite the style to look danger gallantly in the eye the way this party did. What did he know about the handling of guns, anyway.

Ratau said, not unkindly, 'Don't worry, you'll come to no harm. Everything under control.'

The Swedish girl, already seated in the truck with the defensive smile of a terrified child, held to the hand, cold and tough as the feel of a tortoise's foot, of the old gun-bearer who had never before been touched by a white woman.

Twice the party caught up with three eland who threaded images swiftly into the mopane, a disappearing painted ribbon: the exquisite calligraphy of their broad flanks made them seem two-dimensional. Ratau never got within firing range. If he was disappointed, he was not the kind to show his guests the discourtesy of imposing this upon them; the truck bucked off in other directions, where other game had been reported by the scouts. In a natural park between mopane forests, a herd of red hartebeest grazed. They did not see the threat they did not know. The swaying truck did not fit the shape of any predator. The two women in the cab whispered to each other, 'Look! Look!' at the marvel of a pattern of life printed and yet moving glossy russet and cream, prehistory and yet alive (tails flicked, coats twitched at parasites, droppings fell elegantly); the herd progressed like a cloud or the outline of water, changing without breaking.

Ratau was out of the driver's seat, up onto the open truck. His bearers jumped down lightly knee-bent, spilled all round in a criss-cross of guns. He followed the English protocol; each of his guests must have the chance to drop a beast before he would take a shot himself. The air cracked and split over the truck. The ancient alert was marked by the single majestic signal of a horn-swept head. The herd left the way mercury runs, a mass without distinguishable components. Two hundred yards; and then stopped, the lovely masks facing the hunters. In low gear (beside Christine a relative smelling of clothing impregnated with wood-smoke was driving) the truck followed until within range. The guests fired again at their host's instruction. As a piece of rich cloth is grasped at one end and shaken, a shock-wave passed through the herd. They swung away and this time one could hear the wild hobble of their hooves. Some shapes lay on the ground where they had been; 'Five, we got five!' the engineer shouted. 'Six,' Ratau said, putting a hand on the shoulder of another of his friends. 'You aimed too low, old man; you've got him in the leg. Try for the neck now.' Christine and Yolisa had come down from the cab again. Christine had her hands on her hips, gazing. 'One's standing on its own under that tree, there! Look at that!' 'Albert's wounded him, his hind leg's gone.' 'Oh no!' 'Hop back in, there's a good girl.' She wanted to find the photographer and sit with him on the truck but the men, a herd themselves now, pushed past her unseeingly in their excitement and she had to do as Ratau said and get into the cab.

They rolled slowly across the plain towards the acacia under whose thin gauze of shade the markings of the red hartebeest showed cleanly. All eyes were fixed on it and it took the gaze as if waiting for them. It stood perfectly steady on three legs with the fourth, left hind, dangling snapped at the joint. There was only this disarticulation and a string of bright red blood to break the symmetry of the creature. 'A cow,' someone said; and someone else nodded. Ratau stood for encouragement beside the man whose prey it was. No one shuffled. The shot seemed released from the tension of all, and the beast collapsed, but the cry went up—'Still alive!' 'My God, finish it off, man!' Ulla and Yolisa covered their ears. 'Ratau, you do it!' But Ratau, the patient host, was instructing: 'Look, like this—you're point-blank, you can't miss—' Sweating, almost giggling with shame and rage at himself, the guest fired again into his beast that lay there panting, breathing still, looking at him, waiting for the death he owed her. Even that was not a clean shot, though a mortal one. Now she felt herself dying and with the last miracle of co-ordination she could muster drew back her head on the ground and gave a cow's cry, the familiar and gentle, pitiful moo of any clumsy dairy mother. It was as if it were discovered to be true that at midnight on Christmas Eve dumb beasts can speak their sufferings; no one had known that these wild beings could link the abattoir to the hunt, the slave to the free, in that humble bellow. Yolisa and Ulla fled to the cab. Christine stood with the second joint of her forefinger clasped between her bared teeth; she was not thinking of the animal; how horrible this was, he would be thinking, he who had not taken any part, active or vicarious, who had been brought along when what he wanted was to be looking at the Victorian monuments where Ratau's ancestors lay, and watching the council of elders administering the law in the shade of the assembly place, finding sermons in those gravestones and tongues in that tree.

Suddenly she saw he had leapt down from the truck and was walking quickly over to the dying beast. The shorts and veldskoen boots made his small, hard, thin legs look like an ill-nourished schoolboy's, the weighed-down pockets of the bush jacket and the leather straps of two cameras yoked him. He was walking right into the gaze they all decently turned away from. He went straight up to the beast and, down on one knee, began to photograph it again and again, close-up, gazing through the camera, with the camera, into the last moments of life passing in its open eyes. His face was absolutely intent on the techniques he was employing; there was a deep line she had never seen before, drawn down either side of his mouth from the sucked-in nostrils. He placed filters over his lens, removed them. He took his time. The beast tried to open its mouth once more but there was no sound, only a bubble of blood. Its eye (now the head had lolled completely into profile, he could see only one) settled on him almost restfully, the faculty of vision bringing him into focus, then fading, as he himself looked steadily into it with his camera.

He came back to the truck, where Ratau was explaining the reactions of a herd after some of the animals have dropped. She murmured, 'It's still moving'—from afar, the body twitched slackly like a kicked bundle.

'No,' he said. 'She's gone.' He was writing (a date, some figures) in his curling notebook that smelt of tobacco.

The final bag was nineteen—twelve red hartebeest and seven blesbok, most dropped stone-dead with single shots from the host's gun. The eland were not seen again. Yolisa sat in the cab, not looking out, and said, 'All I want is to get back and see if my baby's all right.' Another truck arrived, finding its way in the wake of the first as if along signposted city streets, and relatives collected and flung up the carcasses with tremendous admiration and glee, making a party-cloakroom pile of pelts and blood.

The women said they wouldn't touch any of the meat Ratau promised them that night: 'You'll see, red hartebeest is the best eating of any game.' When evening came, and beneath the mantel photograph of the old Paramount Chief with his looped watch-chain, Homburg hat and leopard skin, the fire spread the delicious incense of burning tambuti wood among the red-wine drinkers, and the hunger of the open air was pleasurable as lust, all ate from the belly-shaped enamel pots a one-eyed relative brought round. 'Should have been hung first'—Ratau referred Christine to the English cuisine they both knew—'But here, with us, nobody wants to wait.' In the kitchen there was feasting, and out in the yard still more people were cooking on a communal open fire. Christine had a lot to drink. She kept an eye on the curiously childlike figure in the old shorts and bush jacket, she was conscious of the smell of his pipe always somewhere in the room, despite the tambuti scent, despite the loudness of the rock music, and she hoped they would get somewhere to sleep alone tonight. She evaded the men who had been dancing with her and found him. 'Are you mad with me?'

He was chatting quietly to an old black man who was trying his tobacco in a home-made pipe. 'Why?'

'Well that's all right then.' She had an urge to kiss passionately that wise-monkey, aesthete's face, to put her hands up under the old khaki clothes and beat her fists at the breast there. He smiled at her affectionately in his appreciation of the old man: she read, 'Go off and enjoy yourself.'

But it was not till the morning that she held his message in her hand. By the time she got up and picked her way among the sleepers on the living-room floor, he had gone with the railway bus that paused, palsied by its sonorous diesel engine, to take on passengers and their small livestock for the capital. He had left a note for her, enclosing another to thank Ratau for his hospitality. Both smelled of proximity to the oilcloth tobacco pouch. 'You'll be glad to know I saw the sun rise from the Great Place today. It's all you said. You've also said there's nowhere else to stay but a Holiday Inn. I'll be based there. For about a week until the 25–6th, I should think. If you should come down, you'll find me queued up at the help-yourself before the curry-and-rice trough, lunchtime.'

She walked through the garden, where butterflies of blossom were alighted on the bauhinia trees and blood-tendoned bones and tufts of hide, dragged from the yard overnight by dogs, littered the oval of ashen winter grass. Flies blundered at her face. Out in the road dust was luxurious as cream underfoot; under the huge tree old men were assembled and a disaffected citizen or two, hat and stick marking formality, awaited the outcome of a long harangue. She hung about, not too near, as if she had only to be able to understand, that's all, and the speaker would have something to say, for her.

TOKAI

Bernard Levinson

Looking back on that night, a sense of timelessness stands out.
And a profound exhaustion. On my knees at the side of her bed,
my hand locked in her womb, I had to nudge the seconds with my
own heart beats. It seems to me now that from the moment I was
woken by the Constable, time had geared itself into slow motion.

"It's the Bezuidenhouts. The baby's coming. . . . ."

I drove for an eternity in the darkness of the Tokai forest looking for their home. Endless black tree-tunnels and railway cot-
tages asleep behind the thick blanket bush in the folds of Muizenberg Mountain. But none with lights on. At moments I could see
the mountain face against the dark sky. A sudden clearing and in
my headlights--rows of grapevines, arms outstretched, cruci-
fied on the supporting wood, the white gables of an old farm
homestead, and immediately trees again, their heads bent together in the darkness.

I recall the feel of excitement and fear I always had going on a
"call." An eager anticipation--and at the very core of this
eagerness a strange dread. Always in equal proportion--my
haste to arrive, to meet this new challenge--and the holding
back, the uncertainty and the fear. Somewhere in this fear was
the pressure of omnipotence. The need of those in distress to
find me certain, all-knowing and magical. I hid my vulnerability in gentleness. My fear imprisoned me. I was never
sure if I could fulfill the role I sensed and read, again and
again, in the eyes of those who suffered.

It was midnight when Kleinman Bezuidenhout waved me in from

the road. I could hear his wife calling--riding the crest of her
pain in a loud cry. We hurried into the cottage.

I was immediately struck by the incongruity of Kleinman's
name. This was not the childhood sarcasm of the tall boy called
Shorty. Kleinman appeared to be short because of the massive-
ness of his chest and shoulders. The impact was of enormous
strength. He was dark-skinned and had a large drooping moustache. A Spanish touch. An air of broooding melancholy. A
heavy silence.

The cottage was dimly lit. Smell of paraffin and camphor. Mrs.
Bezuidenhout lay flat on her back, holding the bars of the worn
metal bod-head. An old soiled sheet partly covered her body.
She was an enormous woman. Her large breasts had fallen
into the hollow of her armpits. They looked tired and collapsed.
Her entire body was wet with perspiration. As I walked in, she
clearly passed into the trough between contractions. She grunted with each breath, her eyes closed. A small baby's hand protruded from the dark cleft between her thighs. For a moment
she looked like a sombre surrealist painting. A baby's hand
gingerly exploring the world between mountainous thighs. My
first impulse was to shake this lonely hand and welcome the
child to the darkness of Tokai and the great sleeping forest
around us. I gently eased the hand and arm back into the dark
cavern. Again the feeling of slow-motion. A dream-like sense
of endlessly, timelessly fingering the small hand back into her
body.

Kleinman arrived with a basin of hot water. He stood silently
waiting, his long powerful arms hanging loose at his side. I
slow-motioned through the act of taking off my jacket, rolling
up my sleeves and washing my hands. In this slow trickle of
time Mrs. Bezuidenhout floundered out of the troughs and again
and again fell on the peaks of her womb's grasp. She was deeply
exhausted. It was impossible to reach her. Impossible to help
her break her painful straining. She filled the room with her
rhythmic grunts, and then gripping the bedhead behind her, she
roared her agony into the night.

The head suddenly appeared. The vagina yawned. With time
frozen I tried to steady the baby's head. Mrs. Bezuidenhout
took a deep breath. The old iron bedstead creaked with her
tightening grip. She put her chin down and began to push deep
inside her chest.

Slow motion.

Kleinman was standing at the side of her bed--her eyes wide.
He leaned forward touching the bed with his massive hands.

"Druk!"

One word. The only word he spoke that entire night. Shot out
at that one overwhelming moment. It burst out like the deep
snap of a heavy rope.

The baby slipped and slithered half turning into my cupped
hands.

Slow motion. Slow motion.

Time-frozen-motion of baby's arms and body stretched, then
folding into legs and joints.

'Don't push! Hold it! Just hold it a moment!"

My voice floated into the dream-motion of cutting the cord. Mrs.
Bezuidenhout was silent and unhearing. Her arms remained
above her head. Her hands open. Her legs had fallen apart,
the knees still bent. Her body glistened in the lamplight.

Kleinman stood at the side of the bed--missing nothing. Silent.
Watching me handle the baby. Watching his wife in exhaustion
asleep. Her heavy limbs asleep and her sagged breasts asleep.
He stood with his arms at his side. Impotent. Waiting.

The after-birth welled out of the darkness, crowned, and eased
into my hand. A dark hot river followed--swelling and bursting
in painful slow motion. I forced my fist into the torrent, slipping deep into her body. With my left hand pressing down on her

abdomen outside, I pushed the loose folds of the womb against
my hidden fist. Slowly the warm flow stopped. Slowly.

It was at that point time stopped completely. It shuddered,
froze, and came to a total standstill. I was on my knees at the
side of her bed. My fist locked inside her. Locked and waiting
in a timeless vacuum. In a series of excursions I grabbed at
my medical bag. A syringe. Ampules. Back to the abdomen,
finding my fist and locking the womb. My feet were cramped
and in spasm. I tried to shift my weight with little relief. I
completed the final excursion with my free left hand and in-
jected her loose thigh.

Kleinman remained at the side of the bed. I could see heavy
beads of sweat on his forehead. His eyes were lamps burning
the dark pool at my elbow.

My fist swam in a deep throbbing. The slow rhythm slowed
through my hand. Hot pulsations blurring the outline of my
fist. My own body picked up this ebb and flow. I closed my
eyes and entered the pendulum beat, hearing my body ache and
strain in time to the slow ripples that flowed from my fist.

Throughout all this endless time Kleinman stood at my side
silent. Waiting. His wife opened her eyes for a moment.
Seemed aware of the force of my hand inside her. Groaned
softly once, and slipped back into her tiredness.

I placed my forehead against her wet thigh. The bed was now
gently throbbing. The dark corners of the room closed around
me. I could feel the night breathing on the cottage walls. In
the forest, the moon climbed out of the trees. I saw her face
at the window pulsating softly. I felt the moon walk on the roof
of the cottage. I felt the slow undulations as she eased herself
on to the edge of Muizenberg Mountain. The mountain throbbed.
And the darkness. The walls of the cottage throbbed.

There was a slight shift of tempo. I listened with the fingers
of my fist. Unmistakably I heard the womb flutter and shift
itself minutely over my fist. Behind the loud rhythmic ache
of my limbs and my body--in the warm darkness, the womb

was waking from its sleep. It turned. Twitched. It lightly felt
out the crevasses between my clenched fingers. It stretched
and gripped. Stretched again and squeezed my fist firmly. I
inched my hand out. A secret dialogue between my hand and the
womb. My blunt fist mute and stolid. The womb excited, chattering and intimately pressing and caressing my hand.

In the moment of utter silence when I withdrew my hand com-
pletely--the seconds took up the pulsation in my body--and time
began to move. I sat on the floor trying to waken my body. I
was aware of Kleinman still waiting at my side, he had not
moved the entire night. I was suddenly aware of how terrifying
it must have been for him watching me at my task.

It was morning when I walked into the kitchen. I leaned on the
half-door and smelt the wet morning air. The heavy scent of
the Tokai forest compounded of damp earth, oak trees and the
sharp edge of pine. In a clearing behind the cottage Kleinman
digging. He had his back to me. I assumed he was about to
bury the placenta. There was something in the way he handled
the shovel that kept me locked to him. He had a way of flicking
the earth to his side, then with a lightning fast spin of the shovel
it was there high above his head--pausing a split second and
then slamming it deep into the soil with incredible force--
flowing immediately into the same rhythm again. He had his
back to me. His legs were apart. Like a dancer repeating his
set choreographed piece, he crouched as the shovel plunged into the earth, then twisted his body and arched himself as though
he were about to leap into the air. Then he snapped into the
deep crouch curling his body around the spade.

Two thoughts struck me at once. The first--that this was a
professional. That he obviously handled a shovel every day of
his working life. It was an extension of his body. He flicked it
and spun it over his head with amazing dexterity. The heavy
silent hands that I had been aware of all night were now singing,
what was for Kleinman, a very familiar song. The rhythm was
unchanging and beautiful to watch. The second thought held me
rooted to the door. Kleinman was clearly not burying anything.
He was already standing thigh-deep in the trench he had dug.

I could see the muscles of his back repeating a pattern of tension under his shirt. His trousers stuck to his wet thighs. He began to dig faster. The shovel cut deeply into the hole tearing out a mound of red clay. The clay had hardly settled on the mountain of earth heaping up at Kleinman's side--when the shovel snapped back into the trench. When he stood waist-deep in the trench, Kleinman suddenly stopped--stepped out of the hole--took a deep breath, and began digging the earth back into the hole. The same precision. The same professional command of the shovel and the flying clods of earth. He dug furiously. He stood astride the loose earth and remained crouching--sweeping the soil back with frantic sharp jabs of the shovel.

There was something ominously aggressive in the entire act. This was an enemy. He was straining to destroy it. With each shovelful the enemy seemed to grow and was instantly matched by his anger and his strength. Now returning to the earth, with the enemy losing, he was sealing his victory with every ounce of strength he had.

I could hear his panting heavily. He was slowly exhausting himself. Then suddenly it was over. The ground was flat. In a final angry gesture he slammed the shovel deep into the soil. He left it deeply embedded and upright. He turned and walked into the cottage. Behind me, in the cool darkness, Mrs. Bezuidenhout still slept. As Kleinman passed me at the door, I could see he had been crying.

"....And He Chose A Mule"

Bernard Levinson

The moment I stepped into the sunlight I collided with the mule.
We stumbled into each other. A series of minor shocks. After
the darkness of the tin shanty, the sun was blinding. The sudden heat struck my face, making me grasp for air--then the
wide, startled eyes of the mule. I reached out instinctively
with my left hand, hitting the side of his face. He jerked his
head away. In a moment it was over. There was room for only
one of us in the narrow space between the hot corrugated iron
walls. I pressed my back against the makeshift wall. Keeping
his eyes on me, the mule inched past. He was painfully thin.
His body was a patchwork of grey scraggy tufts and worn bare
skin.

I waited for Eliphas. While cycling in the township on ob-
stetric calls, I frequently came across Eliphas and his small
grey mule. The old man was always excessively polite. And
always the weird paradox. He would greet me in English. I
would respond in Shangaan. We were both trying to please.

In a moment he was there, shuffling through the heat. In many
ways he resembled the animal. His hair and beard were as
grey and as tightly tufted. His old clothes hung loose, shifting
as he changed his weight from leg to leg. The same slow rolling gait as the mule.

I had just examined a mother and her babe. I had delivered this
child some weeks earlier. She now complained of an abdominal
pain. I examined her and her baby. We watched each other.
Few words passed between us. Her eyes were impossible to
read. She remained totally passive and silent. The baby cried.
I handed the babe to her. She eased a breast out of an old stained

bra and cradled the child towards her. Again the baffling passive acceptance of the hungry mouth. Her eyes never left me
but at the same time denied me an existence. I had no way of
reaching her. I had felt her body. I had listened to the secret
murmurings in her chest--but in no way had I touched her.

I cycled slowly, weaving between the potholes. My stethoscope
swung and thumped my chest. I pass groups of blacks talking.
Laughing. Abrupt silence. The animation in their faces, in
their eyes, ceases. Passivity. I smile apologetically. They
return the smile. The air burns and lifts off the dusty road.
I wonder at their thoughts--

"Who is this man who cycles through our lives? He has a white
coat and a white face. He has a rubber tube around his neck. He
looks at us, but his eyes tell us nothing. . . ."

I cycle on slowly, intensely aware of the bicycle, the deep ruts
in the dirt road, aware of my body, my aloneness and a sense
of trespassing.

"There's another call for you."

Sister Constance Ndlovo wears the white starched veil and uniform of a nursing sister. Her breasts are enormous, bulging
forward without a sign of a cleft. Her bottom recreates the
same configuration.

"You must take the jeep. The driva is there."

I walk across to the police station.

The Gaza Nkulu Township Police Station adjoined the clinic. I
often wondered about this. Although we frequently shared an
interest in the same patient, particularly over the weekends
when the assaults came in, our attitudes to the township in
general, and to the people, were starkly different. An uneasy marriage. At night the young policemen played cards
with the newly-qualified doctors. English was used as a mark
of respect. During the day the relationship formalised. Only
Afrikaans was spoken.

The police van and the clinic jeep shared the same shed. The
station was a heavy red brick structure. A dark red iron roof
covered a long front verandah. The usual blue lamp hung in
front. The clinic was a long wooden prefabricated hut. We
also shared a large open square. The earth was parched. A
solitary palm tree wilted in the centre.

Sergeant Nienaber sat on the stoep of the station in his shirt
sleeves. His face was red up to a clearly demarcated white
fringe on his forehead where his cap squeezed his head. His
fair hair was squashed to one side, still taking the shape of the
inside of his cap.

All this stands out clearly in my mind. The heat, Sister Constance with her majestic breasts and Nienaber fanning his face
with his cap. There was also Izak Lekolane, the driver of the
clinic jeep. He was the first to tell me about the bewitched
black horse. I had picked up pieces of the story on my rounds.

"Come on, Izak, what is this thing about a black horse?" Izak
looked at me solemnly. He was tall and boney-thin. An old
brown dust coat and a black battered peak cap were his uniform
of office. He sat bolt upright in the driver's seat, aware at all
times of his status.

"It is the witchdoctor, my baas. She has put a curse on the
black horse. It runs all over the township."

"Have you seen it?"

"No, my baas," he said slowly. "But it is everywhere."
"Do you really believe that?"

Izak looked at me. My question closed him completely. In an
instant the mask of passivity I knew so well was in place. I
had lost him.

A group of excited children pass. Izak puts his head out of the
cab window.

"Hikwalaho ka yini?"

"It's the black horse. It's there." They point up the dirt road.
Izak looks at me. I nod and he turns the jeep up the narrow
path. More children pass us. Laughter and shouting. There
is a crowd at the first corner. The heat shimmers on the road.
Izak opens the jeep door and stands partly out towering above
the crowd.

"What's happening?"

"Hinci ya ntima. The black horse. He was here chasing the
children. He jumped over the trees and vanished." Izak
slowly turns the jeep. We both remain silent. I can see nothing
in his eyes.

———

The heat remained unbearable all night. It was impossible to
sleep. I listened to the township. Dogs declaring some kind of
territoriality, barked to each other across the sleeping shanties.
Somewhere a police car shrieked at the darkness and rapidly
faded. At four o'clock a faint breeze carried the scent of burning wood and coal. A sour acrid smell. The township was
waking.

———

I met Nienaber at breakfast. The heat had already returned.

"What's this about a bewitched horse, Sergeant?"

"It's the heat, man. This kind of thing happens when it's hot.
They're all restless. It's the heat." He wiped his forehead and
pressed his cap firmly on his head.

"Izak tells me it's the spirit of an Xingomantanda who died.
She's come back as a black horse. Some kind of evil woman."

"She was murdered last year."

"Do you think she's come back in the shape of a black horse?"

91

Nienaber looked at me. For the first time I noticed his eyes.
Do the eyes take on a passivity living and working in the town-
ship? Do the hunter and the hunted develop the identical eyes?
His eyes were blank and silent.

"It's the heat. And we're gonna have another helluva day."

It was no longer safe to cycle. I used the jeep for all calls.
Sometimes Izak came into the homes with me. The township
was restless. The shanties steamed in the heat. Everywhere
we heard stories of the betwitched horse. Eye witnesses had
seen the horse change colour. It was now white. Only a witchdoctor as powerful as this Xingomantanda could so easily turn
herself from a black horse into a white horse.

"She will find those who killed her." Sister Constance nodded
in her starched veil.

It is late in the afternoon when the crowds begin to gather outside the police station. The white horse has been cornered.
We are trying to leave the clinic. We reach the third block away,
and it is clear there is no way to continue. Crowds pour through
the narrow streets towards the police station. The word has
spread. The horse is at bay. Some of the young men carry
rocks. The older men carry their traditional knobkerries. We
inch back to the clinic. The crowd seethes and squeezes around
us. They thump the sides of the jeep with the flat of their hands.
The sound reverberates like pistol shots in the metal cab. We
both look straight ahead. I hold my stethoscope up for all to
see. For the first time I really see my stethoscope--a weak
limp symbol of authority. The heart-shaped ear pieces look
for all the world like the emaciated handles of a trophy. Just
the thin handles trailing a trembling rubber tube. I suddenly
feel ashamed.

Izak revs the engine, slowly forcing a path for us. I am
pleased he doesn't hoot. The jeep bakes in the heat. The air
is thick and burning. Around us the crowd roars. The heavy
staccato of hands battering the jeep. There is something not
entirely hostile in the way they move their bodies. I gradually
become aware of this. There is a great excitement. They

lift their sticks and shout. Their eyes on the police station.

We reached the square at almost the moment the reinforcements
arrived from Pretoria. The square opened up in front of us as
their trucks lumbered in. Izak drove deep into our shed. We
both leapt out and hurried to the perimeter of the clinic. Constance was standing on the flat cement wall looking down into
the square. I climbed to her side.

"Constance! What the hell's happening?"

"The white horse, Doctor." She points into the square. A
horse bobbed and scuffled in the thick crowd. The sound was
overwhelming.

I recognized Colonel Jacobs. He was pushing his way into the
crowd, a handful of police in khaki behind him. I could see
Nienaber at his side carrying a loudhailer. The Africans
squeezed back, opening a path before them. The path rapidly
formed into a tight ragged circle. The horse was pushed in.
The animal jerked free, shivered and slowly rocked from side
to side. A front leg was broken. It swung its head high, the
eyes bloodshot and terrified. Eliphas's mule . The ears folded
back in fear.

Colonel Jacobs takes the loudhailer from Nienaber.

"Miyeleni! Quiet! I want to speak to you!" A sudden silence.
I could hear the mule scuff the ground.

"What shall we do with this animal?"

"Kill it! Nyi dlayeni!" The cry rose with the heat.

"Whose animal is this?"

Nienaber points into the crowd. There was Eliphas. His mouth
hanging open, arms limp at his side--Eliphas in a dream.

"Shall we kill this animal?"

From deep within the dream Eliphas stirred. He must have
realised how easily the "spell" could spread from the mule to
himself. He nodded slowly, staying in the dream.

Colonel Jacobs signalled to one of the men. The policeman
stepped forward, unclipping his holster as he walked.

I placed a hand on Constance's shoulder. Her body drew tight
within the starched white wall of her dress.

The shot filled the square and reverberated again and again
until the lonely palm tree trembled. A deep sigh rose from the
massive crowd. The sigh rippled and flowed out of the square
and through the tightly jammed streets. All Gaza Nkulu sighed.
The township sighed.

Immediately the crowd began to drift away. Colonel Jacobs
handed the loudhailer to Nienaber.

"Man, I've never known such heat as you chaps got in this place."

"Izak! Bring the master some water!"

My last memories of Gaza Nkulu Township were the crowds
silently melting away--of Eliphas, still in a dream--his clothes
loose and limp about him, and Colonel Jacobs standing before a
tin basin held solemnly by Izak. He was wetting his face and
washing his hands.

Beggar My Neighbour

Dan Jacobson

Michael saw them for the first time when he was coming home
from school one day. One moment the street had been empty,
glittering in the light from the sun behind Michael's back, with no
traffic on the roadway and apparently no pedestrians on the broad
sandy pavement; the next moment these two were before him,
their faces raised to his. They seemed to emerge directly in
front of him, as if the light and shade of the glaring street had
suddenly condensed itself into two little piccanins with large eyes
set in their round, black faces.

"Stukkie brood?" the elder, a boy, said in a plaintive voice.
A piece of bread. At Michael's school the slang term for any
African child was just that: stukkie brood. That was what Afri-
can children were always begging for.

"Stukkie brood?" the little girl said. She was wearing a soiled
white dress that was so short it barely covered her loins; there
seemed to be nothing at all beneath the dress. She wore no socks,
no shoes, no cardigan, no cap or hat. She must have been about
ten years old. The boy, who wore a torn khaki shirt and a pair
of grey shorts much too large for him, was about Michael's age,
about twelve, though he was a little smaller than the white boy.
Like the girl, the African boy had no shoes or socks. Their
limbs were painfully thin; their wrists and ankles stood out in
knobs, and the skin over these protruding bones was rougher
than elsewhere. The dirt on their skin showed up as a faint
greyness against the black.

"I've got no bread," the white boy said. He had halted in his
surprise at the suddenness of their appearance before him. They
must have been hiding behind one of the trees that were planted at
intervals along the pavement. "I don't bring bread from
school."

They did not move. Michael shifted his school case from one
hand to the other and took a pace forward. Silently, the African
children stood aside. As he passed them, Michael was conscious

of the movement of their eyes; when he turned to look back he
saw that they were standing still to watch him go. The boy was
holding one of the girl's hands in his.

It was this that made the white child pause. He was touched
by their dependence on one another, and disturbed by it too, as
he had been by the way they had suddenly come before him, and
by their watchfulness and silence after they had uttered their customary, begging request. Michael saw again how ragged and
dirty they were, and thought of how hungry they must be. Surely
he could give them a piece of bread. He was only three blocks
from home.

He said, "I haven't got any bread here. But if you come home
with me, I'll see that you get some bread. Do you understand?"

They made no reply; but they obviously understood what he had
said. The three children moved down the pavement, the two piccanins as silent as the shadows that slid over the rough sand ahead of
them. Once Michael asked them if they went to school, and the
boy shook his head; when Michael asked them if they were brother
and sister, the boy nodded.

When they reached Michael's house, he went inside and told
Dora, the cook-girl, that there were two piccanins in the lane
outside, and that he wanted her to cut some bread and jam for
them. Dora grumbled that she was not supposed to look after every
little beggar in town, and Michael answered her angrily, "We've
got lots of bread. Why shouldn't we give them some?" He was particularly indignant because he felt that Dora, being of the same
race as the two outside, should have been readier than he was to
help them. When Dora was about to take the bread out to the back
gate, where the piccanins waited, Michael stopped her. "It's all
right, Dora," he said in a tone of reproof, "I'll take it," and he
went out into the sunlight, carrying the plate in his hand.

"Stukkie brood," he called out to them. "Here's your stukkie
brood."

The two children stretched their hands out eagerly, and Michael
let them take the inch-thick slices from the plate. He was pleased
to see that Dora had put a scraping of apricot jam on the bread.
Each of the piccanins held the bread in both hands, as if afraid
of dropping it. The girl's mouth worked a little, but she kept her
eyes fixed on the white boy.

"What do you say?" Michael asked.

They replied in high, clear voices, "Thank you, baas."

"That's better. Now you can eat." He wanted to see them eat
it; he wanted to share their pleasure in satisfying their strained
appetites. But without saying a word to him, they began to back
away, side by side. They took a few paces, then they turned and
ran along the lane towards the main road they had walked down
earlier. The little girl's dress fluttered behind her, white
against her black body. At the corner, they halted, looked back
once, and then ran on, out of sight.

A few days later, at the same time and in the same place, Michael saw them again, on his way home from school. They were
standing in the middle of the pavement, and he saw them from a
long way off. They were obviously waiting for him to come. Michael was the first to speak, as he approached them.

"What? Another piece of bread?" he called out from a few
yards away.

"Yes, baas," they answered together. They turned immediately to join him as he walked by. Yet they kept a respectful
pace or two behind.

"How did you know I was coming?"

"We know the baas is coming from school."

"And how do you know that I am going to give you bread?"

There was no reply; not even a smile from the boy, in response to Michael's. They seemed to Michael, as he glanced
casually at them, identical in appearance to a hundred, a thousand,
other piccanins, from the peppercorns on top of their heads to
their wide, calloused, sand-grey feet.

When they reached the house, Michael told Dora, "Those stukkie broods are waiting outside again. Give them something and
then they can go."

Dora grumbled once again, but did as she was told. Michael
did not go out with the bread himself; he was in a hurry to get
back to work on a model car he was making, and was satisfied to
see, out of his bedroom window, Dora coming from the back gate
a few minutes later with an empty plate in her hand. Soon he
had forgotten all about the two children. He did not go out of
the house until a couple of hours had passed; by then it was dusk,
and he took a torch with him to help him find a piece of wire
for his model in the darkness of the lumber-shed. Handling
the torch gave Michael a feeling of power and importance, and

he stepped into the lane with it, intending to shine it about like
a policeman on his beat. Immediately he opened the gate, he
saw the two little piccanins standing in the half-light, just a few
paces away from him.

"What are you doing here?" Michael exclaimed in surprise.

The boy answered, holding his head up, as if warning Michael
to be silent. "We were waiting to say thank you to the baas."

"What!" Michael took a step towards them both, and they
stood their ground, only shrinking together slightly.

For all the glare and glitter there was in the streets of Lynd-
hurst by day, it was winter, midwinter; and once the sun had set
a bitter chill came into the air, as swiftly as the darkness. The
cold at night wrung deep notes from the contracting iron roofs
of the houses, and froze the fish-ponds in all the fine gardens
of the white suburbs. Already Michael could feel its sharp
touch on the tips of his ears and fingers. And the two African
children stood there barefoot, in a flimsy dress and torn shirt,
waiting to thank him for the bread he had sent out to them.

"You mustn't wait," Michael said. In the half-darkness he
saw the white dress on the girl more clearly than the boy's
clothing; and he remembered the nakedness and puniness of her
black thighs. He stretched his hand out, with the torch in it.
"Take it," he said. The torch was in their hands, and there was
nothing else he could give to them. "It's nice," he said. "It's
a torch. Look!" He switched it on and saw in its beam of light
a pair of startled eyes, darting desperately from side to side.
"You see how nice it is," Michael said, turning the beam up-
wards, where it lost itself against the light that lingered in the
sky. "If you don't want it, you can sell it. Go on, take it."

A hand came up and took the torch from him. Then the two
children ran off, in the same direction they had taken on the
first afternoon. When they reached the corner all the street
lights came on, as if at a single touch, and the children stopped
and stared at them, before running on. Michael saw the torch
glinting in the boy's hand, and only then did it occur to him that
despite their zeal to thank him for the bread,they hadn't thanked
him for the torch. The size of the gift must have surprised
them into silence, Michael decided; and the thought of his own
generosity helped to console him for the regret he couldn't help
feeling when he saw the torch being carried away from him.

Michael was a lonely child. He had neither brothers nor sisters; both his parents worked during the day, and he had made
few friends at school. But he was not by any means unhappy in
his loneliness. He was used to it, in the first place; and then,
because he was lonely, he was all the better able to indulge himself in his own fantasies. He played for hours, by himself,
games of his own invention--games of war, of exploration, of
seafaring, of scientific invention, of crime, of espionage, of
living in a house beneath or above his real one. It was not long
before the two African children, who were now accosting him
regularly, appeared in some of his games, for their weakness,
poverty, and dependence gave Michael ample scope to display
in fantasy his kindness, generosity, courage and decisiveness.
Sometimes in his games Michael saved the boy's life, and was
thanked for it in broken English. Sometimes he saved the girl's,
and then she humbly begged his pardon for having caused him so
much trouble. Sometimes he was just too late to save the life
of either, though he tried his best, and then there were affecting scenes of farewell.

But in real life, Michael did not play with the children at all:
they were too dirty, too ragged, too strange, too persistent.
Their persistence eventually drove Dora to tell Michael's mother about them; and his mother did her duty by telling Michael
that on no account should he play with the children, nor should
he give them anything of value.

"Play with them!" Michael laughed at the idea. And apart
from bread and the torch he had given them nothing but a few
old toys, a singlet or two, a pair of old canvas shoes. No one
could begrudge them those gifts. And the truth was that Michael's
mother begrudged the piccanins neither the old toys and clothes,
nor the bread. What she was anxious to do was simply to prevent her son playing with the piccanins, fearing that he would
pick up germs, bad language, and "kaffir ways" generally from
them, if he did. Hearing from both Michael and Dora that he
did not play with them at all, and that he had never even asked

them into the back yard, let alone the house, Michael's mother
was satisfied.

They came to Michael about once a week,meeting him as he
walked back from school, or simply waiting for him outside the
back gate. The spring winds had already blown the cold weather
away, almost overnight, and still the children came. Their
words of thanks varied neither in tone nor length, whatever Michael gave them; but they had revealed, in response to his
question, that the boy's name was Frans and the girl's name
was Annie, that they lived in Green Point Location, and that
their mother and father were both dead. During all this time
Michael had not touched them, except for the fleeting contact
of their hands when he passed a gift to them. Yet sometimes
Michael wished that they were more demonstrative in their expressions of gratitude to him; he thought that they could, for
instance, seize his hand and embrace it; or go down on their
knees and weep, just once. As it was, he had to content himself with fantasies of how they spoke of him among their friends,
when they returned to the tumbled squalor of Green Point Location; of how incredulous their friends must be to hear their
stories about the kind white kleinbaas who gave them food and toys
and clothing.

One day Michael came out to them carrying a possession he
particularly prized--an elaborate pen and pencil set which had
been given to him for a recent birthday. He had no intention of
giving the outfit to the African children, and he did not think
that he would be showing off with it in front of them. He merely
wanted to share his pleasure in it with someone who had not already seen it. But as soon as he noticed the way the children
were looking at the open box, Michael knew the mistake he had
made. "This isn't for you," he said abruptly. The children
blinked soundlessly, staring from the box to Michael and back
to the box again. "You can just look at it," Michael said. He
held the box tightly in his hand, stretching it forward, the pen
and the propelling pencils shining inside the velvet-lined case.
The two heads of the children came together over the box; they
stared deeply into it.

At last the boy lifted his head. "It's beautiful," he breathed
out. As he spoke, his hand slowly came up towards the box.

"No," Michael said, and snatched the box away.

"Baas?"

"No," Michael retreated a little, away from the beseeching
eyes, and the uplifted hand.

"Please, baas, for me?"

And his sister said, "For me also, baas."

"No, you can't have this," Michael attempted to laugh, as if
at the absurdity of the idea. He was annoyed with himself for
having shown the box, and at the same time shocked at them for
having asked for it. It was the first time they had asked for anything but bread.

"Please, baas. It's nice." The boy's voice trailed away on
the last word, in longing; and then his sister repeated the word,
like an echo, her own voice trailing away too. "Ni-ice."

"No! I won't give it to you! I won't give you anything, if you
ask for this. Do you hear?"

Their eyes dropped, their hands came together, they lowered
their heads. Being sure now that they would not again ask for
the box, Michael relented. He said,"I'm going in now, and I'll
tell Dora to bring you some bread."

But Dora came to him in his room a few minutes later.
"The little kaffirs are gone." She was holding the plate of
bread in her hand. Dora hated the two children, and Michael
thought there was some kind of triumph in her voice and manner
as she made the announcement.

He went outside to see if she was telling the truth. The lane
was empty. He went to the street, and looked up and down its
length, but there was no sign of them there either. They were
gone. He had driven them away. Michael expected to feel
guilty; but to his own intense surprise he felt nothing of the kind.
He was relieved that they were gone, and that was all.

When they appeared a few days later, Michael felt scorn towards them for coming back after what had happened on the last
occasion. He felt they were in his power. "So you've come
back?" he greeted them. "You like your stukkie brood, hey?
You're hungry, so today you'll wait, you won't run away."

"Yes, baas,"they said, in their low voices.

Michael brought the bread out to them; when they reached for

it he jokingly pulled the plate back and laughed at their surprise.
Then only did he give them the bread.

"Thank you, baas."

"Thank you, baas."

They ate the bread in Michael's presence; watching them, he
felt a little more kindly disposed towards them. "All right, you
can come another day, and there'll be some more bread for you."

"Thank you, baas."

"Thank you, baas."

They came back sooner than Michael had expected them to.
He gave them their bread and told them to go. They went off,
but again did not wait for the usual five or six days to pass, before approaching him once more. Only two days had passed,
yet here they were with their eternal request--"Stukkie brood,
baas?"

Michael said, "Why do you get hungry so quickly now?" But
he gave them their bread.

When they appeared in his games and fantasies, Michael no
longer rescued them, healed them, casually presented them
with kingdoms and motor-cars. Now he ordered them about,
sent them away on disastrous missions, picked them out to be
shot for cowardice in the face of the enemy. And because something similar to these fantasies was easier to enact in the real
world than his earlier fantasies, Michael was soon ordering
them about unreasonably in fact. He deliberately left them waiting; he sent them away and told them to come back on days when
he knew he would be in town; he told them there was no bread in
the house. And when he did give them anything, it was bread
only now; never old toys or articles of clothing.

So, as the weeks passed, Michael's scorn gave way to impatience and irritation, irritation to anger. And what angered
him most was that the two piccanins seemed too stupid to real-
ize what he now felt about them, and instead of coming less frequently, continued to appear more often than ever before. Soon
they were coming almost every day, though Michael shouted at
them and teased them, left them waiting for hours, and made
them do tricks and sing songs for their bread. They did everything he told them to do; but they altogether ignored his instructions as to which days they should come. Invariably, they would
be waiting for him, in the shade of one of the trees that grew

alongside the main road from school, or standing at the gate
behind the house with sand scuffed up about their bare toes.
They were as silent as before; but more persistent, inexorably
persistent. Michael took to walking home by different routes,
but they were not to be so easily discouraged. They simply
waited at the back gate, and whether he went into the house by
the front or the back gate, he could not avoid seeing their upright, unmoving figures.

Finally, he told them to go and never come back at all. Often
he had been tempted to do this, but some shame or pride had always prevented him from doing it; he had always weakened previously, and named a date, a week or two weeks ahead, when
they could come again. But now he shouted at them, "It's finished! No more bread--nothing! Come on, voetsek! If you
come back I'll tell the garden-boy to chase you away."

From then on they came every day. They no longer waited
right at the back gate, but squatted in the sand across the lane.
Michael was aware of their eyes following him when he went by,
but they did not approach him at all. They did not even get up
from the ground when he passed. A few times he shouted at
them to go, and stamped his foot, but he shrank from hitting
them. He did not want to touch them. Once he sent out Jan,
the garden-boy, to drive them away; but Jan, who had hitherto
always shared Dora's views on the piccanins, came back muttering angrily and incomprehensibly to himself; and when Michael
peeped into the lane he saw that they were still there. Michael
tried to ignore them, to pretend that he did not see them. He
hated them now; even more, he began to dread them.
But he did not know how much he hated and feared the two
piccanins until he fell ill with a cold, and lay feverish in bed
for a few days. During those days the two children were constantly in his dreams, or in his half-dreams, for even as he
dreamed he knew he was turning on his bed; he was conscious
of the sun shining outside by day, and at night of the passage-
light that had been left on inside the house. In these dreams he
struck again at the children with weapons he found in his hands;
he fled in fear from them down lanes so thick with sand his feet
could barely move through it; he committed lewd, cruel acts
upon the bare-thighed girl, and her brother shrieked to tell the

empty street of what he was doing. Michael struck out at him
with a piece of heavy cast-iron guttering. Its edge dug sharply
into Michael's hands as the blow fell, and when he lifted the
weapon he saw the horror he had made of the side of the boy's
head, and how the one remaining eyeball still stared unwinkingly
at him.

Michael thought he was awake, and suddenly calm. The fever
seemed to have left him. It was as though he had slept deeply,
for days, after that last dream of violence; yet his impression
was that he had woken directly from it. The bedclothes felt heavy
on him, and he drew them off. The house was quite silent. He
got out of bed and went to look at the clock in the kitchen: it was
early afternoon. Dora and Jan were resting in their rooms across
the yard, as they always did after lunch. Outside, the light of
the sun was unremitting, a single golden glare. He walked back
to his bedroom; there, he put on his dressing-gown and slippers,
feeling the coolness inside his slippers on his bare feet. He
went through the kitchen again, quietly, and on to the back
stoep, and then across the back yard. The sun seemed to seize
the back of his neck as firmly as a hand grasping, and its light
was so bright he was aware of it only as a darkness beyond the
little stretch of ground he looked down upon. He opened the
back gate. Inevitably, as he had known they would be, the two
were waiting.

He did not want to go beyond the gate in his pyjamas and dressing-gown, so, shielding his eyes from the glare with one hand,
he beckoned to them to him with the other. Together, in silence,
they rose and crossed the lane. It seemed to take them a long
time to come to him, but at last they stood in front of him, with
their hands interlinked. Michael stared into their dark faces,
and they stared into his.

"What are you waiting for?" he asked.

"For you." First the boy answered; then the girl repeated,
"For you."

Michael looked from the one to the other; and he remembered
what he had been doing to them in his dreams. Their eyes were
black to look into, deep black. Staring forward, Michael understood what he should have understood long before: that they came
to him not in hope or appeal or even in reproach, but in hatred.
What he felt towards them, they felt towards him; what he had

done to them in his dreams, they did to him in theirs.

The sun, their staring eyes, his own fear came together in a sound that seemed to hang in the air of the lane--a cry, the sound of someone weeping. Then Michael knew that it was he who was crying. He felt the heat of the tears in his eyes, he felt the moisture running down his cheeks. And with the same fixity of decision that had been his in his dreams of violence and torture, Michael knew what he must do. He beckoned them forward, closer. They came. He stretched out his hands, he felt under his fingers the springy hair he had looked at so often before from the distance between himself and them; he felt the smooth skin of their faces; their frail, rounded shoulders, their hands. Their hands were in his, and he led them inside the gate.

He led them into the house, through the kitchen down the passage, into his room, where they had never been before. They looked about at the pictures on the walls, the toys on top of the low cupboard, the twisted white sheets and tumbled blankets on the bed. They stood on both sides of him, and for the first time since he had met them, their lips parted into slow, grave smiles. And Michael knew that what he had to give them was not toys or clothes or bread, but something more difficult. Yet it was not difficult at all, for there was nothing else he could give them. He took the girl's face in his hands and pressed his lips to hers. He was aware of the darkness of her skin, and the smell of it, and of the faint movement of her lips, a single pulse that beat momentarily against his own. Then it was gone. He kissed the boy, too, and let them go. They came together, and grasped each other by the hand, staring at him.

"What do you want now?" he asked.

A last anxiety flickered in Michael and left him, as the boy slowly shook his head. He began to step back, pulling his sister with him; when he was through the door he turned his back on Michael and they walked away down the passage. Michael watched them go. At the door of the kitchen, on their way out of the house, they paused, turned once more, and lifted their hands, the girl copying the boy, in a silent, tentative gesture of farewell.

Michael did not follow them. He heard the back gate swing open, and then bang when it closed. He went wearily back to his bed, and as he fell upon it, his relief and gratitude that the bed should be there to receive him changed suddenly into grief at the knowledge that he was already lying upon it--that he had never left it.

His cold grew worse, turned into bronchitis, kept him in bed for several weeks. But his dreams were no longer of violence; they were calm, spacious, and empty of people. As empty as the lane was, when he was at last allowed out of the house, and made his way there immediately, to see if the children were waiting for him.

He never saw them again, though he looked for them in the streets and lanes of the town. He saw a hundred, a thousand, children like them; but not the two he hoped to find.

Light Dark

Rose Moss

There was always something mysterious about them and the
way we lived with them. There was something between us that
meant we couldn't really see them when we looked at them, they
were hidden like a leg inside a stocking, or the living face behind the cardboard faces children put on at Halloween. It's
something I find difficult to explain, but sometimes people who
grew up in the South know what I mean.

Once when I was a child we had duck for Sunday dinner. I
saw it before it was cooled. It was in a bowl on the step outside
the kitchen door. Raw, yellow. Everything grown-ups and servants did had reasons, their reasons. I didn't ask anyone why
it was out there. Perhaps Beauty still had to singe the pin feathers off the way she did with chickens, or perhaps she had to
clean out the intestines and lungs. My mother used to tell her
to be very careful doing this because if the gall bladder breaks
it taints the whole bird with bitterness.
I was on my way to the backyard where there were things I
used to do with stones and bits of stick. I loved the white
quartz stones that half let light through like an egg. Once when
I read a story about how Leonardo painted pictures as a child
and used colors pressed from flower petals I went to the front
of the house and picked red and yellow cannas, but no Verrochio
saw my sun on the whitewashed wall or said, "Come, be my apprentice. You will be a painter." Perhaps Beauty saw my sun,
or Isaac the garden boy, or maybe Beauty's husband Philemon,
who visited her on weekends.
I don't know why I turned round to look at the duck lying there
in its white enamel dish. Ants were coming out of the hole where
the neck had been chopped off. The whole cavity was creepy
with them coming in and out in a ribbon like a spill of black,

glittering blood, beads of jet like the lines picked out on dressy
ladies' dresses, splashed all over the costumes of nightclub
singers. The ants poured down into the basin like a pool. I
ran inside to tell Beauty or my mother, but they were talking
to each other about the cake and didn't want me to make a fuss.
I went outside again and looked. I suppose I was feeling the
naive horror of a city child who has never seen a corpse before.

There were guests at dinner and everything was served ele-
gantly--the herring on little glass plates, the radishes cut into
flowers, and the butter rolled into dewy balls. When Isaac
brought the duck to the table it was golden brown, lacquered
and shining like Russian tea in a glass with a silver holder. All
round it on the platter were golden roast potatoes and ponds of
brilliant green peas. I opened my mouth, but my mother stopped
me before I could say anything.

So it became hidden, in that place we hide things we were
taught as children not to talk about.

At high school I hated the big framed Rembrandt reproduc-
tion outside the principal's office. Every morning we lined up
to go to assembly and outside the principal's office we had to
stop to wait for the other forms that filed in before us. It feels
as if it were always dark there where we had to wait, and the
prefects saw to it that we couldn't talk, we just waited for all
the forms to go in in the right order. I didn't know what I was
learning there under the picture of Rembrandt's general wearing
a gold helmet, though there was something in his surly, decay-
ing face that felt like the word "policeman," and I connected it
with all the things I hated, respect for authority, school spirit,
neatness and ladylike manners. I couldn't have found words to
explain the connection, so it remained half hidden from me and
weakened me. I wore my black gym, and filed in to assembly
in my proper place, and listened when the principal read a passage from the Bible and then school announcements, and I sang
a hymn and the Lord's Prayer before we all filed out in our
black lines. Although my gym was often defiantly dirty, when
the prefects stopped me and told that I disgraced the school I
felt ashamed. Even though I despised what they stood for.

Because the imagination's rivers running underground sometimes flow as if away from logic, I will say that I hated the Rembrandt because of the duck. I felt that those yellow-brown

landscapes and portraits done in oils stood for the manners of
the upper classes and their catchwords like duty and honor, and
for years I couldn't look at a Claude, or Lorraine, or even
Constable, and see what anyone found lovely there. Though I
found out about Rembrandt because when I got to college a
teacher showed us that picture of a carcass hanging from the
butcher's hook.

When I met my mother-in-law I thought she blamed me for
taking her son away to live in a foreign country. She said,
"I'd never vote for the Nationalists, but no government's perfect." She often says, "You have to close your eyes to some
things."

She has three sons. The youngest was born eight years
after Eric. Her husband enlisted as soon as the war started
and was away for six years. One day when we were looking
through the family photographs, Eric showed me a studio portrait of him wearing his uniform. It was the only picture of
him by himself. In all the others he was with his boys or part
of a family picnic or wedding. There were his own wedding
pictures with her in her white dress and veil.
    In ten years I've heard her mention him once. She was ask-
ing Eric whether he remembered a little trick with a handkerchief that amuses children. Her voice sounded alive and happy.
    When I asked Eric whether his parents were happy together
he said, "I don't know."
Sometimes he thinks there was another woman those years
away during the war.

It's not as though I saw things no one else saw. There were
always empty lots where you could see a picannin or two with a
soccer ball belly and a bud of green snot in one nostril, playing
with nothing to play with and no grown-up in sight. Everyone
had servants coming and going in the backyard, making too much
noise, everyone said, and getting arrested for something to do
with a pass or smoking dagga. All the houses had thick burglar-
proof netting over the windows, or burglar-proofing like curled
cast-iron decorations because there were always some who
wanted to come in and steal and murder. There were other
things they would do too, but those were so terrible no one

talked about them at all. There were always friends with me
on a Saturday afternoon when we came out of the bioscope still
thinking about Clark Gable or Gary Cooper, and the deformed
things were there outside waiting for us, they had a few pennies
and silver coins spread out in the bowl of a felt hat, shining
like ringworm. Sometimes they called out, "Missus," although we were still children, "Penny, Missus."

Children our own age or younger than we danced on street
corners to the music of their own clapping or piping on a penny
whistle, and then we gave them money. Even in winter they
didn't wear shoes. Newsboys sometimes wore men's jackets
and fumbled for change in the pockets at their thighs.

Everyone saw these things and heard the clink of milk bottles in
the dawning street   where the delivery boys were riding tri-
cycles. Everyone gave when the school collected pennies for
charity, the clinic in Alexandra, milk for the school feeding
scheme, clothes for the refugee children in Europe.

When I was fifteen Beauty was sick. My mother went to her
room with medicines, and her husband came to visit her every
night. He ate supper with the garden boy. One evening when I
was bored and went into the kitchen forgetting that Beauty
wouldn't be there, I saw him sitting upright on a straight chair
against the wall. He was wearing a dark brown suit and dark
brown shoes, and a grey felt hat. I didn't know what to say to
him. Afterwards he was there when I brought medicines to
Beauty and saw his white shirt glare in the light of a bare electric bulb. I can't think where I've seen that effect in America.
Perhaps in a lighted supermarket parking lot late at night when
it's empty except for the snow piled high at the corners. In
Europe I've seen it in the deserted platforms of midnight railway stations and in the shabby waiting rooms. An effect like
the chiaroscuro in Rembrandt's paintings: light dark.

What my mother-in-law did want me to see was the Barberton daisies growing wild near the mountains of Swaziland in the
springtime. She said, "There's nothing like them in the whole
world." Other people told about them too, the slopes covered
with wild daisies, red, pink, yellow, orange. In New York I
sometimes see Barberton daisies in flower shops.

At a party once I met a keen gardener who said,"I wish I
could go to South Africa. "

"Why?" I asked her.

"Flower catalogues are full of the most beautiful flowers
that just grow wild there. "

"You mean daisies?"

"And gladiolus, and freesias, and amaryllis. It must be a
beautiful country. "

"Yes. "

When Eric and I set off driving towards the mountains it was
a time of drought. There's always drought before the spring
rains in October, but this year it was worse than usual and
some of the white newspapers were showing pictures of the des-
sicated cattle lying on cracked ground, either dead or near
enough. The vultures must have feasted, but family newspapers draw the line at showing some things.

One day there was a picture of a dune of oranges on the
Weenen farm, the largest of the huge citrus plantations in the
Transvaal. There was a glut, and orange prices were too low
to make it worthwhile to send any to market. After that there
were letters in the paper about how the government should buy
the oranges and give them to African children. People who
read the English press in South Africa know that black children
are always starving.

But we didn't really see that the drought was worse than
usual until the car broke down about two hundred miles from
Johannesburg, in the middle of nowhere. We hitchhiked to the
nearest place with a name and a garage and had the car towed.
They said, three days, four days. They couldn't do anything
without a new part.

There was one hotel. There was a new car salesroom. A
cafe with two pinball machines. Three churches. A retail
store with a display of men's woolen socks in one window and
a pyramid of toothpaste boxes in the other. Inside on the
counter there was a display of Kodak film featuring a pretty
girl with hair in a windblown style that could remind someone
who had travelled or looked at art books of Botticelli's Venus.

Eric remembered that one of his school friends had become
a missionary and that the mission was as near to Stoffberg as
to any other place.

Julian said he'd come and fetch us, so we waited in the cafe.
We drank cokes and watched the high school boys killing time
with the pinball machines.

On the way to the mission we saw that this part of the country
was really dry. It looked worse than the Karroo where some
species of plants and animals have adapted to near desert conditions. In the Karroo after a rain the flowers open and the
desert becomes a fairyland. Here, when it rained, the loose
soil would just pour down the gullies. It was flying about now in
the wind, the sky was dirty and grey looking without any clouds.
When we came to a big gully wide enough to be a river in summer
we saw a settlement of Africans. They'd been moved out of
their old homeland, Julian told us. It had taken police, because
they wouldn't go peacefully. Their new settlement, in this desig-
nated black area, was on the banks of the steep ditch where we
couldn't see any water, though there were some women down
near the rocks at the bottom with tin cans. We couldn't see much
because as we were crossing the bridge children picked up stones
and threw them at the car.

At the mission there was a hospital and a school as well as a
church and a monastery. When we wanted to visit the hospital
Julian put us off, but before we left he did tell us the story. I
think it was preying on his mind. There'd been an outbreak of
measles, and when children are starving and get measles they
die of it, or go blind, or deaf, sometimes mad. The white doctors were trying to prevent the epidemic from spreading and
wouldn't let the children out. Their mothers were gathering
outside the hospital, sitting on the ground all day, all night,
begging to have their children back.

In those days they were still begging a lot.

But the white doctors said, no. They said they must keep the
children or everyone would get measles.

"I shouldn't really talk about it," Julian said.

When the car was fixed we didn't want to go to Barberton
to see the flowers, so we turned round and went back to Johannesburg.

My mother-in-law was disappointed. She's always loved
flowers and her own herbacious border used to win prizes
every year. This year, though, all the flower gardens in Johannesburg were suffering because of the drought and the regu-
lations against watering. My brother-in-law's roses were in

danger, and the newly laid swimming pool was beginning to
crack. It needed to be filled.

But as she said herself, you can't worry about everything.

She didn't have her own flower garden anymore. When her
husband had died, three years before, she'd moved to a flat. It
was more convenient, though there was a problem about finding
a room for Susan, the maid who's been with her for fourteen
years. Most of the servants in the building have to share a room,
but my mother-in-law insisted on Susan's behalf, and managed to
get a room Susan doesn't have to share. Of course she pays
more, but she's always been generous. She's helped Susan for
years with extra money for uniforms and boarding fees so that
her son could go to high school. A flat is much more convenient
now that she lives alone. She travels a lot now. She went on
her first trip to Europe a year after her husband died, and since
then she's been to Asia and Latin America, and on a tour of the
United States that allowed her to stop with us in New York for a
few days.

When we visited Johannesburg four years ago, it was around
the time of her birthday. The sons arranged that they'd all take
her out to dinner. On the way to her flat we stopped to buy
flowers. They sell them on street corners in South Africa,
lovely tiers of bloom so cheap that for only a few dollars you
get so many you carry them like a child cradled in arms. I've
never seen anything like these flower sellers in the United
States, and I said to Eric, "Let's get a picture of that."

When the Coloured flower seller saw us using the camera
she said, "Where do you come from, master?"

"The United States."

"America?" she asked in a voice that made me think she'd
never spoken to anyone who'd actually been there.

"Yes. New York."

"Please baas, master, take me with you. Just me and my
little boy, baas, my baby. I'll be your servant for seven years
master, you needn't give me any pay, just food and a room to
sleep. Please master. Only, in seven years it's time for me
to make the pilgrimage to Mecca."

I don't think she understood why we said no, we couldn't. As
though her terms weren't good enough.

We didn't tell my mother-in-law what had happened.

It was her birthday. Eric figured out that she must be turning sixty-six.

So I sent this memory down to that place where there are things ripening in the dark.

After the Soweto riots her oldest son came to visit us here in New York. One day when we were alone in the apartment together he took out a newspaper clipping and showed it to me. He'd cut it out a month before, when he first arrived in San Francisco, on the other side of the continent. It was about how political prisoners are treated in South Africa. When I'd read it through he said to me, "What do you think?"

"It's really shocking."

"Yes, isn't it. I'm appalled that they'll publish such lies without checking the facts! What a bunch of lies!"

He's her son, I thought.

But then he folded the clipping and packed it carefully in his suitcase under the clean woolen socks, so that it wouldn't get damaged when he took it home with him.

Now he's decided to leave South Africa, with his wife and three children. He's found a job in Phoenix.

The youngest brother's gone also. He found work in England, and left last month with his wife and two children.

That leaves her alone, except for her friends. We'd be worried about her living alone like that without anyone, but Susan's going to stay. Her son's just finished high school, so she's offered to help Susan send him to college. He'll go to one of the universities separate for each tribe. This one's called the University of the North.

The campus is quite near the Weenen citrus farms.

She fell a few months ago and broke her hip. Susan looked after her and friends came to visit. Eric flew over to see that everything was all right. I went to meet his plane today. When I asked, "How is she?" he said, "Fine."

"Is she afraid of dying?" I asked.

"She doesn't talk about it."

"And the political situation?"
"She doesn't talk about that either. As long as Susan stays
with her there's no problem."

Section 11

Other Routes

from The Keep

Jillian Becker

    Africa had not been a place of survival for all of them. After
all, out of the quite considerable number which had arrived from
Russia, only the Kronowskys and Great-Aunt Lydia were extant.
The rest, even here, had come to dust. Their grandfather and
grandmother, and the rest. Dead and gone, long ago. And this
was odd to think of, because, to Josephine, Africa if it was anything was here and now. Europe was a tale of war and death,
but Africa was pervading certainty, like the sunlight, not particularly to be noticed but the general condition of being. Africa
was not a word that had to be seen through. Africa, though almost totally inapprehensible, suffused and supported, overlay
and underlay. Only at some points it stuck out at you, with
something, and you could feel its special feel, see it, smell it.
There was the sprawling thorny shrub that grew against the wall
of the kitchen garden at home, flaunting on its dry sticks, very
occasionally, such blooms, so perfumed, that the English wall-
flowers secluded between the pea-rows and even the twelve tulips which Mrs. Leyton had the gardener coax into rigid existence every spring in the wall's shadow, were humbled into a
modesty that golden-brown and purple could never ordinarily express. At such times it incited admiration. But at others it
merely looked savage. Twice Mrs. Leyton, visiting her tulips
in the seedling stage, before its evil glamour had begun to cast
its own unconquerable spell, had ordered its destruction. But
either its roots went too deep, or the gardener was in league
with it, for twice it rose again, stretched out, clawing at the
pea-vines, and again, in due season, shamed the tulips. Except
that there was a unanimous certainty of its being indigenous,
nothing was known about it and nobody could put a name to it:
not even Uncle Fred, who had made a study of local flora and
fauna, and had his own "indigenous collection."
Uncle Fred's African studies had begun when he'd "smoused"
through the Free State and the Transvaal with the customary

donkey-cart (that motif of the pioneering days so common that
along the frieze of the century it fits between the oxwagons as
a Greek triglyph between the metopes). They had continued
when he had turned prospector, exercising his hopes with a
sluicepan, and they were given their widest scope when, after
making his fortune in partnership with the owner of a mining
store who'd had a side-interest in brandy and a side-door which
the mine boys preferred to the other, he had gone with a party
of intrepid men into the bushveld and shot his subjects dead.
More recently they had been pursued chiefly through books,
museums and camera lenses. But throughout, their chief purpose had been to assist Fred Kronowsky in fixing his claim to be
a True Man of Africa.

"Jews," he instructed the children, "have always had to be
adaptable. You can't say a Jew's like this or a Jew's like that.
The most typical example, of any nation, on this earth, that you
may care to name, is its Jew. The most Russian Russian. The
most German German. And so on. Maybe not the Esquimaux.
All right, about Esquimaux I'm not arguing. But Indiannns,
Chineeeese, I'm telling you. And in the Middle East, like it or
not, there are Jews as black as kaffirs. Blacker, if you'll excuse me. I'm telling you if we had to live among leopards, we'd
come out in spots. All you've got to do, you've got to put a Jew
in a New Country, and you've got a New Man."

It was something to do with his being a New Man that kept the
"Great"from growing on the "Uncle" like an old man's beard.
He was their great-uncle from being married to their great-
aunt, who was older than he, but he would not be venerable. And
it was because of his newness and trueness that his library con-
sisted of so many books about Southern Africa, and his walls
were hung with the heads of beasts; with maps, tusks, and, faded
to reddish lines on yellowish grounds, framed round photographs like sick eyes. If one looked very closely at these one
could make out hatted, moustachioed cronies. Among this lot,
his fellow Uitlanders, he had stood and booed President Kruger
at the Wanderers Ground when that rheumy old tyrant had dared
to come to Johannesburg. (As he'd passed in his open carriage,
Fred Kronowsky had been able to see little more than his top
hat, for being a short man and his confederates tall, he had done
what he could with his teak periscope to witness the historic

event.) Before the eyes of this lot he had brought his hippo
down. With these he had celebrated the Jubilee. In himself,
to himself, he seemed a piece of history, and as triumphantly
resultant as any other current event.

OUR WAR

BARNEY SIMON

About Us and Our War

WELL, this is about our war. Whenever I complained about it, the noise and the dirt and the stinking and the dying, Mama used to say, "Listen, Leiba, be grateful for what you've got. That you're not in London or Moscow or New York or somewhere. Be grateful you're here where things always happen easier." When I got upset about Lily Fine losing her leg, she said, "So, but she's still got her head." And when our house went up in the second bombardment (which was famous for the first usage outside of Asia and the Middle East of .22238 Ziggmutt Mortars) and we built a shelter and it rained all those October days, the way she behaved you would've thought that it was the Christmas holidays and we were on holiday at the Imperial Hotel in Muizenberg. But if you think I was a moaner, you should've heard Rochella. She cried if there were lumps in the mealie-meal porridge or hair on the soap. She wouldn't wear a dress if it was dirty and if there was skin on the milk (when there was any) she'd rather go thirsty. When the mortars got going and there were blasts and quakes and screams, she complained that she couldn't go to sleep. But to be fair, that was toward the beginning.

One Sunday, which turned out to be the day of the eighteen hour blast (the fourth time in the whole world an entire ground-to-ground operation was carried out by the crews of Donnizetti rocket units) the Mizroch family, Zaidah Mizroch,

Mrs Mizroch, his daughter-in-law, and little Mitzi and Mike all went to collect what firewood they could from Gilooly's Farm, and when they hadn't come back by Friday, we moved into their house which was a little small for us, but still.

About Mama

Mama worked at the Bertha Solomon Social Centre, which was used as a hospital and house for old people since our war began. She did shift work, sometimes at night, sometimes during the day. She cleaned and scrubbed and nursed and sometimes she even helped in the surgery. She didn't like us to come there, but once I did. There were old people all over. On the verandah, on beds, on mattresses, on the floor, all calling her Malka, which is her first name, and asking her to sing. She didn't have a good voice—you know, she never got the tune nicely, but everybody used to ask her to sing because she knew nice songs with nice words. Then they asked her to tell them a joke. It wasn't so good but when she told it she was laughing so much she made us all laugh too.

Old Mr Lapinsky said that she had hands of solid gold. Everybody called for her to turn them over or rub them or massage them where they were sore. Especially Mr Lapinsky whose eyes were all white, and when he died, he left her his watch. At first we thought it was real gold, but when we took it to Maishke, he said it wasn't gold, just golden.She had friends who worked there too, like Mrs Pinchuk, Mrs Maganoff and Bessie Finestein. They weren't friends like she had in the old days like Pearl Reichman, but they were nice all the same.

At home our best times were when she made us potato sweets, and night, when we used to push our mattresses together and lie there in the dark. If you got there first, you lay next to her. First nobody talked and we just breathed. And then she told us about how she was a little girl in a little village in Lithuania and how she was scared of ice-skates, but she used to 'glitzzzz' on her shoes across the ice and how she used to find strawberries in the forests that smelt as sweet as flowers and covered her whole hand and how they used to sleep on the stove (that was always Mendel's favourite) in winter and how when she came here her best friend was the beauty queen and whistler Pearl Reichman and how they used to copy the movie stars' make-up with luscious lips and gypsy eyes, and how when she first came she thought the traffic cop stopped the traffic for her to cross the street and what a nice man she thought he was to do that (that was Rochella's favourite) and how once when somebody asked her to make a bet, she said she could make her own bed thank you (that was mine). Laykella had her own bed-time because she slept in a little hammock and went to bed early. Her favourite story was about the Reb and the Rebbitsen. But that's too long to tell now.

How we lost Hindella

Three days after we moved into the Mizroch house, we lost Hindella. There was some street fighting, no mortar or artillery, just rifles and a grenade or two. God knows what was happening in Pandora Street. It sounded like hell. Anyway, we were all lying flat on the lounge floor because we were all going out when it started and it didn't sound bad enough for the cellar when Hindella, God knows why, got up, peeped out of the window and plop was down with us again flat on her back with a bright red spot between her eyes.

After that, even before the funeral, Mama couldn't stand the Mizroch house any more, so she sent me out to Auntie Ada in Greenside where we heard it was pretty quiet to ask if we could move in with her and also to tell her about Hindella and her funeral, but when I got there, her house was full of other people who said they didn't know where Auntie Ada was and we couldn't come. So we just stayed on at the Mizroch house and Mama and Rochella spoke and cried in their sleep every night. Mendel and me mind you went on sleeping like logs and Baby Layka of course just went on snoring like an angel.

121

Hindella's Funeral

We buried Hindella in the cemetery that had been made on the soccer-field in Rhodes Park. On the way there, Rochella asked me to pinch her or something if she started to giggle because she always does. It was a hot day with a very blue sky. Mrs Maganoff, Mrs Katzen and Mrs Pinchuk, who worked with Mama at the Bertha Solomon Social Centre, were there, and Mama and me and Rochella and Tiny Yiddel from Belgravia Shul (he's the one Chesterfield's Circus wanted but he wouldn't take the job and kept his old one opening the Shul in the morning and locking it at night and setting out the prayer books) and Rabbi Spitz with his yellow-and-black beard. He was there to say the prayers, but before he did, Yiddel and me dug the grave, and when the service began, we were covered with orange dust. Rabbi Spitz first sang a song and then we put Hindella's coffin into the hole and then we all began to say prayers and old Mrs Pinchuk started crying and Mama lent her her hanky and she started crying too and the wind came up and blew the dust into our faces and when Mama stepped back from Mrs Pinchuk, some ground gave way underneath her and she nearly fell into Hindella's grave. Then Rabbi Spitz took off his torn coat and gave it to Yiddel, and he had on a nice shiny one underneath and Yiddel gave him his prayer-shawl and he put it on and then he took of his black hat and handed it to Yiddel and he had a little yarmulka on the back of his head and then Yiddel handed him his prayer-book and he was ready, with Yiddel holding everything behind him. I tip-toed over to Yiddel and asked him if I could help him, and he said he was fine, but did I hear about the saltenossas he made. When he starts talking about saltenossas it's the end of you, so I tip-toed back to Rochella, and Rabbi Spitz began to talk about the ten plagues of Egypt and how the worst of all was the plague that caused the plagues—the hatred between men, the hatred that rises when we forget about God. Mama was dusting herself off and she asked him to stop talking and just help bury Hindella and Rabbi Spitz said why was he asked to come then and Mama said she never asked him to

come, Mrs Pinchuk did, and so Rabbi Spitz took his hat from
the top of Yiddel and put it back on his head over the
yarmulka, and then he put his prayer-book where the hat had
been on Yiddel and he took off his prayer-shawl and began to
fold it and Mrs Pinchuk said he should be ashamed to leave
the grave of a Jewish child and Mama said, "Look at us, look
where my child is—and he talks about Moses and the ten
commandments!"

"The ten *Plagues!*" Rabbi Spitz shouted.

"What's the difference?" Mama screamed, "don't talk to
me about God. *This* is the place they should bomb and his
churches and his shuls—let *him* know what it's all about."
Little Yiddel was standing on the tips of his toes holding onto
the prayer-book and the prayer-shawl and helping Rabbi
Spitz struggle into his coat. I could feel Rochella shaking
next to me, so I pinched her arm. Mama got onto her knees
next to the grave and she picked up a pile of sand in her arms
and threw it onto the coffin—"There!" she shouted in
Yiddish, "Nuh!" and she picked up more, and threw and
threw shouting "Nuh! Nuh! Nuh!" The dust was flying all
over, covering her face and her body and all of us. Mrs.
Pinchuk and Mrs Maganoff and Mrs Katzen also ran to the
grave and started throwing sand too, all together, and Rabbi
Spitz, still fighting with his coat, started to run away across
the field, with little Yiddel following on his little legs, still all
orange, carrying the prayer-book and the prayer-shawl.

Mama, Mrs Katzen, Mrs Pinchuk and Mrs Maganoff went
on throwing, tearing at the ground when the dug-up sand
was finished, until there was a mound on top of Hindella's
grave. Everybody was cursing and crying, turning the dust
to mud on their faces, and beside me I felt Rochella still
shaking.

"Stop laughing!" I shouted, and everybody stopped in the
dust and stared at us and Rochella began to cry.

About Pearl Reichman

Pearl Reichman was Mama's best friend from long ago. She
used to live down the street when we lived in Troyeville.

Sometimes she used to go to the movies with us, to the musicals. She had black hair and a shiny mouth which she always painted red. She was famous as a whistler. People said she should be in Hollywood and when Tyrone Power came to visit South Africa she was one of the girls they took his photograph with at the airport. The publicity men put her third from the left, but when Tyrone Power had to kiss someone on the cheek for a photo, he chose Pearl, and she had to pretend to faint and when she did it was marvellous and then she had to pretend to whistle and she *really* whistled, her speciality, a canary whistling Swannee, and Tyrone Power got a real surprise and asked her to do it again so she did a whole performance there in the airport and her picture was in every paper, him kissing her on the cheek and her whistling and everybody thought now she must go to Hollywood because there'd never been a whistling movie star—singers yes, like Jeannette Macdonald, Kathryn Grayson, Jane Powell, Illona Massey, Rise Stevens, Carmen Miranda or organ players like Ethel Smith playing 'Tico Tico' and there were rumours that Pearl was leaving any day so people began to get her to whistle at Bar Mitzvahs and weddings and birthday parties and over the radio once and once when Mama and me were in town with her somebody stopped her in the street and asked her to whistle what she whistled for Tyrone Power so she whistled her speciality, Swannee like a canary, and everyone stood around us and when she finished we all clapped and a woman and a little girl and a boy, all separately asked her for her autograph. Anyway then one summer she went on a tour of all the holiday places like Port Elizabeth, East London, Durban and Mossel Bay and she married a Mr Salzman in Durban who had a shop near the dock which sold everything from a thimble to an elephant (which was his motto, the elephant being a brooch actually) then once when we were in Durban on holiday we saw her at a concert at the Jewish Club and after the concert we went back behind the curtain to see her and everything. But I don't remember much about her there except that her arms were very white and she had a gold filling in her side tooth and a rose in her hair because I had bad sunburn and that was what was really worrying me. Then when our war began and there was a big bombardment of the Natal coast, Mr Salzman's shop went up and him too and Pearl came back to her family, old Mrs Reichman, the only one left. She called herself Pearl Reichman again and used to walk around in her nightie because she said it was an evening dress. Even Rochella could understand but couldn't explain to her that a nightie isn't an evening dress. Anyhow, the nightie was how we first knew she was going funny and then it just got worse and Pearl got thinner and thinner and then old Mrs Reichman died of natural causes not just our war, and the Reichman house got mortar-blasted and Pearl lived on the verandah swing seat and all the time she went up and down the street looking for food and whistling and sometimes it was beautiful and sometimes it got on your nerves. Then one day we found her in her backyard, dead. It was after the rain and she was lying on her back with her eyes open and her mouth open and her nightie was wet and you could see everything. That's what happened to Pearl Reichman. When Mama came home and I told her how we found Pearl Reichman, she cried and I asked her why. She never cried when Jossel Hurwitz died or Cousin Lily was blown up and lots of other people and she said I didn't know Pearl when she was beautiful and dreaming all the time and Tyrone Power kissed her and she wore her ruby red evening dress at weddings and Bar Mitzvahs. God, Mama said, what dreams she had—sequins and gold handbags and Hollywood and look how she died—dreaming of bread!

The Reb and the Rebbitsen,
Laykella's Favourite Story told by Mama

Every morning Laykella was the first one up. She used to climb out of her hammock and then into Mama's bed and then into mine and each of us had to tell her a story and she would tell us one back.

The Reb and the Rebbitsen

Once upon a time (Mama used to say) there was a Rabbi and his wife, the Rebbitsen. They had lots, l-o-o-o-ts of little children. The biggest one was called Leibella, the next was called Laykella and there were many more, whose names are too many to tell, but the last one, the very, very last one was called Mottel. He was tiny. Tinier than Yiddel of Belgravia Shul, tinier than Laykella. Maybe he was as tiny as the Englishman Tom Thumb (Laykella always used to say that) maybe he was the tiniest boy in the world. Well, one day the Rabbi put on his yarmulka and his black top hat, and the Rebbitsen put on her shaitel (her wig) and her pink flower-hat and they went to shul where everybody said how nice they looked. But before they went, the Reb and the Rebbitsen said, "Children we're leaving you alone at home. Whatever you do, don't open the doors for anyone. No matter what they say, what they play, don't open the door." And the children all said, "No matter what they say, what they play, we won't open the door!'

Well, there they were, laughing and happy and playing games and singing songs when a big white bear came to the door. "Kinderlach, konderlach, lost mir arein," the bear said, "children, children, let me in—I'll give you honey and sugar."

"Nein!, Nein!" The children called, "Mir haben alein! We have our own!"

"Kinderlach, konderlach," the bear began again, "lost mir arein—ich et dir gebben putter mit breit! Butter and bread!"

"Nein, nein mir haben alein!"

So the bear gave a graiser forts—a big fart— which blew down the door and he ran in and swallowed all the little children. All except little Mottel who hid in a bottle. And when the Reb and the Rebbitsen came home, he in his tall black top hat and she in her pink-flower hat, they found the door broken down and all their children gone. All except Mottel who was banging on his bottle. Well, they helped Mottel out of the bottle and he told them what had happened. How the bear with one graiser forts had broken down the door and then swallowed up all their children. The Rebbitsen was very clever. If you've swallowed so many children what do you do? You take a drink of water and you lie down in a cool place. So she took off her pink-flower hat to disguise herself and she took her scissors and her needle and her cotton and she went down to the river. And there under a big shady tree was the bear with a graiser boich—a big stomach—fast asleep. So she tiptoed up to him and cut open his stomach with her scissors and she took all her children out and then she got some smooth warm stones from the river-bank and she packed them where her children had been and sewed the bear's stomach so neatly together that he never noticed a stitch. And soon the children were all home again, laughing and happy and playing games and singing songs, and when the bear woke up he stretched and yawned and went to look for honey.

How We Lost Laykella

One morning, on the 16th of April, we all slept late, mostly because Laykella hadn't woken us. I went in to see Mama at about nine o'clock. She was sleeping with her arm over her eyes. Laykella was still curled up in her little hammock. I tiptoed up in case she was pretending and I could give her a fright. I swung the hammock up and down but she didn't move inside it. I twanged the strings but she didn't pretend to snore or bark or poop or anything. I tickled where her backside was and waited. Then I slowly pulled the sides apart and peeped inside. Her face was very white, the skin around her mouth was very blue and her eyes were half-open. Her lips were moving. I shouted and Mama jumped up and grabbed Laykella from me and put her on the bed and pumped her legs up and down and kissed her feet and her face. She pulled a dress on and rolled Laykella up in a blanket and picked her up and ran into the street, her feet bare, her hair all over her face. I ran behind. There was a doctor's house on the corner of Phoenix Street and Roberts Avenue. The door was locked and the windows closed. I ran around to the back. It was burnt out. Only one room was left and it was black with soot.

There was a dinner-wagon with plates still inside against one wall. I opened the door from the inside and Mama thought it was the doctor and she started to cry when she saw that it was me. We ran ten blocks to the Sanatorium shouting for help and for a doctor all the way and Laykella flapping in our arms and people running away when they saw what she looked like.

First we came to the side of the Sanatorium. There was a line curled around and around the stairs, the garden and the pavement, sick people and wounded people were sitting around crying and calling and there was a stink like rotten mangoes. Nobody took any notice of us there. A man in a dirty white coat told us to stand in the line. He wouldn't listen when I told him about Laykella, so we went to the front where nobody was supposed to go and I banged on the doors then Mama gave me Laykella and she banged even harder and then a woman in a brown overall and a white nurse's hat opened it and said what did we want and Mama showed her Laykella and the nurse said yes, it was typhoid but she couldn't do anything we should try the General Hospital. Behind her I could see people lying on benches in the passage and on the floor and there was the same smell of mangoes. Mama said please to just show Laykella to a doctor and the nurse said what doctor and slammed the door. Then suddenly Mama wrapped up Laykella tight and put her down on the top stair and pulled me up and we ran across the street and as we were about to hide behind a wall, the door opened and the woman came out screaming at us—"What are you doing?" she shouted, "Leave me alone!" and she burst into tears and slammed the door shut again. We went back to Laykella on the stair and Laykella was dead. We couldn't give her a proper family funeral like Hindella because she had to be buried in a special typhoid place on the other side of Cyrildene.

Yiddel, Saltenossas and Mama

On Thursday, the 26th of July, I was out in Pandora Street with Rochella, looking for wood. Pandora Street had gone down in the big four day bombardment around about the time Hindella was shot. They used the new A40A bazookas for the first time, but if you looked hard enough among the rubble you could find some floor boards and cellar beams. It was very cold and we were wrapped up with everything we could find, like blankets and sacks and old socks on our hands, so it was hard to even move. Rochella kept complaining, and then she found some marbles and some pieces of a jig-saw puzzle with flowers on it and she started to play with them so I left her, as long as she was quiet.

Anyway, I was climbing all over, pulling and pushing around deep in the cellar, when I heard her calling again. I looked up, and there against the sky was tiny little Yiddel of Belgravia Shul.

"Mrs. Pinchuk wants you," he said.

"What for?" I asked.

"I don't know," he said, "but, she said you must come now."

"Okay," I said, "I will."

"No," he said, "You must come now."

"Okay," I said, "you go and I'll come."

"It's all right" he said, "I'll walk with you."

I couldn't think of anything more to say, so that was that, I was stuck with him and his saltenossas, there was no way out. All he talks about is the saltenossas his late mother used to make and how he got those eggs that time when somebody, a stranger, came to the shul and gave him two and he got some flour and milk which isn't as good as cream (which is *really* what you're supposed to bake saltenossas in) but still good enough when he does them, and he made his own saltenossa lokshen, and how yellow they were because he used *real* eggs, not like the white lokshen he used to buy. "Egg lokshen they used to call them," he said sarcastically, "but what does that mean? Egg lokshen have to have *eggs* in them, otherwise don't call them egg lokshen!" And then he described how Mrs Pinchuk gave him a little white cheese and how *thin* his lokshen were because he rolled them so hard and he had to use a vinegar bottle because somebody had stolen his late mother's rolling pin (for firewood most probably) and then when he put it all in the oven and he baked them, how the milk bubbled and how beautiful and brown they were on top, and the *smell*,—with his eyes closed, he was in his late mother's kitchen, waiting with his plate. Everybody, he said, the whole street, smelt his saltenossas and Mrs Pinchuk, when she smelt them, said to herself (she told him after) "Es gezunterheit Yiddel, eat in good health." and he did! He always laughed at the same point and grepsed on purpose. That's a story you can hear once or twice, but if you hear it too much it can get on your nerves. And then when we were passing the shul he started to look for the key that hung from a pin on his coat but he couldn't find it so we stood there while he pulled his pockets inside out and stuck his fingers through the holes until he saw the door was open and he remembered he had given the rabbi the key. Then while he was pushing his pockets back in, he started to tell me how he only wore tennis shoes on Yom Kippur before our war, but now they were all he had and he showed me how they were glued together with rags and cardboard. Then he asked me if *I* knew where there were some eggs, and if that is what we were *really* looking for up there in Pandora Street. He was sure he heard a chicken when he was coming up the road. I said it must have been Rochella playing with the marbles and he said why should she sound like a chicken when she's playing with marbles and that he noticed feathers among the bricks, and I tried to get him onto the subject of birds in general and how even the sparrows had gone in our war, but he shot back to eggs and saltenossas again, and then just when he got to the part about the milk and how it was bubbling, we got to the Pinchuk's house and old Mrs Pinchuk was waiting outside and Yiddel said "Here he is." And Mrs Pinchuk squeezed me and took me into a room and there was a body on the floor covered with sacks and she bent down and lifted some sack from the head and it was my mother's face. Somebody had just washed it. It was very clean and the hair was wet. Mrs Pinchuk said somebody had started shooting at the corner of Marshall and Browning Streets and my mother got shot. Mrs Pinchuk asked me if I wanted to kiss my mother and I said no. My mother's feet were showing at the other end of the sacks. They were dirty. Mrs Pinchuk asked me if I wanted to bring Rochella and Mendel to see her and I said no, so she walked with me down the street to Head-quarters where she said we must see the Captain. She had her hand at the back of my neck and some people were staring at me.

The Captain

The Captain was eating stew. There was a little left. I could see some potato, beans and meat and something red. He stopped when Mrs Pinchuk said who I was and he showed me my mother's papers that they found on her when she was shot and he said she was forty-two.

"That's right," Mrs. Pinchuk said.

"She misses category 627VX/A by seven months and four days," said the Captain, "luck of the game. If she'd been born that much later or killed that much earlier, she would've been IN. Yesterday there was a case—mother of two—who made it by one single day."

"I think I know who it was," said Mrs Pinchuk, "Is it a Mrs Katzoff by any chance? Two girls—Maisie and Lynette."

"How many children?" the Captain asked me, but I was watching the stew.

"How many?" he asked Mrs Pinchuk.

"Five," she said. He wrote down five.

"Sorry," she said, "is it in ink? Two dead."

"So that's ..." he calculated, "two living..." he scratched a two over the five.

"Sorry," Mrs Pinchuk said, "I think it's three."

"Five—two—" the captain said, "You're right—three." He blacked out the five with the two over it and wrote a three beside.

"Names?"

"Leiba—that's him—Rochella and Mendel."

"Ages?"

"Twelve, seven," Mrs Pinchuk said, "and ... and how old's Mendel?"

"Five," I said.

The Captain looked at me. "Do you want some stew?" he asked.

"Yes," I said. I took the socks off my hands and rolled them together into a ball. Outside, a siren was going, but none of us took any notice. I could hear people running. He gave me his plate and spoon and they watched me finish what was there. I ate fast, staring down at the plate and listening to every chew and swallow in my head and every scrape of the spoon on the plate.

"Your relationship?" he asked Mrs Pinchuk.

"We worked together at the Bertha Solomon Social Centre."

I licked the plate.

"Did you deal with Mrs Maganoff?" Mrs Pinchuk asked, "I was with her too. That sniper got her in Flossie Street."

"...C-e-n-t-r-e..." The Captain was still writing. I put the plate back on his desk.

"Now," said the Captain, "we've got to add a little, multiply a little and divde by three." He scribbled on a piece of paper. I noticed a streak of gravy still left on the stew plate, so I picked it up and licked it away. The Captain was adding next to a doodle of a girl's face.

"One times one is one and one is two. Twenty-eight pounds thirteen and sixpence. Let me check. Three children. Forty-two years old. Category 627VX—B. Right. You see, if she'd made "A". it would've been *thirty*-eight pounds."

"You can't do anything more?" Mrs Pinchuk asked. "They're lovely children."

"How do you want it?" the Captain asked, "In cash?"

"I suppose so," Mrs Pinchuk said, "what do you say, Leiba?" I didn't say anything.

"Do you want me to keep it for you?" Mrs Pinchuk asked.

"No." I said.

"So then how do you want it?"

"I don't know."

"I'll give it to you in notes and silver." the Captain said.

He took money out of a metal box and counted it into a paper-bag. "Five—ten—twenty—a   five—one—two—three—in notes—Good—now—two (silver clinked) four—

six — eight — ten — one — two — three — thirteen shillings—and—six—pence! Do you want to check?"

I didn't say anything and Mrs Pinchuk said, "Don't worry, we trust you." He gave me the paper-bag.

Mrs Pinchuk was on her way back to the Bertha Solomon Social Centre, and it was on the way home, so I walked with her. She put her hand on the back of my neck again and I was carrying the paper-bag.

At the gate of the Bertha Solomon Social Centre she asked me if I wanted to come in with her. I said no. There were some old people on the verandah and I thought I saw Mr Lapinsky among them and I was about to say hello when I remembered that he was dead, but I waved anyway and the other old man waved back. Then Mrs Pinchuk squeezed me and kissed me and told me to look after the money and the children and she went in and I started to walk home.

I went first to Pandora Street, but Rochella wasn't there any more, just little Yiddel looking for eggs where we had been. There was nobody at the house either. I didn't want to go inside. I called Rochella's name and Mendel's, walking up and down the street. The all-clear had sounded half-an-hour before, but nobody in the street had returned. I seemed to be the last person left on earth. I went back to our house, but couldn't stay there. I called their names from the door. Rifle fire began again in the distance. It was an evening sound, like trains shunting or children calling long ago. I went up Highlands Road, now just saying Rochella and Mendel's names. I turned down a side-street, stopping to kick around among the bricks and ashes of a ruined house. Suddenly I heard a bird. Only a bit of a sound, but real and clear. I stood still for a long time, hardly breathing, waiting for it to come again. The rifle-fire was getting heavier, somewhere deep in Hillbrow. I moved to where the bird sound had come from and came to a big curly-iron gate still standing between two burnt black pillars. I walked around them into a broken garden, the trees twisted and scattered, the house a pile of rubble glistening with glass. Beyond, I suddenly saw more trees, green and straight, forgotten by our war. I climbed over the house to reach them and when I got there I didn't know properly what to do. I just touched them a bit, the fir needles and the bark. I began to cry and I tried to remember my mother. I tried to remember her living but it was hard. Whenever I concentrated on her I saw her dead, and when I didn't concentrate I saw only the trees. I called again for Rochella and Mendel and then I remembered the bird. I stood still to hear it again, but there was no sound of one.

I went back to the street. It was full of people now and when I got to the house, Rochella and Mendel were waiting for me at the door. When I told them about Mama, Rochella started to cry and Mendel wasn't listening properly. And when I told them about the money, they asked to look into the paper-bag and I let them. Then Rochella said she wanted a cardigan like Leila Schlossburg's and Mendel went outside again to play.

The next day I bought:

    5 lbs. mealie-meal porridge
    3 lbs. sugar
    3 chops (I don't know what kind)
    2 loaves of bread
    1 tin Golden Syrup
    2 tins Captain Albert's Sardines
    3 marshmallow fishes
    4 carrots
    1 package salt

Oh yes, and the cardigan for Rochella. A white one. That really got on my nerves. But she wouldn't stop crying for it.

KNOWLEDGE

When Felix wrote a story about a bridge-builder that showed he knew nothing about the building of bridges, Mr de Waal said, 'No! Look . . . look . . . You've never built a bridge, have you? If you want to write a story about something you don't know from your own experience, you must find out about it. You must look it up. Otherwise it will lack authenticity. Look, haven't you got an encyclopaedia?'

'Not really,' said Felix. 'Actually only an old set that's incomplete.'

Mr de Waal wanted to see the set. It began at AND to AUS. Then the volume between BIS to CAL and DEM to EDW was missing, also the next but one, just before EVA to FRA and five others.

'There's plenty for you to find out about in all these volumes.' Mr de Waal smiled. 'Even though they're old — hey? — you'll be quite well-informed if all you read is this part that isn't lost.'

'Twenty-two volumes,' Felix said.

'Yes. Only twenty-two volumes. I think they should keep you busy for a little while.' Mr de Waal laughed out loud and Felix joined in. 'Yes. Pile them up over your desk and use them. Read about bridges and boats and China and magic and painting. Look up whatever you want to write about — make sure you know about whatever you're referring to.'

Wanting to understand, to get things right, to please, Felix asked, 'But what if the volume I want is missing?'

Mr de Waal smiled, shrugged, fiicked his hands apart like a spread of wings, turning the problem free. 'You can't know everything . . .'

So that was how Edwin Shaver's twenty-two volumes came to be stacked on Felix's desk, where his eyes rested on them as he pondered while writing and the legends on the spines became embedded in his memory: ITA to KYS, MUN to ODD, ODE to PAY, VET to ZYM. . .

Felix and Edwin had first become friendly, like a pair of disciples, through their interest in what Skipper Ross had to teach. Once he had gone from the Home there was no one to share it with beside each other, and that also went for their interest in education and other vaguer ambitions beyond. Felix now admired the self-assurance he had resented when Edwin was a new boy. He found his high style of speaking half ludicrous and half enviable, but he was altogether impressed by his determined ambitiousness.

Like Felix, Edwin was a spastic, though his pattern was different — his speech was easier and he could trot at almost a running pace and make his way without help in the swimming pool as long as he could hold the side. He seemed to have a way of using the need to control the rigidities and spasms of his body, making something purposeful and implacable out of involuntary jerkiness and slowness. He moved like a lordly machine. His left arm would swing outward in a reflex stiffening in moments of stress, but he turned it into a commanding gesture. When his limbs sprung him into a stumble or other mishap, he righted himself immediately, adjusting his glasses with a fierce stab of his forefinger to the bridge of his nose, while the tremble of his drawn-up chin and taut mouth expressed only indignation.

'My ambition,' Edwin announced during break at school one day when he and Felix and one or two others had chosen to stay in the class-room, 'is to know everything there is to know. Because knowledge, my boys, is power.' He was perched on top of his desk, the way he always sat when he had to write without his typewriter, practising his signature on the back of an exercise book: E. Shaver, E. P. J. Shaver, Edwin Peter Jarrold Shaver, Edwin P. Shaver, E. Shaver, Esq. . . With his left arm held rigid he was anchoring the exercise book alongside his leg while, with the fingers of his right hand knotted around the pencil, he designed signature after signature, trying to make each one show as little as possible of his tremble.

He continued, with one of his diplomatic little dips into slang, 'And I'm willing to bet any of you guys anything you like that it can be done.'

'Hundred pounds,' one of the others chipped in.

'A million pounds to one pound!' Edwin went on, absorbing cynical giggles with a serene nod of his head. 'That's what I'm prepared to bet that it can be accomplished. All it requires is determination . . .' — he wrote 'DETERMINATION!' in the midst of his signatures — 'application and persistence, provided one possesses the ability to assimilate data and, of course, to understand intelligently whatever one memorizes. That — poof, poof! — that ought to go without saying, actually.'

'What is data?' Felix asked.

'What? Oh! Haw haw haw! Good joke, good joke!' Edwin bellowed, miming a pat on Felix' head. 'What *is* data, indeed!'

'But I want to know,' said Felix.

'Do my ears deceive me, dear boy? You really don't know? Such ignorance, tut, tut! Well then, I'll tell you with the greatest of pleasure. Data is the plural of datum. Hm . . .?' He paused, long enough for Felix to begin, 'But . . .', then continued, 'And a datum is definable as a relevant fact. "Relevant" is the operative term, you understand? Therefore, data equals relevant or apposite facts, or indeed — let me rather say and/or — figures in any field of study. There you are! Elementary! Q.E.D.! And you ought, speaking grammatically, to have asked, 'What *are* data?' Hm . . .?'

By this time Felix couldn't remember what had been said about data in the first place. But he had been learning many things from Edwin, who was two years his senior though they were in the same class at school. (Edwin had hinted that he had had to fight a way through neglect, illness and even cruelty in earlier years, but preferred talking about the future.) Those two extra years seemed to have equipped him not only with more learning than Felix possessed but with other kinds of knowledge and strength that he felt he never would possess.

The Britannica was Edwin's, one of the unusual possessions he had brought with him when he first came to the Home. His portable typewriter was another. He had a watch and there were some other books and two boxes of what he called 'my therapeutic equipment and personal effects'. It was all far too much to go into a bedside locker, and he was allowed to keep it in a cupboard in the supervisor's office — perhaps because he was an orphan and The Home was his only home. In any case, all the particular things about him — the possessions, the cupboard, the many letters he wrote and received, the judge who visited him three or four times a year, his quick expertness at Scouts over Morse and the theory of First Aid and knots and staves, his way of speaking, and all the information he was able to give when showing visitors around the boys' section — all belonged to what made him seem more important than just another inmate.

Another thing was money — not so much any money he had as money he needed and somehow found. To Felix a shilling or two seemed a lot, but Edwin spoke of, obtained and spent as much as several pounds at a time. It was once when he needed money that he offered the incomplete 1910 Encyclopaedia Britannica to Felix for two guineas. 'You must appreciate that it is printed on India paper and bound in calf leather, dear boy. I'm sure that I could get more for it, considerably more, if I made further enquiries. But with your interests I am confident that you would make excellent use of it.' Grumbling at the age and incompleteness of the set, Dad only reluctantly agreed to buy it and Felix felt as he handed the money over that he had done his friend a favour.

The tall, neat volumes with their scuffed gilt-lettered spines were loaded on the back seat of Dad's car one Sunday and taken home. During the next few school holidays Felix now and then pulled one of them out to see what the Encyclopaedia Britannica was like or to read about Chess or Hypnotism or Mind (He was looking for Mind Over Matter) or to stare at the nude female figures that illustrated Sculpture. Dad also occasionally looked up something like Palestine or Potato or Money, but when the wanted volume was missing he said, 'What's the use if it's incomplete!' When the war ended, Felix wrote to the publishers to find out what it would cost to complete the set. The quotation was two guineas per volume, so he gave up the idea and somehow never told Edwin about his enquiry. The set was stored in a low cupboard whose door tended to swing ajar. One day the cat sharpened her claws on the spines, scratching away more of the finish on several of them and rawly ploughing up the soft leather on BIS to CAL, REF to SAI and SAI to SHU.

After Felix left the Home, Edwin stayed on and soon after was appointed assistant to the supervisor of the boys. It was the first time an inmate had become a member of staff. Mainly to see him, Felix would visit the Home from time to time. Edwin accepted occasional invitations to visit Felix for a few hours of talk and chess and a meal.

Felix had been accepted at a private college in town where he could finish his schooling. He was surprised one day nearly two months after starting, to find Edwin in the class-room. He attended regularly after that, though it was never explained what arrangements had been made for paying the college fees or over permission from the matron of the Home to take the necessary hours off every day. All Edwin cared to say about it was, 'One has to matriculate, dear boy, which evidently is something you well understand. Matriculation is a necessary, or let me rather say unavoidable hurdle if one intends taking a university degree. I intend taking, initially, the Bachelor of Arts degree, the B.A., and after that, Honours and an Ll.B. or a Master's, and ultimately a D. Phil., that is to say a Doctorate of Philosophy. Quite. Quite. Hm . . .?' He signed his name: E. Shaver, B.A.(Hons.), Ll.B., M.A., D. Phil.

For the time being, Felix could not look forward with anything like the same composure. He was still recovering after the steep step up from the commercial Standard Eight he had passed at the Home school to the academic matriculation level of the classes at the college. The aloofness or shyness that isolated him from his fellow students was not all that made him feel out of place at first. He had joined the English class a few days late and found himself plunged into the roisterous obscurities of a play the teacher called 'Henry IV', and only discovered after several more lessons that it was by Shakespeare. As for poetry, he was surprised to be told he was right when he guessed that 'Intimations of Immortality' was about a baby growing up.

But it was his rawness that allowed him a virgin excitement when he was introduced to Keats. 'The Eve of St Agnes' and 'Ode to a Nightingale' made him feel for the first time how much more there was to poetry than the rhyme and metre he had been triumphant over in his own verses, written about one a month since Standard Five or Six. He begged a neglected volume of Keats from a cousin's bookshelf and read for his own pleasure, and when he wrote yearned toward the same poignantly sweet pitch. The power of poetry became a mystery he longed to understand.

A hint that there were those who, for all their familiarity with poetry, still felt this mystery urgently for themselves, came one day when an English lesson was given by a new teacher. It was a man with apprehensive looks and a soft hesitant way of speech. His hands moving somehow pleadingly and defensively, he set about explaining not facts about the set-work but feelings about poetry itself, which, with reverence, he pronounced 'poietry'. Everything about him invited derision from the raucous class, which it expressed with mocking inattentiveness. Habitually respectful of teachers and even more of newcomers, Felix was ashamed of this rudeness. But despite his curiosity about what the man might have to tell, he found his presentation unengaging. Not surprisngly, he gave no more than that one lesson. But his manner had been unusual enough to leave a little legend and a nickname, Old Poytry.

Felix thought he saw him later several times coming or going in the vicinity of the college. At least he saw a man who usually walked with the Afrikaans teacher, her husband presumably — a man who moved in a way that combined shyness and jauntiness, carried a folded magazine tucked under one arm, and always wore a hat tipped rakishly to one side but with the brim drawn down as though to shelter his eyes. Because of the hat Felix could not be certain that he was Old Poytry.

To Edwin, attendance at the college meant that he had to make his way between the Home and town by tram and by foot. As the months passed and the examinations grew closer, the number of extra classes for revision was increased and sometimes lectures ended late in the afternoon. Climbing the path up the koppie toward the Home one evening after dusk, he was set upon by a prowler who pushed him down, causing his glasses to smash, and robbed him of his watch and money. When after missing two days, he returned to college with grazes on his hand and temple, he explained, 'If the scoundrel had not sprung on me from behind I might have got my special grip on his neck and over-powered him by applying pressure on certain neural paths. There is a way of producing complete immobilization. Nothing to it if you know the technique, nothing to it at all . . .'

But the attack had left him pale and over-tense, and not long after, his college attendance was threatened because he began to suffer from an inhibition over crossing streets. The trouble was brought under control through a course of treatments by the college principal, Mr Franklin, who held an American degree in psychology and was an expert hypnotist, and Edwin was able to continue at college and to sit the examinations.

He and Felix, permitted extra time and the use of typewriters, were given a room apart to write in. When the results gave them as both having failed in the same two subjects, which did not match their picture of their respective strengths, it was natural to wonder if some of their answer papers had not gone astray. Nevertheless, Edwin arranged to sit again at the earliest opportunity, and then passed.

Felix had been several days late in learning his result, because Dad and Moh at first contrived to keep the news of his failure from him. His outrage when he discovered their ploy blurred his disappointment in the result itself. 'How dare you keep the truth away from me,' he shouted, 'the truth about myself! I'll die if I have to be ashamed of my own truth and hide away from it. I have to know . . .'

Despite his anger they resisted his wish to push on as Edwin was doing, insisting that the papers must have been lost and that it would be wrong if he had to go through the ordeal of writing again. The re-mark Mr Franklin applied for brought no change in the result, and it looked as though Felix was in a cul de sac as far as his education was concerned. Mr Franklin showed the way out. He knew of Felix's ambition, and told Mr

Greenspan he could recommend as a suitable 'creative writing coach', Mr Johan de Waal who was the literary editor of The Monthly Review.

It was Old Poytry Felix found in the principal's office on the day he went there to meet his coach. Mr Franklin was not present to introduce them and they waited a few moments in uncertainty. Then the man said, 'Are... you... Felix?' thrusting each word out with deliberateness as though to propel it across the barrier of his hesitancy, but reminding Felix of how some of his solemn pronouncements and quotations in his lecture of months ago had been paced. Their identities confessed, Mr de Waal suggested that they make their way to his office for the first lesson. But after walking a few yards in the street he decided that the journey of several blocks would be too much for Felix. So the lesson took place in a café near the college. One of the two people at a nearby table was the college art teacher. Mr de Waal greeted the couple heartily and with a kind of flourish made a one-sided introduction: 'This is Felix. He's going to be a marvellous writer.'

It was, of course, a joke, gently satirising Felix's aspirations. At the same time, it was acknowledgement and even encouragement of those aspirations. Felix became flushed with excitement. Mr de Waal had been given a handful of his writings by Mr Franklin, and as he now commented on these Felix began to realise that he had infinities to learn. But there was a phrase here and there that pleased Mr de Waal, and it was his way of acknowledging this pleasure that intoxicated Felix. Each successful touch was hailed with extraordinary signs of excitement and with laughter. Felix sniggered helplessly with pride and pleasure at being praised and celebrated in this overwhelming way. It was difficult to identify the present Mr de Waal with the teacher who had been paralyzed with awkwardness in the face of that class-room of impatient boys and girls, dificult to know how such a person could have seemed unengaging.

As Felix grew familiar with him over the following months, it was Mr de Waal's laughter that came to seem perhaps the most extraordinary thing about him. Though hearty and free it somehow carried all sorts of serious implications. Like a bolt of lightning or a ceremony, it illuminated and altered what it touched. But even without laughter he produced an aura which had a way of intensifying the moment. His eyes had something to do with it, the eyes he so often hid along with the breadth of his brow under the wild tilt of his hat. They were vividly blue, and tangled sandy eyebrows contributed to their expressiveness. When they weren't flashing excitement, awe, apprehensiveness or moments of secretly explicable terror, they were beaming tenderly shrewd amusement that could take off wildly into hilarity or deepen to a look that cherished whatever or whomever it was resting on. And his hands also played their part, dancing with the meaning, shaping and reshaping it, as he spoke.

The drama of his expressions seemed to refer back to things experienced. A secret history — his broad shoulders, lopsidedly hunching a little toward his vulnerable neck, carried the weight of it — predisposed him to receive each word or situation or piece of writing with a warmth that magnified its significance, or to shrink as though it implied a blow, an affront. The last, for example, was in his comment as he returned Matthew Kahn's little book to Felix who had brought it to him as a discovery: 'No, look . . . When I'd finished reading it I threw it across the room. You see, if there wasn't a whole school — hey? — a whole university of followers of T. S. Eliot, then one might find some time for this stuff — one might suspect that there is something real in it.' And Eliot was no favourite of Mr de Waal's, as Felix knew. It never became possible for him to predict with certainty whether an expansive or a negative response would be forthcoming. The clues were guarded by a personal reticence: polite curiosity about himself was one identifiable thing Mr de Waal would shrink from.

Yet there was something lavish in the way he shared his excitements, such as his personal joy over any illumination concerning creativity. 'Look . . . Look . . . Listen to this!' he urged one day as soon as he had sat down with Felix. The knuckles of one hand came up in front of his smiling lips as if to hide or restrain the busy-ness of his mouth, while the other fist pummelled his thigh like a gavel. 'Yes. Yes. Yes. Yes . . .' he almost hissed, and it seemed that his thought was still unfolding in his imagination. 'Look . . . If a farmer goes to a scientist, he can say: "I have this piece of land. Now, if I sow this quantity of seed, and if I put in this quantity of such-and-such fertilizer, and I give the field so-and-so much irrigation, how many bags of mielies per morgen will I reap?" And the scientist will be able to tell him: "Under those circumstances you can expect to reap so many bags per morgen." But if the farmer goes to God — hey? — and tells God about his land and his seed and his fertilizer and his water, and asks God, "How many bags of mielies per morgen will I reap?" — God will say, "I don't know. But, go ahead. Try it. You'll get a *lot*." '

Mr de Waal's creed, for which the college English class had lacked patience — all those inspiringly surprising tenets to which Felix clung with hard faith as each became identifiable —, concerned not poetry alone but all of literature, the writing of which was not separable from responsive reading, and the whole of which, with the other arts, was tied up with life. 'Art and life and God are one,' he affirmed. Felix had never guessed art could be taken so seriously, or life so religiously, or God so earthily. Imperative behind all art there were 'the eternal verities', there were venerable traditions and secrets of art, and yet all was essentially known only in the heart, so everything was thrown back on the artist's self, the flux of his feelings rather than the predictabilities of the mind, his own experience of life, his individual style.

Groping to understand how he was to achieve his style, his personal voice, his known subject matter, Felix once asked, 'Should I write about my own life?'

Mr de Waal pressed his knuckles nervously against his mouth. 'No . . . Look . . . If you mean your physical disability, that isn't going to allow you your imaginative detachment, not so? It sets you the trap of self-pity, and other traps nearly as bad. But — hey? — in any case, it's too obvious — yes? yes? — too easy to be of any artistic significance.' In this form, Felix saw, art was going to require on his own part, too, a certain reticence.

The lessons were interrupted after a few months by Felix's last and longest stay on the farm with Skipper Ross. One day he repeated some of Mr de Waal's comments on Dickens to Skipper: 'His approach is sentimental and didactic, so he makes a lot of his characters either all good or all bad, instead of mixed, like real people.'

'But you have to have a clear picture of what is good if you're going to give an illustration that explains truth,' Skipper answered. 'The only books that are worthwhile are those that can teach us lessons about goodness. The rest are only distractions that prevent people from seeking the truth.'

Felix said nothing. What Skipper was saying was in keeping with what he had been teaching all along, but now Felix knew that as far as literature was concerned, as he was trying to learn about it from Mr de Waal, there was something wrong with Skipper's argument. He tried to forget about it, but an uncomfortable feeling of being at odds recurred for a moment from time to time as long as he remained on the farm. His stay ended when he finally discovered that he could not live up to Skipper's expectations. Something prevented him from ever telling Edwin about his failure, and although once he'd left the farm he never visited or wrote to Skipper again, Skipper's ideas were, in a way, kept alive for him by Edwin.

Mr de Waal did not drive but came by tram to the Greenspan's house to give Felix his twice weekly lessons. One day not long after they were resumed, he arrived soon after Felix had begun eating a belated lunch. In the place of the food he had to leave, Felix took a handful of almonds which, one by one, he pushed into his mouth and munched as the lesson got under way. Mr de Waal was talking about a book called 'Masters of English Literature' which he had brought for Felix to read.

'You can leave out the chapters on the Age of Reason,' he was saying. 'The spirit of poetry has got nothing to do with logic and reason . . .' Then, as Felix manipulated the fourth nut through his lips, he broke off and in a sharpened voice said, 'No . . . No, look! Throw that away! Hey?'

Shocked, Felix silently emptied his hand into the waste

paper basket. For a few minutes harsh resentment deafened him to the progress of the lesson. How dared the man so rudely vent his irritation on him! Who was he, anyway? The teacher who received a few pounds a month from Dad for these lessons ... A magazine journalist whose own bits of writing lacked the polish and dignity of real literature ...

This anger could not survive Mr de Waal's celebratory warmth as the lesson went on, and as it receded Felix began to see that his tutor's snappishness had not come of some nervous response to the ungainliness of his movements as he nibbled the nuts, but was a demand for due respect to the subject they were engaged with. It was not much after this day that his judgement of Mr de Waal as a writer also began to alter. Reading more of the stories and essays that appeared in The Monthly Review, he grew gradually to appreciate that they were more than the rough, light pieces they had at first seemed because of their colloqial style and open humour, but were brilliantly original and magical. He began to understand that, however thrillingly he was being inducted into his apprenticeship as writer, Mr de Waal was only incidentally his teacher, out of the same brute necessity that made him work on The Monthly Review and other publications as sub-editor, proofreader and seller of advertising space: he was primarily an author in his own right, one of rare attractiveness and power, and a master of art and wisdom.

The rules of his thinking were less easy to define than Skipper Ross's, and Felix tottered precariously as he strained to share a viewpoint in which the moment's feeling, or humour, or art could always give un unpredictable shape to the truth. In time he realised that in fact there were no rules. Paradox could be just as false as banality. The important thing was to be open to experience, to recognize the fascination of human life together with all its imperfections, of people, without wanting to improve them, and to follow one's heart.

Mr de Waal's way, into the marvels of art, was as much of a flight as Skipper's way had been, yet it was also a return to the human earth. When, among the columns of a story Mr de Waal was showing him in a magazine, Felix noticed a cartoon depicting a tight-rope walker performing without a rope, captioned 'Mind over matter,' he said, 'That's something I believe in. Anyone can really do that if they use the powers of the mind.'

'Oh, yes . . .?' said Mr de Waal, only glancing at the cartoon. He looked uneasy and was siezed by a fit of coughing. When it stopped he laid one hand on Felix's shoulder and with the other slapped his own leg. 'No, look . . .' he said eagerly. 'It's enough when there is a rope. Hey?' A loud laugh burst out of him and he thumped his thigh. 'Even when there is a rope and a net underneath, it's enough. Because . . . Look!' He broke off, laughing wildly, pressing his knuckles to his mouth as though to quell his mirth. 'It's enough, *because* — hey? hey? — when there is a rope, you *can* fall off.'

Felix laughed to applaud the joke and let the subject go. He felt a little disconcerted but knew it was no use trying to insist or explain the belief to Mr de Waal. Arguments were not his way of dealing: he would either turn them into jokes or shrink from the arguer in a way that seemed almost frightened. But soon there was a different feeling, a kind of relief at the dismissal of Mind Over Matter. There could be an end of uneasy feelings about seeing the powers and attractions of matter. And there was more to it than indulgence: Matter had its own ways of being important for writing. Apart from inspirations and fantasies and jokes, there were facts, techniques and disciplines that had to be given their due. Mr de Waal told Felix to take a daily walk and pay attention to his surroundings as he did so, to forfend the danger of becoming absorbed in introspection. And he insisted on a solid background of knowledge to whatever one chose to write about. If a writer had an inspiration, that was manna, but he must always remain humble enough to check the validity of what came into his head by the facts of his own experience or else by the dictionary, the encyclopaedia or other authoritative sources. This was the insistence that led to the rescue of Edwin's Britannica from its obscure cupboard, to be stood, with the gilt of Syllables like GIC to HAR, VET to ZYM and MED to MUM glinting its promise of resource, closest to Felix when he was at work.

Edwin was one of the people to whom Felix tried to convey an idea of Mr de Waal's uniqueness. 'Just to show you how he looks at things,' he explained on one of the now infrequent occasions when they saw each other, 'he told me the other day about meeting an artist friend of his who said something he liked very much. He told Mr de Waal he had had an exhibition which had been very successful. When Mr de Waal asked him if he had sold many paintings, he answered, 'No, not one. But . . . one man *spat*.'

'But, dear boy,' Edwin protested, 'why should anyone regard such a rude gesture as a sign of success?'

'Well, it proved that he hadn't painted so as to please people, but so as to move them.'

'Evidently it proved that,' Edwin argued on, 'but as a consequence of not pleasing his public, he sold none of his paintings.'

Felix shook his head urgently. 'That's not what matters. What matters is art for art's sake.'

'Art for art's sake?' Edwin mused. 'What does that imply?'

'Well, it's creating because you believe in it, not just for money or fame.'

'In an idealistic way, hm? I see. Well, that's quite commendable.'

'But at the same time the artist must be humble. Mr de Waal says he must approach everything, other artists, his own work, the whole of life, in a spirit of humility — otherwise his creativity will go sour.'

'Well, I daresay a modicum of humility would serve as an appropriate safeguard for most sorts of people,' said Edwin, losing interest. And Felix realized that he had chosen an inappropriate line.

In the city reference library, where he went to read some of Mr de Waal's earlier work, Felix was moved to discover that humility could not always have been an article of his credo. There had been a stage when his poems and essays contained wild assumptions and proclamations about the superiority of his calling and his standing among men. What moved Felix was the certainty that pain, if not calamity, must have intervened to displace that romantic arrogance, and the thought that it might easily have been replaced by bitterness instead of the graciousness and warmth that had come.

So these qualities seemed even more gift-like than before and a dimension was added for Felix when, for example, Mr de Waal one afternoon brought a large bouquet of red roses for Moh. The romance of such a gesture was incongruous in terms of Moh's life, but the writer saw things in the light of a different world and cared to claim her from the drabness of hers for a moment.

Again, when Mr and Mrs de Waal visited the Greenspans of an evening, Dad expanded and glowed in the warmth of a delighted audience for his prodigiously rambling anecdotes about his earlier days. No one else, no one in the family at any rate, had ever had much patience for them. Whatever enrichment and order Mr de Waal's imagination was bringing to the stories, Felix also had to credit him with generosity and gentleness.

After about eighteen months Mr de Waal declared that he had nothing more to teach Felix. Was it one of his jokes? Dad wanted a visible sign of Felix' training and at first pressed Mr de Waal into continuing the lessons. But a few weeks later there was a visible sign, when the Monthly Review accepted a story of Felix's for publication. Moreover, a publisher had engaged Mr de Waal for a project which required him to move to Cape Town.

The regular formal lessons ended, but Felix's tutelage continued unchanged in his own mind even if disrupted by circumstances. He wrote to Mr de Waal and sent him his next completed story, and received a reply that sustained him. In fact he had come to the state of needing his acknowledgement for something much more than guidance. He could not regard the new piece of writing as real at all until Mr de Waal had read it, as though till then the type might have vanished from the paper. So it was a happy thing for him that the Cape Town project failed and the de Waals returned to Johannesburg after a few months. He could again see his mentor from time to time, and such encounters — whether Felix took his newest story to

Mr de Waal at his new place of work, or whether the de Waals paid a friendly visit to the Greenspan's house — were always prime occasions for Felix.

His excitement had partly to do with a kind of acceptance, which after all he was even less used to for himself than for his father. This was something he found also in the de Waal's circle, at the occasional parties they invited him to — twice when a new book of Mr de Waal's was published. In other company, even in wider family gatherings, Felix often sat silent after bidding in vain for a hearing or getting in a remark that won a flat response, himself bored by the conversation and unable to think of anything to say that might command attention. But at the de Waal's parties, where many of the guests were writers, artists, actors or publishers and the conversation — given its centre and level by the host — dazzled Felix with its brilliance and fun, he found himself listened to and answered and his jokes laughed at.

But there was more to it than congenial acceptance. It was as though, when he was in Mr de Waal's presence, sharing through propinquity in his fantastical enriching vision of whatever came into view or into mind, accepted by him as a novice of the creative brotherhood, Felix was endowed with wings with which to soar above whatever made existence mundane, solemn, dull, ordinary.

'Oh, Lord, Felix! I think you're so brave to go into all that.' Mrs de Waal exclaimed when Felix came to her husband's office with the news that he was accepted as a student at the university.

'My God! Think of all that still to go through!' Mr de Waal took the idea up. 'And then, afterwards . . . Hey?'

'Afterwards! Oooh . . .' Mrs de Waal moaned and laughed simultaneously over a preposterous memory. 'The confusion! I was never so confused in my life. Do you remember what it was like, Johan?'

'Yes! Yes! We knew, once we had graduated, that we had been educated to a high level. But it took us a long time to discover — hey? — that it was a high level of . . . of . . .' He broke off, laughing.

His wife supplied, 'Ignorance! Oooh...!'

'Yes! Yes! Or of — hey? — a high level of *silliness*...'

'And I,' said Felix, only half mock-ruefully, 'have got to study for three years before I get up to that level!'

'Ah, no, shame, Felix!' Mrs de Waal protested when the laughter subsided. 'I was only remembering how confused I was.'

In fact Mr de Waal had long before made the point that as a writer Felix could benefit by the experience of university and some academic background and had provided a testimonial to help gain him a matric exemption. By the time he entered university, Edwin had been taking university courses in psychology and economics by correspondence for some years. They had seen each other once or twice during this time and Edwin had talked about the lecturers and fellow students he had been able to meet through a summer school. There was a note of intensity, of pride and unburdening, in what he had to say of a girl student who had accepted him as her lover. 'What is particularly beautiful and delightful to me is the way she wants me to bring her breasts into our love-play. She likes to have them stroked and squeezed and kissed and even gently nibbled. I knew, of course, that the breasts were erogenous zones, but she has taught me what an important role they can play in erotic contact.'

Felix had never dreamed that a real girl could be like that, especially not a university student, yet here was Edwin with first-hand knowledge. 'Edwin,' he pleaded, 'what did she...? I mean, how did you...?'

'How did I get her to love me, old boy, is that what you want to know?' Edwin flicked a finger and thumb, like signalling an easy command or turning a switch. 'Just positive thinking, dear chap. Nothing to it, really, when you practise consistently. I always form a clear and vivid mental image of what I want, and then it's just a matter, so to speak, if you'll pardon the pun — haw haw! —, of mind over matter.'

Felix nodded as though it were explained, but the picture of the girl wanting those caresses was so fantastic that he did not know how to fit it into his reality, and when at later encounters

Edwin did not refer to her again he did not know how to re-open the interesting subject.

When Uncle Lewis died, even death was shown in a surprisng aspect by Mr de Waal's light. On the evening of the very day, the de Waals paid the Greenspans a visit which had been previously arranged. They received the news and gave their condolences ceremoniously enough, but after Dad went off to be with his widowed sister-in-law, Mr de Waal, who had once met Uncle Lewis but, as he had told Felix, had not cared for his cleverness or his way of showing it, became as fanciful and jocular as usual. 'Why don't you have a drink as well?' he said to Felix as he accepted his own. 'We could have a little wake — hey? It's the right time to get tipsy and tell stories of all the things you can remember about your uncle — especially the funny things. It's right that the best sort of parties, the most light-hearted sort — hey? — should happen when somebody dies.'

For a moment thinking of Dad's loss — his brother had been his hero — Felix felt chilled at this playfulness. Surely it was callous? But Mr de Waal was *his* hero and was being consistent with himself as well as acting out a piece of his own wisdom: the obvious was never to be trusted, and to have respected mournfulness and solemnity at such a time would have been to have acted obviously. The laughter was a means of dispelling the gloom in the house, but there was also a threefold challenge in it: apart from the challenge to convention, Felix himself was being challenged as to his imaginative agility and his courage, and death was being challenged.

Felix was disappointed with University from the first, because the choice of English set-works did not accord with the canon Mr de Waal had introduced him to. Later his dissatisfaction increased when he found the books being subjected to an unimpassioned analysis, as though they were codes of some sort, instead of living miraculous things as Mr de Waal had let him know them. Besides, he was finding scarcely any time for writing. Early in his second year, when the process was beginning to be applied to 'Humphrey Clinker' which he had read with particular pleasure on Mr de Waal's recommendation, he decided that he would stand no more of the solemn vandalism and gave up the university.

Dad, who believed that a degree behind an author's name would help to sell his books, was disappointed, but helped Felix mitigate his failure by creating a job for him in the office of his timber yard. Felix typed letters, filed invoices and absorbed the atmosphere of the fierce scramble for livelihoods under the looming power station cooling towers. Something in it all, the cluttered sprawl of the yard, the noise of machines, traffic, work, voices, the variety of people who came into watching and listening distance of the cubicle where he worked, excited him, enlivened him with urgent inspirations of all sorts, which mostly had dissipated by the time he got home to his quiet room where he was free to write.

'No, look . . .' said Mr de Waal when Felix complained to him, 'If the muse flirts with you in Newtown, you must be glad, even if she plays hard to get in Kensington. If she's kind to you in Newtown — Newtown, you know? — then she's interested in you. And if she spurns you in Kensington, that's all right. She wants you to get to know something about her.'

'But I'm getting so little writing done,' Felix pressed.

'I've told you before, it's not the quantity that counts. It's the genuine inspiration of what you do, coming out of a knowledge of life. That's all that matters.'

A girl named Daphne who had been at the Home worked near the timber yard and took to dropping by for a chat with Felix. A friend of hers worked at the Home so she sometimes had an item of gossip to impart. It was she who brought the news that Edwin was ill, seriously enough to have been moved from the Home to hospital. Felix got Dad to take him to visit his friend a day or two later. Edwin was scarcely recognizable, unbespectacled, prostrate, and unable to utter more than a breathless word or two by way of distraction from the malady that commanded his attention, swelling his abdomen and making him moan and ceaselessly writhe in the bed.

A few days later Felix found himself at one of the de Waal's parties. It was the first in the small house they had moved to —

before that they had lived in hotel rooms and a succession of flats — almost a year before, since when Felix had scarcely seen them, understanding that Mr de Waal had been working at an unusual pitch that required him to go into a sort of retreat. Some remnant of quietness still seemed to hang on him during the party, but it did not amount to a damping of his vivacity nor make him, for Felix, anything less than the vibrant centre of things.

'Old Johan is settling down and turning bourgeois these days,' Felix was shocked to hear another guest remark to him. 'Giving house-warming parties! He's chaining up the demon I used to know, trying to be safe and ordinary now that he's getting a reputation as a respectable author.'

The speaker was drunk and Felix put his words down to envy, mischief and blindness. All the same he answered him: 'Well, I don't know what he used to be like but I've never come across anyone more alive and free than he is.'

'Ag, come off it — you don't really mean that?' the other said with a heavy wink.

'Of course, I do.' Felix was indignant. He was about to go on to assert, 'A genius knows better than anyone else how to run his life,' but held his tongue rather than provoke more sozzled sarcasm, and the exchange ended with a cynical shrug from the man.

A heavy storm took place during the evening, and afterwards when some of the guests were preparing to leave they found that their cars were bogged down in mud in the yard and along the unmade street of the new suburb. Some pulled away, but there were several, including the one Felix was in, which no amount of engine-racing or pushing could dislodge. At one point Mr de Waal appeared, having changed into khaki shorts for muddy work, and by the light of headlamps through which still streaked a few flecks of rain, set about digging one of the cars free. But though strenuous his effort was vain, and the guests trooped back inside to resume their seats and eventually try to sleep.

It was known that Mr de Waal had to be at his job in town next morning, yet he and his wife remained in the front room with their guests and tried to rest by bedding down on a table which offered the only sufficient space. Felix saw this as a remarkable courtesy, which some of the other guests, still tipsy and high spirited, seemed not to appreciate, as they went on wisecracking and laughing deep into the night. Mr de Waal meanwhile registered the agonies of fractured sleep with spasmodic and violent jerks and twists on the table, which Felix watched with something like an empathetic agony.

Quiet came at last, and the host was still sound asleep when daylight showed that the ground had dried sufficiently for the cars to move and the gritty-eyed guests drove away.

On the Monday morning following the Friday of the party, Felix and Dad were eating breakfast and listening to the broadcast news before going to work. Toward the end of the bulletin came the words, 'The death has occurred unexpectedly of the well-known South African author, Johan de Waal . . .'

Felix stiffened and took in the remaining words that pressed the message into reality, before he dropped his fork and started wailing: 'We killed him . . . Oh, my God! we bloody-well killed him . . .'

The news was not new to Dad and Moh. Mrs de Waal had telephoned the previous day to say that her husband had collapsed and died late on Saturday afternoon. They had not known how to break the news to Felix, had meant to prepare him for it.

'I want to go and see her,' Felix demanded. So it was arranged that, though incapable of work, he would come to the office and Dad would drive him out to Mrs de Waal in the afternoon.

At mid-morning Daphne appeared. Her message was, 'Edwin died on Saturday.'

The cemetery was too new to be mitigated by trees. Stretching to the foot of a low bald ridge, it lay open to the sky. The ridge drew the horizon suffocatingly close and emptied the view of everything but raw veld. It was a place without answers or mysteries, with nothing but bare dumb earth, ready to swallow everything human. No wonder the speeches of tribute to Edwin, one each from a member of committee and an inmate, sounded of nothing but futility. And no wonder none out of the many articulate people by Mr de Waal's graveside cared to speak a word of praise in that place.

Standing at the second of the afternoon's two burials, Felix dully noticed Dad's head, unaccustomedly bared for the gentile rituals, and remembered his fear of sunstroke. He moved a step or two to where he could, with a raised hand, cast a shadow to shield the vulnerable scalp. But for himself he could think of nothing that was left now to temper the blatant emptiness of the sky, the flat banality of the earth.

Moving away from the funeral scene through the following days and weeks, he could not shed that impression. Flat banality seemed to infect the earth since Mr de Waal no longer existed on it. There was the terrible sadness of wasted hope in Edwin's death, and bewilderment and spite in the coincidence of the two deaths — one so closely appertaining to the self his body made him, the other to the self he aspired to be —, but it was Mr de Waal's death that deprived him of his point of reference and cancelled the colour of the world and the possibility of meaning.

He could not write. Not only was his validating reader gone, but so was any reason for writing. But after some months a kind of restoration was started, through the richness of memory itself. A journal invited his recollections of the dead author and he was able to write this article. He became a fascinated audience for reminiscences of anyone else he met who had known Johan de Waal, which piecemeal revealed a history fully as extraordinary as his personality. There were several unexpectedly sombre strokes in the picture: originality pitched to the point of mental illness, intensity carrying over into criminal violence, and the exacted price of such eruptions. But if Felix discovered these with a feeling of disturbance, he absorbed that feeling into the amazement with which he contemplated the whole brilliant and increasingly mysterious legend.

It was Dad who one day filled in a passage that for a while disabled Felix from holding the image together. 'Do you know what I heard about your Mr de Waal from someone in town

156

today? During the war he wrote a letter to a newspaper saying nine million Jewish refugees from Poland wanted to come into this country and they should be allowed in. But he wrote it to make trouble. It wasn't true, he knew there never were so many Jews in Poland. Anyway, his letter caused an outcry, and afterwards the government passed a Bill to stop most refugees from coming here.'

'Who told you that?'

'A Mr Kaplan, a journalist.'

Kaplan was one of the people Felix had met who had known Mr de Waal. Besides, the round-about thinking and grandiose scale of that mischief seemed to bear a recognisable stamp.

'Ah, it's bad!' Dad said. 'If I knew he did a thing like this I would have had nothing to do with him.'

The gentle words — gentle, Felix knew, for his own sake — had the force of a curse on behalf of their injured race. But it was not only that that disconcerted him, nor even the cruel group-selfishness that Mr de Waal was accused of serving with his wit and mordant insight: he could somehow leave the horror of this to his father and others. What confused him more was that Mr de Waal had put his hand to a political machination at all. This was a contradiction that touched something deeper than his morals, which were already complicated beyond the range of judgement. It touched his imaginativeness, his insistence on an individual reality. It robbed his character of some of its unique originality, which was its essence, and for the moment left Felix feeling bereaved of Mr de Waal for the second time.

He went to his room and sat a long time at his desk, staring numbly at the broken encyclopaedia that stood dominant there because of Edwin and Mr de Waal who had never known each other — he could not remember whether Edwin had been present at the 'poietry' lesson. As for himself, the double or triple knowledge of death that had come through them to him left him feeling that he was irremediably alone and as incapable of using anything he had been taught as if he knew nothing and there was nothing to be known.

'I know nothing ... I know nothing ... I know nothing ...' he muttered, over and over again, until the compulsion of his eyes on the spines of the jumbled volumes affected his tongue, and he began to intone, 'L to LOR, SHU to SUB, HAR to HUR, HUS to ITA...'

The Night Motke Behr Danced

Bernard Levinson

Doornfontein. It doesn't sound in any way like Sholem Alei-
chem's Kasrilevke. And yet, who knows. . . . The night Motke
Behr danced in his backyard, I have no doubt that he was at that
moment living in Kasrilevke.

Standing on my bed I could see him dancing in the darkness.
His white hair and his long white nightgown flapping against his
bare legs. My first impression was that this was quite naturally a ghost. We had an old clock on our mantle. The face was
surrounded by two lethargic Victorian angels. Underneath, em-
blazoned in gilt were the words "Take it slowly." Somebody
had--and not a fingerprint or a sign of the intruder. I was satisfied that our clock was stolen by a ghost--though I was never
sure of the motive. One look out of my bedroom window convinced me that the ghost had returned. Then it called out in
Yiddish--"Neyn! Vos is dos? Neyn!" And I knew this was a
special ghost. Not a Golem, nor a dybbuk. But Motke Behr
dancing in the moonlight.

If I jumped on my bed I could follow him to the wall of wooden
crates that filled at least a third of his yard. The crates were
piled as high as a single story house.

I adored these enormous wooden boxes. This was my secret
jungle I spent hours exploring, the endless square caverns and
dark passageways. While the world of Kasrilevke, up and down
the whole length of Upper Ross Street teemed with pedlars'
carts, women's voices and children calling--I sat in a dark
wooden uterus, deep in the body of crates in Motke Behr's yard.

159

In one corner was our club house. It was the largest crate we
could find that was still deep enough and hidden from view.
There were twelve members of the club. Louie the 'greiser,'
Louie the 'kleiner,' Rosalie, eight white mice and me. Louie
the 'greiser' was a large loose-jointed boy who rarely spoke.
He had a way of bobbing his head from side to side.

Although he said little, he gave the impression of active involvement with his incessant head movements. I never knew
what he was thinking, but I liked addressing remarks to him--
his vigorous head movements gave me the encouragement I
needed. Louie the 'kleiner' was his younger brother. As silent as his older brother but with serious intense eyes. He had
a stab of ginger hair rising to a point above his head. This enhanced his earnest appearance. When he was not literally
hanging on to my shirt--he hung on to my words. To him I
addressed my most passionate speeches. His eyes were my
answer.

Rosalie joined the club late. She had a wonderful waterfall of
black curled hair cascading on to her shoulders. Each of her
curls was bound in a small tight bandage. There were bows on
her dresses. She was an apprentice Jewish Princess. I could
never take my eyes off her.

Then of course there were the white mice. The original mother
and father had long since merged with sons and daughters. Their
health, well-being, and recreation made up the agenda of every
meeting. They were the reason for our meetings. Even before we used the wooden world of Motke Behr for our club
house, we met to discuss the raising of white mice. Those
were the days before Rosalie joined us. We were then the
"Susie Street Tennis Club." None of us played tennis. We
would meet in the guttering surrounding the tennis courts in
Susie Street and air our white mice. Rosalie could see us from
her house. She had a morbid fascination for the mice. I waited
patiently meeting after meeting knowing it was only a matter of
time before she would join the club. In my dreams she was
Esther and I was Ahasuerus. I held her hand. We sat on a
throne in a tiny square crypt. No sooner had Rosalie joined
the "Susie Street Tennis Club" when I suggested we move to the

wooden underworld of Motke Behr's yard.

We crawled into the clubhouse and sat compressed together. It
was essentially a hopeless situation. Louie the 'kleiner' never
took his eyes off me. I was agog with ribbons, curls, and the
softness of Rosalie. And she sat wide-eyed, watching the
white mice.

Sometimes we adjourned to the Alhambra bioscope. On these
occasions I carried the eight mice inside my shirt. They per-
formed a unique accompaniment to my fragile emotions. Rosalie brushed her curls against my shoulder. My heart somer-
saulted in my chest seemingly carried by thirty-two tiny feet
. . . .and once--when she touched my chest with her small
hand and asked if 'they' were all right--my heart turned over
without any help. The serial was more spellbinding for Rosalie
than were the white mice. We were all enchanted by the weekly
serial. When Louie the 'kleiner' had a wee in the aisle, he
never took his eyes off the screen once.

On one occasion I was alone with Rosalie in the club house. We
were a quorum. An exact minyon. Eight white mice, Rosalie
and me. Without the mice she would never have come. We
squeezed into the wooden chamber of the club house. We had
great difficulty in finding a position for our feet. I was drunk
with the smell of her hair, I kept sighing in the darkness.
"Rosalie, can I hold your hand?" "Are you going to put a mouse
in my hand?"

We each had our own obsession. I have wondered since then if
our obsessions were not in fact very similar. But who could
have understood then. . . .At about this time my mother began
to call. Her voice had to traverse the intricacies of the wooden
labyrinth. She had a voice that could do that. . . ."You are
going to be late for Cheder! Z--will kill you if you come late
again!" There was a shattering ring of truth to this statement.
I had to go. I looked at Rosalie squashed and huddled at my side.
She was staring at a white mouse, in the cup of her hand. "Here,
Rosalie," I said, "take them all. I must go to Cheder." I ran
all the way down to Beit Street.

Once--only once--I actually held Rosalie's hand. That was
the time she came with me to the Shochet. It was my duty to
take our chicken to the Shochet. I refused to carry the chicken.
Not that I was ashamed to walk down the street with a chicken
under my arm--I just had a feeling that in hand-to-hand combat
on a fight-to-the-finish basis, I might be defeated by the chicken.
Its legs were tied and it was placed in a basket. Only its head
protruded, pivoting wide-eyed at the passing world. The "Club"
always came with me. The white mice were never taken on
such outings. Louie the 'kleiner' walked closely by my side.
Louie the 'greiser' carried the basket, his own head movements
not unlike the jerky bobbing of the chicken's head. Rosalie
walked serenely behind us. Occasionally the bird would flutter
frantically in the basket. We all stopped while Louie the
'greiser' shook the chicken back into stillness.

I handed the chicken to the Shochet. He never looked at me or
at anyone else. His eyes were partly closed and he mumbled
to himself. He was also living in Kasrilevke.   I wondered, if
I handed him Louie the 'kleiner,' would he go on mumbling and
cut his throat. The chicken's neck was arched in his hand and
he plucked a few straggly feathers. This is the moment when
the Shochet is asking the chicken if it has one last wish. Is
there any final thought it wished to express. Rosalie is holding
my hand. Or was it I who held her hand? Our palms are sticky
and hot. Around us, slaughtered chickens lie in grotesque
heaps. Some have just ended their final blind epileptic dance.
But we only have eyes for our own chicken. Rosalie squeezes
my hand. Louie the 'kleiner,' his butt of red hair standing
fiercely upright, stares fixedly at the Shochet from behind the
folds of my old jersey. Louie the 'greiser' holds the empty
basket, his head a nervous metronome. Our chicken begins its
last frantic dance.

On the way home Louie the 'greiser' imitated the dying chicken.
We were all too diminished to laugh. Besides I was holding
Rosalie's hand. In no way would I break the spell. Louie the
'greiser' continued: Flapping his arms and dancing his macabre
convulsive chicken-in-death.

When Motke Behr danced in the darkness of his backyard there

was something in the urgency of his movements that held me
rooted to the window. His leaps and twists were joyless and
frantic. I was gradually aware that he was not alone. I could
hear him shouting in Yiddish and then unmistakably I could
hear a horse neighing. Motke Behr was dancing with his horse.
His horse was consumptive, thin. A dreamy deeply turned-in
creature, never known to speak--or to complain. But now erect
on its hind legs--its tail lashing the wooden crates, it looked
majestic and wild. Motke Behr also looked majestic and wild.
He faced the horse and they both jumped in unison. They
leapt and stumbled on the small stage of the backyard.

Standing on the window-sill in my bedroom I watched this
strange pas de deux. Motke Behr, beard flowing, arms
thrashing, and the horse, upright--all eyes and teeth. When
the moon twisted its way out of the clouds and blinked into the
yard, for one brief moment I caught a glimpse of white mice
scampering between the dancers.

from Another Year In Africa

Rose Zwi

*B*erka Feldman spat out the nails from between his lips, cleared the table of leather, tacks and thread and left the shoe on the last, to be repaired the following morning. It was only ten to five. He seldom left the workshop before six, but today he felt restive. After an oppressively hot morning the sky had suddenly darkened and distant thunder had rolled like wagon wheels over rocky ground. Ripped by forked lightning the clouds emptied themselves over the suburb then drifted away, leaving a brilliant sunset and steaming streets.

From the doorway he watched the water gurgle down the gutters towards the Dip. He drew a deep breath. His lungs caught sharply on the smell of damp concrete and a sudden yearning for the wet-straw smell of the veld washed over him. He longed to be on his wagon again, enclosed in the silence and emptiness of the veld, with only his voorloper to lead the oxen. In summer he had watched the grass bend and sway like Jews at prayer while he hummed the half-forgotten songs and psalms of his childhood. In winter he listened to the susurrus of the wind through the dry grass, rising to a mournful swell as it swept over the veld. Towards evening a thin spiral of smoke might appear on the horizon. He savoured his solitude, certain that it would end. Soon he would walk into a mud-walled farmhouse filled with the smell of coffee and griddle cakes baking on an open fire. Hanging from the rafters of the reed-and-thatch roof would be cobs of dried mealies, twisted rolls of tobacco and strips of biltong. From the earthen floor into which peach pips had been beaten would rise the faint sweet smell of cowdung . . .

How free, how lonely that life had been.

He took off his leather apron, washed his hands in the cracked basin at the back of the shop and rinsed out his mouth. The taste of nails persisted. Only a drink would remove that metallic taste, but if he came home on a Friday evening smelling of beer, Yenta would have another weapon in her armoury of abuse. He put his cap over his thick grey hair and walked out of the shop, squinting up at the sun which hung low over Main Street.

From where he stood he could see the eastern part of the suburb; from the top of Main Street he would see the rest. The city lay to the east, its tall grey towers rosy in the dying light, a coppery blaze piercing the eye as the sun reflected off glass and steel.

To think that forty-five years ago it had been little more than a miners' village with row upon row of tin shanties, rough men, horses, ox wagons. Berka shrugged his shoulders at the miracle of its growth.

His shop was a mile and a half from town, but the Dip brought the buildings nearer and they towered like a fortified city over a village at its gates. Although he might yearn, occasionally, for his carefree days as an itinerant cobbler, he had lived in the shadow of the city for so long that he gladly accepted the boundaries of his world: The sun rose to the east of Main Street, and set over the hill, to the west of it.

Berka recalled clearly his arrival in South Africa, early in 1892.

'It's a bad time to have come,' his uncle reproached him. The pogrom should have coincided with a boom in South Africa. 'There's no gold in the streets nor, it seems, in the mines,' he continued crossly as he led Berka into a small room at the back of the Concession Store. 'You'll have to work hard. I pay five pounds a month with free board and lodging. If you want to get rich, save.'

For several years Berka sold blankets and trinkets to black miners. On week-ends he helped in the Kaffir Eating House attached to the store. The smell of burned entrails and cooked meat clung to his clothes and cleaved to his nostrils. His cousins sniffed fastidiously when he came to his uncle's house for an occasional meal.

In his sparsely furnished room he studied English from a tattered grammar book. The bar was his elocution class. From the English miners he acquired a Midlands accent which, coupled with impeccable Yiddish inflexions, made his teachers roar with good-natured laughter. He read voraciously. This improved his English, widened his knowledge and assuaged the loneliness of his years as a kafferitnik. He worked for long enough to buy the tools of the trade he had learned in the old country, then started on his life of wandering.

His uncle never forgave him his ingratitude.

'If you'd remained with me instead of running off into the veld like a wild chatas,' he said to Berka, 'you'd have been a rich man. Today you don't even own the house you live in.'

'Property is theft,' Berka had replied. 'I want nothing that I haven't earned with my own labour.'

They never spoke to one another again.

Berka stood at the corner of Main Street and Lovers' Lane. Wherever he looked he saw Uncle Feldman's possessions. He had become a man of property over the years. But Uncle Feldman was not a happy man; he had little joy from his sons. They had not gone beyond Standard Seven in school and proved equally inept in business. He would be lucky if they said a decent kaddish for him when he died — at a hundred and twenty years, please God. Berka chuckled. He could think of no greater punishment for his sons.

Uncle Feldman had moved out of Mayfontein twenty years ago but he retained his Concession Store, the source of all his wealth. He hired a manager and although he was almost eighty, he still went to the business. At irregular hours, Berka thought grimly, so that he could catch the manager stealing. Uncle Feldman was certain that everyone stole from him.

Berka spat into the gutter.

Uncle Feldman was one of the few people towards whom Berka could not extend tolerance, an attribute which he valued above most others. Yenta, who had never really understood him, claimed that his tolerance stopped at his own front door.

He began walking up Main Street, aware that his tall bulky figure was as much an institution in Mayfontein as the headgear of the mine, the white dumps on its outskirts or the bar. As he walked to and from work every day he was hailed from all sides.

His heart swelled with emotion: He was the friend of Jew and Gentile, the arbiter in disputes, the consoler in sorrow. In short, he was loved.

'Feldman!' came a deep voice from the smithy across the road. 'Why do you stand there in the middle of the street, smiting yourself on the chest, smiling, spitting, shaking your fist?'

Leib Schwartzman emerged from the smithy. He was a stocky man whose powerful shoulders gleamed with sweat under his grease-stained vest.

'Are you sick that you're shutting shop so early, or has your uncle written you into his will?' he asked with a grin.

'Neither. I calculated that if I worked an hour less today, I'd become a millionaire that much later. How's business?'

'Bad, bad.' Leib wiped his forehead with the back of his hand. 'Cars, trams, bicycles. Where have all the horses gone?'

'To the Free State, to become rabbis like that ass Benjamin,' Berka said.

'Don't blaspheme against the servants of the Lord. What will happen when you have to account to Him one day?'

'If God is just, as you claim he is, he'll distinguish between those with kosher stomachs and unkosher souls. I may not get to heaven but neither will my reverend brother-in-law Benjamin. The only trouble is that I'll probably meet him in the Other Place.'

Leib laughed. He had studied Law in Kovno but influenced by the workers' movement he had given up Torah for a trade. The future of society, after all, lay in the hands of the proletariat. But he had retained his love for Jewish tradition and went to shul, to synagogue, regularly. Opiate of the masses, he'd exclaim angrily when Berka defined religion for him. What's a worse opiate? Going to shul or going to the bar? Meet my learned friend Bernard, he would mock. He's so thirsty for Justice that he's been called to the Bar.

'When I saw you packing up early I thought perhaps you wanted to get to shul in time,' Leib smiled.

'Don't joke,' Berka said gloomily. 'I'll probably land up doing that to please Ruth. It's not easy being an honorary grand-father. Ruth's afraid I'll land up in Hell because she once heard me say that there was no God. She wants me to look for Him in shul.'

'Strange child,' Leib said rubbing a grease spot off his arm. 'Last week your sister-in-law sent Ruth to borrow a pot from us. "Mrs. Blackman," says Ruth to the wife because she's speaking English now so the name's Blackman not Schwartzman, "mine grenny vants to lend your big bleck pot." Why doesn't she speak Yiddish to my Chaya? They're both a pair of English scholars, Ruth and Chaya.'

'Because she doesn't know Chaya well and to strangers she speaks only English.' Berka looked angry, upset. 'I must be getting along. I'll stop off at the bar to chat with our local proletarians.'

Leib put his hand on Berka's shoulder.

'Don't be angry with me, Berka, I know how fond you are of the child. But to whom can one speak? To her father the dreamer? Or her mother who's always wrapped up in Vicks and cottonwool?'

'Ruth's not strange, Leib. She's got too much imagination and too few friends. The kids tease her because she doesn't speak English properly. She'll learn. She begins school on Monday where she'll mix with other children. Have a good sabbath. See you at the poker game on Sunday night.'

The sun had almost disappeared behind the Main Street hill and Berka stepped up his pace. He wanted to see it set behind the mine dumps. There were few sights he loved more.

Poor Ruthie. She'd have to learn to live in the present. A child of six burdened with a consciousness of tragedy and persecution, with memories that weren't even hers. He himself was guilty of telling the story of his family's massacre in her presence. He had broken down that time and shouted:

'There is no God!'

Berka coughed to clear the heaviness on his chest. He hummed tunelessly for a while then remembered the song about the drunkard:

> When they write my epitaph
> It'll read 'Here lies a drunk',
> And I'll answer with a laugh,
> 'There's no brandy here, I'm sunk!'

He must sing that for Yenta. She said that real Jews didn't booze. Yet here, immortalised in a Yiddish folk song, was the lament of a Jewish drunkard. Let her explain that one away. Berka walked on, humming the jaunty tune.

There were few people in Main Street. The Jewish house-wives were at home preparing the sabbath meal and the miners' wives shopped on Saturday morning. Haggard, often toothless, their hair perpetually in curlers, they trudged across the veld in their slippers from the mine's Married Quarters to do their weekly shopping. There was little enough in their purses after their men had stopped off at the bar and at the bucket shop on Friday evenings. Their children, thin and snot-nosed, ran wild through the suburb.

Harsh men, these miners, yet who could judge them? Here he was, walking in the clear rain-washed air while they were thousands of feet below surface, drilling into stubborn rock, breathing in poisonous fumes, stumbling through the tunnels that honeycombed the earth beneath his feet. Underground was Hell. Dark tunnels of damp rock, slippery passages, unbearable heat, pressure bursts, rock falls. Could these conditions produce gentle compassionate men? And what was it all for anyway? They wrested a few grains of gold from tons of rock, then buried it again in underground vaults.

He had watched the men come off shift, their faces pale with dust and fatigue, tin hats in one hand, carbide lamps in the other, blinking in the unaccustomed light of day. They washed down the mine dust with drink and beat up their wives, their children and the hapless mine kaffirs. To them, the blacks were barely human.

Every year Berka watched the black recruits arriving at Mayfontein Railway Station clad in loin cloths and blankets. They were tall sturdy men, selected for their strength and good health. For two shillings a day, a pot of mealie meal and kaffir beer, they travelled hundreds of miles from their kraals and their families to live in crowded mine compounds and to do the hardest work underground. When their nine months' contract ended, they might be a few pounds richer, wear trousers and a shirt, and carry away with them, under their gay blankets, a lung disease.

And the white miners organised unions to protect them-selves from the blacks' cheap labour, but left them to be slaves to the mine bosses.

'Berka! You look as though you're carrying the world on your shoulders,' a gentle voice said at his side. 'And all the way uphill too.'

'Reb Hershl! Just the man I need to see.' Berka stopped at the bakery door and sniffed. 'Ah, you perfume the suburb. There's such comfort in the smell of fresh bread. Little wonder I've got such a big nose. All my emotions are filtered through it.' He put his arm around Hershl's shoulders and walked into the bakery with him. He had time. There would be another sunset tomorrow evening. Such a pessimist he wasn't. A few words with Hershl would remove the metallic taste from his mouth and the ash from his soul.

Hershl took off his floury apron and hung it on a nail behind the counter. The bakery was small. The front portion had been divided off from the wall ovens at the back by a thin wooden partition. There was a glass-fronted counter which displayed iced cakes, buns and several kinds of bread: rye with aniseed, special sabbath kitkes and sandwich loaves. Through the opening in the partition came a surge of hot air as the iron doors of the wall ovens swung open to receive another load of bread. A loud crash of metal trays and bread tins drowned the first part of Hershl's sentence:

'. . . the last lot of loaves for the night,' he said as the noise died down. 'Dirk will lock up. Since I took him on I can go to the synagogue on Friday evenings.'

'How's business?' Berka asked.

'Excellent, improving all the time. It paid to take on a trained baker. Faigel works up front now and only does the confectionery for special occasions. I bought a horse and cart this week. The deliveries were getting too big for my bicycle.'

'Leib will be pleased to hear there's another horse in town,' Berka said. 'He thought they'd all gone to the Free State.'

'Free State?' Hershl looked puzzled. He did not always understand Berka's jokes. 'Did I tell you I'd made an offer for Sharp's delicatessen? It's much bigger than my shop and I can build in extra ovens. Now that I've got contracts with a few Concession stores I shall need it. I saw Uncle Feldman the other day,' Hershl added. 'For two reasons. To get an order for the bakery and to ask for a donation for the Refugees' Fund.'

'Let me guess,' Berka said drily. 'The order you got at cut

prices. And if you did get a donation, you had to sweat blood first.'

'You know the man. He denied he was stingy. All rumours, he said. People thought he was mean because he didn't advertise his charitable deeds as others did. He gave anonymously.'

'So anonymously that he doesn't even sign his cheques.' Berka retorted. 'Let's talk of cheerful things.'

'Cheerful things?' Hershl's face dropped. 'There's nothing cheerful in 1937. Look at Germany: Jews thrown out of jobs, property confiscated, schools closed, people shut up in ghettos. That's cheerful? And suddenly the world's too overcrowded to take in a few Jewish refugees.'

'They let some Jews into South Africa from Germany.'

'And are drafting the Aliens Act to keep the others out. They hate the Jews as much as the Nazis do.'

'But what's happening in Germany couldn't happen here,' Berka persisted.

'You've been saying that for years, Berka. This isn't the same South Africa you knew in the old days. All those stories you tell of Boer hospitality and respect for the people of the Book. When they're in the Book they're all right, but when the farmer's crops fail and he comes to borrow from the Jewish storekeeper at interest, it's a different matter. When the Jew was a smous, a pedlar, they tolerated him. When he holds the purse strings or he's in competition, they fear him. And where there's fear, there'll be persecution.'

'Nonsense. There may be hotheads among them but has there ever been a pogrom here?'

'What do you think the Greyshirts are planning, a Purim party?'

'So, where's it better?'

'Where's it better he asks,' Hershl appealed to the ceiling. 'Berka, we need a home of our own, without Aliens Acts and without anyone's kind permission to exist.'

'Spare me the Zionism. Bought any good stands in the sea lately?'

Hershl laughed, not without embarrassment. I shall die in Jerusalem, he predicted when he argued about Zionism with Berka. That I can believe, Berka would reply. To live there is another matter. Emissaries from Palestine had an easy time with Hershl. Two years earlier an imposing man with a dark flowing beard and side curls had sold Hershl a stand in Palestine. A few months later he discovered it was situated a mile off the coast of Jaffa, in the sea.

'Nu, in Lithuania I was a Hebrew teacher,' Hershl said. 'Here I am a baker. In Palestine I'll become a fisherman. Remember how furious Faigel was? She doesn't understand how I feel about Palestine. Buying trees, making an annual contribution to Zionist funds, sending other people, that she doesn't mind. But the idea of settling there is beyond her comprehension.'

'And mine. It's too remote and strange to me. How's the family?'

'Fine. Daniel starts school on Monday.'

'So does Ruthie. It's a pity they don't play together. It'd help if Ruth had friends her own age.'

'Daniel's also shy. Children of immigrant parents have a hard time. Torn between different ways of life. If we lived in Palestine . . .'

'There he goes again,' Berka said walking towards the door. 'I live in the present and you live in an impossible dream of the future. It's better, I suppose, than living in the past like our Dovidke. Come here, Hershl. Look at him standing there at his window, dreaming of the old country no doubt, where the fields were greener and the fruit sweeter.'

'He often stands like that,' Hershl said looking up at Dovid Erlich at his workshop window over the road, gazing sightlessly into the distance. 'He's got problems. Not much work coming in, mostly alterations. And Sheinka is a nagging wife.'

'Is there another kind?' Berka asked.

'Poor Ruthie. She's caught in the middle. They can't be easy parents to live with. I wonder what went wrong? Sheinka was a lovely woman when they came out from Lithuania eight years ago. A little melancholic perhaps, but charming. She's grown bitter over the last few years.'

Berka was looking up at Dovid. From his first floor workshop, he thought enviously, he can see over the ridge of the hill where the sun will soon set. And he's not even aware of what he's seeing. Berka turned to leave the bakery.

'Have a good sabbath, Hershl. Come over and kibbitz on Sunday night. Leib and I have arranged a game of bloff. Low stakes.'

He shook Hershl's floury hand warmly. He loved the man; he renewed Berka's faith in humanity.

Main Street was shining after the rain. A tram car clambered heavily up the hill, packed with people returning from work. Their faces looked soft and warm in the golden light. Berka loved them all. Even that thief Steinberg who gave short weight in his butchery; and Chidrawi, the swarthy Syrian who was arranging a pyramid of yellow peaches in his window; and Levin the outfitter who stood in his doorway, a tape measure around his neck. And all those children outside the fish and chips shop watching wistfully as Ronnie Davis sprinkled vinegar over someone else's chips. He even felt a fleeting affection for the miser Pinn who owned the second-hand shop. His wife stood in the doorway, fluffing her hair this way and that, before embarking on what must be a two-hour journey home. She stopped off all along Main Street, garnering the news of the day, which she then embellished and disseminated among the housewives of First Avenue. She often knew better than they what was happening in the house next door. Some people were entirely unlovable.

Berka looked into the dark interior of Nathan's Drapery Store where his daughter Raizel worked. She was probably cashing up now. She had worked for the Nathans for four years, since she matriculated. At first she was a counter hand, measuring out elastic, hair ribbons and dress material. Today she practically ran the business. Mrs. Nathan spent most of her time in the city, drinking tea at the Corner Lounge, or walking about from shop to shop. Getting ideas for the trade, she called it. Mr. Nathan was almost blind. My eyes, he called Raizel. My heart, Berka murmured as he passed the shop.

The barbershop next to Nathan's was crowded with miners. Not, God forbid, having haircuts, but placing bets for the dog races.

Friday Night is Wanderers Night,
Night for Greyhound Racing.

read a poster on the wall. Next to it hung a framed picture

173

of water-waved ladies. And Wednesday night was Wembley Night, yet another night for dog racing.

Berka walked resolutely past the hotel bar. The Siren-sounds of clinking glasses and loud laughter would not tempt him tonight.

From the bar onwards Main Street ran a flat course for half a mile towards the large bluegum plantation which flanked the suburb on the west. The plantation stretched from the end of Main Street southwards towards the mine dumps. Below the dumps was a small dam into which water was pumped from underground. If Berka had seen snow-capped mountains, pine forests and an inland lake as he turned the corner from Main Street into First Avenue, he would not have been happier. He remembered when the first saplings had been planted. He had watched the mine dump grow as the coco-pans crawled up its sandy slopes depositing yet another load of finely crushed rock onto the chalky hill. And next to it the yellow slimes dam also grew slowly, hardening towards its final shape as a truncated pyramid.

He never tired of this constant yet ever-changing scene. On rainy days the dump stained deep yellow, the trees washed a lighter green and the leaden skies reflected dully in the cyanic dam. Under the clear winter skies the dam sparkled like a jewel, and the whiteness of the dump was blinding. He loved it most at sunset, however, when the dump became a mountain of gold dust and the dam liquid amber.

They could keep their gold bars in their vaults. He was satisfied with the refuse. From the top of First Avenue he surveyed his kingdom. King of the Rubbish Heaps, he thought with a smile. Beyond the veld which separated Mayfontein from the mine, the wheels of the headgear turned ceaselessly and the stentorian voice of the crushers echoed throughout the suburb, day and night, week after week, year after year, until it seemed to be the very breath of the suburb. He breathed in unison with it.

At this time of the day the rows of the red-bricked semi-detached houses glowed like live coals and the whole suburb caught fire. Only the plane trees cast a cooling shadow across the hot sandy roads. Yanka the fruit vendor came into view, driving his horses hard in his effort to reach home before the sabbath. Billowing clouds of red dust rose in his wake. Like the cumulus clouds which hung over the dump, like the dust raised by Boers on commando.

'This is my world,' Berka sighed as he walked down First Avenue towards his house, 'and I'm glad of it.'

*D*ovid looked towards the mine dumps over which the sun was setting. It was all so ugly: The sun like an evil eye in the red sky; the yellow sand; the turgid water. Even the birds recoiled from that foul-smelling pool and the silent bluegum plantation at its edge. The trees were dull green all year round and smelled of eucalyptus. Like Sheinka. They did not shed their leaves in winter nor put out new ones in spring. Like everything else in Africa they looked artificial. Here the earth seemed governed by laws which did not respond to a benign nature. Forests were planted, mountains built from mine refuse and lakes pumped up from hell. Dovid shuddered. And that infernal headgear just kept turning and turning. One's very soul felt lashed to its wheels.

Out of the corner of his eye he saw Berka walking into the bakery with his arm around Hershl's shoulders. Berka loved the country. Johannesburg's not Africa, he frequently told Dovid, describing the rolling grasslands, the mountains, the valleys. But Johannesburg does have a beauty of its own, he said. Perhaps. Dovid could not see it. If his father, Red Yehuda, had remained in Africa twenty-five years ago instead of returning to the old country, Dovid might have grown up with a different view of Africa.

Yehuda, like other Jews from Lithuania, had come to the diamond diggings in 1912 to seek his fortune. He went for one year but stayed two. "Noch a yahr in Africa," he wrote to his wife, prolonging his stay. Another year in Africa, in exile. He returned to Ragaza with two hundred pounds and a golden brooch for his wife. South Africa, he told her when she suggested emigrating, had no future. After the gold had been extracted from the earth all the adventurers would leave and the veld would come into its own again. How could he take his family to a land where the earth was sour from the gold in its veins, where the hills were rocky and bare and where the rivers ran shallow and brown? Nowhere had he seen green fields and forests like those of Ragaza nor a river which flowed through such fragrant banks.

Eighteen years later Dovid, under pressure from Sheinka, was the only member of his family to emigrate. Yehuda had not lived to see him go. Dovid found Johannesburg as bleak and as bare as his father had described it. But Yehuda had been wrong about one thing: South Africa, it seemed, did have a future. Whether or not Dovid wanted to be a part of it was another matter.

Dovid pressed his head against the cool glass. His family in Lithuania did not understand what life was like in Africa. They believed that the streets were paved with the proverbial gold. I hear, his mother wrote bitterly, that in addition to your wife and child you also support Gittel. For your own mother, however, you haven't got a few roubles to send. You've forgotten how I slaved into the small hours of the night to support you and your brothers while your father was seeking fortunes in Africa . . .

Would they believe him if he wrote that last month he had to borrow three pounds towards the rent from Steinberg the butcher? He sent money home when he could. As explanations proved futile his letters to his mother became less frequent. But one day he'd go home again and the need for explanations would cease.

He glanced away from the mine dumps. Berka and Hershl were standing outside the bakery looking up at him. He pretended not to see them. Only when Berka turned homewards did he look down the road in the direction of Nathan's Drapery Store. It was ten past five. Raizel was probably cashing up. He had time to sew the buttons onto the jacket.

Crazy, he was absolutely crazy. Here he was, thirty-one, with a school-going daughter, an ailing pregnant wife and her parasitic family to support and what was he doing? Daydreaming like a lovesick adolescent.

He walked angrily across the wooden boards and pulled off an unfinished suit from the hanger. The left lapel needed adjustment. His perfectionism maddened Sheinka. You could turn out two extra suits a month if you weren't so meticulous, she complained. Look at Yaakov Koren. A rich man he's becoming from his tailoring.

He looked at Yaakov Koren; a mere haizenschneider, a trouser maker, who couldn't even sew a sleeve into a jacket.

His hands shook as he wound the cotton onto the bobbin. He threaded the needle with difficulty and placed the lapel under the presser foot. For a while he sat staring at his old Singer machine, with his foot poised over the treadle, then he got up and went to the window again.

'Raizel, I love you,' he whispered fiercely against the window, misting it with his breath. So. He had said it at last and the skies had not fallen onto his head.

She had been a child of fifteen when he arrived in Johannesburg, a lively precocious girl who had giggled at his English. He dismissed her as an unpleasant child but was stung by her laughter. He watched her grow out of her adolescent gawkishness into a rounded young woman whom all the neighbourhood boys pursued. He often walked into Berka's house to hear the gramophone blaring out a tango and was pained to watch some young lout bending over her as he led her through the intricate steps. His pain was for Berka, he had told himself. One day he would have trouble with that girl. She's only a child, he reproached himself afterwards. And he clung to this comforting phrase which allowed him to ignore her blossoming womanhood.

One cold winter's evening about eighteen months ago, Dovid had been sitting in front of the coal stove with Ruth on his lap. He was alone. Gittel and Sheinka had gone to visit Yenta. In the glow of the sabbath candles Dovid sang Yiddish songs for Ruth. He sang of workers who built mansions for the rich but themselves lived in hovels; who sewed for the idle and wore rags; who ploughed the fields but owned no land. There were songs about families parted by war, by poverty, by persecution; about refugees herded in cattle trucks, going into exile through snowy wastes. He sang of lonely orphans in a hostile world, and about crossed lovers. There seemed to be no other lovers in Yiddish folklore.

'Sing "Oyfn Pripetshok",' Ruth requested. Dovid sang about the Rabbi who teaches his pupils, with the first letters of the alphabet, that the world is a vale of tears:

> . . . As you grow older, dear children,
> All too soon you'll learn,
> How many tears the eye holds
> And how to weep and yearn . . .

'And now about the man who doesn't know when it's his birthday,' she said sleepily.

He sang about the man who had nothing by which to measure his years. The rich man measures his days by his money, the happy man by the passing hours. If misery were the measure of life, he would be ancient; if happiness were, he is not yet born.

> Eib leben heist laiden, dan leb ich shein lang,
> Dan hob ich genug shein die yahren,
> Eib leben heist heren fun glick chotz ein klang,
> Dan bin ich noch garnisht geboren.

Ruth knew all his songs. They took the place of bedtime stories. At least part of his heritage would live on, he thought gratefully as she slept in his arms.

What was he doing in this harsh alien land where he would always be a stranger? His life was bound up with der heim, the old country, where he was born, where his family lived, where his father lay buried. His fate was linked with theirs. Like his father before him he longed for the pinewoods of Ragaza, and for the river which flowed through such fragrant banks.

As he wiped away his tears, he heard a light step across the floor. He turned around, startled. Raizel stood behind him in the flickering candlelight with tears in her eyes. She bent down quickly, kissed him full on the lips, then fled.

Had it really happened, he wondered afterwards, or had it been a wraith from one of his songs? From Raizel he had no sign. She remained as lively and as provocative as ever. When she was not looking he searched her face, he hardly knew for what. For traces of tears he had seen in the candlelight? But

he sensed she had changed, that she was conscious of him.
Once, when Ruth asked whether only Jews lived in Russia,
Raizel laughed and said that as a child she too had thought
that Russia was a Jewish country; it was der heim for everyone
she had known. Then she herself began to ask Dovid questions:
about der heim, about Jewish festivals, about Jewish history.
And the previous year she had offered to give him English
lessons, to correct his pronunciation.

As the religious man works and battles through the week
towards his soul's repose on the sabbath, so Dovid yearned
for Sunday nights when he would sit at Berka's kitchen table,
his books in front of him, listening to Raizel. Like this, she
would say putting her tongue against her even white teeth.
He turned from her with a hammering heart. You put your
tongue so, then blow out: 'th', not 'd', this thing, not dis ding.
Hey, you're not watching. You'll never learn if you keep your
nose in the book. Look at me!

And when he turned to look, not at her mouth shaping a 'th'
but into her eyes, he found what he was looking for.

Dovid moved away from the window and began to clear
the room feverishly. He must hurry, he must hurry. He tore
the jacket from under the presser foot, threw it over a hanger,
then grabbing his own jacket, rushed out of his workshop down
the flight of dark stone stairs, into the street.

• • • •

Hitler's march on Moscow stemmed, Berka read. But Smolensk lies devastated, he thought wearily, and Kiev had fallen. Chmielnicki's hordes have risen again with perfected means for death and torture.

He looked up from his newspaper into the haunted eyes of Dovid. Like a spectre from the grave. Berka nodded, then turned away his eyes from the thin, pitiable figure on the corner of Lover's Lane.

Enough work. Berka looked with wry amusement at the untouched shoe on his last: Mrs. Melamed could wait until Monday. Now for the real work of the day, the walk up Main Street hill. Every year it grew steeper.

He folded up the newspaper and left it on the workbench. It was good only for wrapping up old shoes. He no longer charted the course of the war. His map hung untouched on the wall between the yellowed patches where Yenta's relatives had simpered and smirked in sepia.

He should hang Ruthie's drawings up in the lounge and cover up the ghosts of the past, he thought as he walked around the shop slowly, stopping now and then before a dog-eared drawing. Here was one of him on an ox wagon with Zutzke, kindly lent for company. She had captured the feeling of desolation so well. Loneliness is grey, she had said. Even his moustache drooped wearily. And here was a picture of people huddled under a tree while a plane spat fire from the sky.

'Words', she had said gravely when he asked after her first day at school what she most wanted to learn. Her drawings were more eloquent than any words she would ever learn. Poor child. His heart ached when he thought of the toil, hope and disillusion that still lay ahead of her.

He walked out of his shop and took a deep breath. Spring. The first rains had washed the mine dust from the air and through the smell of damp concrete, exhaust and Hershl's fresh bread, he thought he smelled blossoms. By now the veld fires had charred the grass to black stubble, the farmer had taken to his plough and a new cycle would begin.

Perhaps on the land life had retained some meaning. Or perhaps there too it was reduced to the monotonous cycle of birth, growth, death and rebirth. It wearied him to'think of it.

There was definitely a smell of blossoms in the air. Berka drew in another deep breath and his lungs caught on the smell of exhaust. Spring. It was a season for lovers, farmers and warlords. For old men it was a mockery.

He looked beyond the Dip towards the city and mourned for its transience. A few bombs and it would suffer the fate of older, nobler cities. Like a proud fortress it towered over the suburb at its gates and he had never suspected its vulnerability.

Yet life went on. He viewed it with detachment, surprised at his former involvement and passion. Along the same arteries flowed the old with the new: the miners' wives he had pitied; the black men whose lot he had lamented; the hungry children he longed to feed, and the shoppers who arrived in their shiny cars from other suburbs.

There would always be poverty and oppression alongside of wealth and greed, whether he hammered away at his last all day or whether he sat back to read the chronicle of daily disasters.

He walked slowly up Main Street, stopping for breath only when a jagged pain pierced his chest. Tolerance, he thought. It was a word whose meaning he had forgotten. For him the line between tolerance and indifference had become smudged. In the shadow of death one became obsessed with one's mortality. Not that he was afraid of dying. It was a process which one experienced throughout one's life. If a man could live in isolation, without emotional bonds, without love or hate, he might live forever. As it was, his life was tied up with that of others and was diminished by each death, withdrawal or rejection.

But when he looked into the dark interior of Nathan's Drapery Store, he was surprised to find that the shell of his being still ached with longing and nostalgia.

It was some time before he sensed the excitement in Main Street. Everybody seemed to be hurrying in the direction of the mine dumps.

'What is it?' he asked a group of miners who stood outside the bar, talking earnestly among themselves.

'That crazy Bolshie Koren drowned himself,' one of them replied. 'Just walked into the dam and disappeared into the slime. They're looking for his body.'

Berka walked past First Avenue towards the plantation. People were converging on the dam from all directions. He paused at the top of the hill and looked about him. The mine dumps shimmered palely in the warm spring sun and the bluegums hung sadly over the dam. In the distance the headgear turned ceaselessly and the roar of the crushers reverberated throughout the suburb.

'My kingdom,' he thought grimly, and breathing heavily, made his way down to the dam.

Section 111

A Name in Africa

A Name in Africa

Write one song every day:
try for that
at least.
Say you weep,
tell Africa of your tears,
speak of holiness and weep again.
With whom have you joined hands?

    Here they prefer to ask:
    "What do people call you?"
    Very few ask:
    "What's your name?"

They did that in another time.

Knowing now, that I always will,
I long for Africa even more--
I call her by name,
I know what people call me there.

Denis Diamond

Here is Nowhere

Rain beats down on the shebeen;
the iron roof is its cowhide drum.
Soaking the grey-blanket-smoke of huddled chimneys
rain drowns township music.
Music of despair
music everywhere;
rain music, train music, mine music
home music. . . . . .
Here is nowhere.

Home is the huts on the hills
the green hills;
the wheels of the plough
the rain in the fields
Kaffir-boom,
Umbrella thorn
fish in the rolling river
and the cry of herdboys bringing cattle home.

But the young ones, they don't care. . . . .
"Halal, Umamedala! There is no money there."

Joan Jacoby

Homecoming

I come back
you huts on the hills;
flat umbrella-thorn, banana palms,
I come.
Umbogentweni, Mkababa, Mkababa, Mkomaas
the train says.
A big bird beats its wing in my chest.
Mfolosi, Mfolosi,
great muddy-water-snake, I see you
through the waving-finger-sugar-cane---
Sakabula bird,
I come home!

Joan Jacoby

<u>**Anniversary**</u>   by Helen Segal

i.
When I was young
I wore my hair
in plaits,
for plainness
I said,
before I learned
to doubt
my best intention

great twisted bands
of hair
over my shoulder
to chew as a child
or play coquette with

the movement
of my hand
as it flattered
the bands
of hair
was matched
by the movement
of eye

I was looking

not so much
for the chance
as for a hero
for my hair

ii.
a man
who could talk
so well
so long
about peanuts
required
more
than attention

not information
like data
of growth
and variety
but the meat
of the nut
ready
for my teeth

I bit

not green
in judgement

iii.
the body
in the head
head
in body--
there was no separation

each
taking
its chance
on the other's
yes

the eiderdown
on the floor
by the fire
was our winter
home

time reduced
when and why
into
an instant
moment

186

and I couldn't
care less
for consequences

the integrity
of the
very young

iv.
Three hundred
and sixty five days
to a year

I played
Muzetta
up to a point,
sipped coffee
in cafes
with bearded
gentlemen
and their current
problems

mostly
landlords;

the world
must have spun
on its axis
while I digested
the protein
in the peanut
and learned
the value
of vitamin
through
the flesh

v.
Two wedding parties,
one for family
and friends
of pre-historic days,
and one for acquaintances
after

the second
was most unexpected
we didn't recognize
a soul,
but there was wine
of course
and berets
so we had
familiar
landmarks

I had
to buy
a special dress
for the other
"What's _this_
got to do
with _us_?"
I yelled.
It'll make
my mother
happy
he said

Aha. . .
. . . .
vi.
It doesn't matter
about money
we said.
Food and clothes
and roofs
weren't money.
They were
food and clothes
and roofs.

The empty fridge
was an insult
or a threat.
So I cut
my hair.

Responsibility
came
in stages

We sacrificed
the coffee
in the cafes
and, little by little,
our time

there were
a few
disbelieving moments
when we comprehended
reality--
the bread and butter
kind

and the baby
did
the rest

vii.
it cried

long and loud
and, being given
to abstractions
--labels are always safe
                    they say--
we had a name
for every pitch;

it's tired
too dry
too wet
and settled
on cosmic despair
relieving
the sense of duty,
but not
the sense
of strain

I developed
an aversion
to peanuts.
They tended
to give me
bile

viii.
We were
no great shakes
at making money
but we had
enough.
Not enough
to pretend with
but enough
to stay healthy

The lack
kept
my head.
I was given
to romantic
ostentation
of the worst kind;
not him--

He was not
corrupted
by visions
of splendour,
at heart
as sound
as a nut

I lived
in my head
for a while,
my skin
not touching
the outside

i x
After the first one
I said
that's enough--
a little coy
and girlish.
We had
accomplished
our miracle
and my physicallity
was tender

a year later
I said the same,
not quite
so girlish;

weakness
finds
its strength
in the test;

my bones,
too soft
I had thought,
cradled
the third one
most kindly

for four years
was confused;
looked at the man
my mate
and wondered
who'd
let him in

x.
simmered down
and took
my sights

School days--
to live
all that
again;
and three
birthday parties
a year

God help
the intellectual
confronted
by three pairs
of dirty hands

constantly

who has
to learn
forgotten alphabets
of doing
and being
in everyday
terms

and the mothers
of the other
boys
at school.

I couldn't be
so precious
at not
playing a part--
my surfaces
were
too shabby

xi.
the long
winter nights
are too short,
the cat-tongued fires
can never purr
enough;

applying the technique
of his approach
to peanut,
my husband
explains
the universe

satisfactorily
I think

and the children
all sleep
through the night

while, tender
in the age
of my flesh,
I am running
and jumping

and twist
through my fingers
the long strands
of my hair

To Mark On An Anniversary

So how do you like
the fire in the hearth
hey my old tom-cat,
and the six o'clock saucer
of milk?
How do you like
the mince
and the mash
and the very few innovations--
not so much old
as house-trained
at last
after twenty-two years
of habit
(I would do it again
I would do it again)

Once you zipped trees
up and down,
your cut-out cat shape
black
on a branch of the moon
your eyes
were signals
in the sky.
Now there is milk
on your whiskers
and you don't
turn your head
when I kitty-kat
the room

Our claws tucked away,
we are polite
to strangers
and unexpected guests
our tails lash out
only at thunder.
You allow fleas
to walk
through your fur
and your interest
in birds
is academic

oh I like you
my anniversary man
I will do it again
if I can

It's all
very well
to be happy
he said,
but
for people
like us
who've waded
too deep
in pain,
peace
can be
too shallow

can only swim
beyond
our depths
where
crazy waves
may spin and spit
but never
shift
our balance

keep
an edge
to our stroke

he said

Continental Shift

At 6 a.m.
the sun comes
with the tea
to waken
A.D. Adam
for his fall
from innocence,
to waken
empires
which have known
a better day
or two,
to cockrow 4th and 5th
a half a dozen worlds
(and so forths
and so on)
backing out
or coming in
at any moment now

All over the world,
scattered
like ants
on a leftover bun,
black people and yellow, white
and brown
stretch and yawn
prepared
to meet
the day
for what has all this
got to do
with them

To John Berryman: His Toy, His Dream, His Rest

            and what
            you did
            to the language pal
            making us search
            the verb
            and adjective
            until meanings
            clicked
            like moments
            of truth
            and no not never nor nor neither
            nodded their yes
            in our dark rooms;

            the rhythm
            of your speech
            new
            as the blues
            to the darkies was
            not to mention
            an Association
            of Ideas
            that made
            us word-men
            word-men

            I had
            to run
            to nearly
            catch you gone O
            the way
            with Sexton
            Jonker
            Plath
            to say a
            a few

Bernard Levinson

Dear Anne

When I go from breakfast to madness
dear Anne
with the clouds clutched tight in my hand
and my frail books
filled with worn-out words--
I tell the nurse
this is a rest home for retired spies
cranky characters
talking back to the their chairs.
And we both laugh
to ease my pain
and hide for a moment
the sleep walkers
who pace their mops on the burnished floor.

Charles

I think of Charles
who hanged himself
from the lintel of his door.
On the surface of my mind
a single dry leaf floats.
Now it is a hand calling--
now a rusty raft. . . .
I listen--
there are no demands
no call for help
only the Autumn wind crying

195

Kineret

Lake Kineret
I know you
I watch your firefly-fishermen
move in your darkness
awaking a memory deep in my soul.

Kineret
I remember you
for four thousand years
the fires of your fishermen
burn in my blood,
and the nets
drag their fish
to my own secret shore.

Kineret
only now
when I stand in your silence
I know who I am.

Massada

I want to climb Massada--
not the easy way
like a Roman --
But like a Jew
I want to struggle with the east wall.
It's not enough to arrive--
This must be handled like a woman
slowly, holding back the moment.
I'm afraid
of being unable to lose myself.
I'm afraid
I will never find myself

For Fran
        who died at the age of 17

Isaac
bound on the altar
waiting for the miracle
that always comes--
I place your trust
in a locket.
It hangs from my neck
like a stone.
For I am Abraham
bent by the weight
of your eyes.
Talk to me--
I want to forget
There are flowers
bursting from your pocket

In Your Darkness

In your darkness
where the sick sleep
curled in their blind beds--
There is a splinter of moon,
a surgeon's needle threading the stars
through the wide window of the ward
winding the day's madness
into a long narrow sleep.
Come my friend
there is no need to stand
at the side of your bed
living still your day's dream
while the moon sews the night
into a small dark fist.
Put the voices away
and let this womb accept you.

Riva Rubin

Process

The house is eating itself--
lightening from the inside,
hollowing as a tree hollows
for its own reasons,
lending itself to wide-eyed night
things with a tendency to swoop
or claw or peck or snap the back of squealing
flashes in the dry
weave and mat of the field
no one plays anymore.

Ladder

        Even though you sleep on stones
you dream.
        Behold a ladder--and I am
among them.

Sequins

Sequins
on the ruff of your new dance dress,
mother of the dove-blue
boys of the R.A.F.!
And on the silver screen Zombies
with panoramic eyes in
the Dachau horror-show!
Like the Gates of Mercy
shut the White Cliffs of Dover
and the prices of David's House go down
with their burning boat in Haifa Bay
and Tipperary's a long way away!

Sequins
on the pockets of your re-cycled jeans,
pink-chested pink-nose in the heat wave,
sons of the R.A.F.!
And in swinging Chelsea see

The Rocky Horror Show!
And Freedom Killers at the Olympic Games!
Liberated Aquarian
seeks sheik for the winter!
Oh, Peter Pan is Trendy, again!
He's in! And Chaimberlain!
And the Black Theatre of Prague, Czechoslovakia!

Sequins
on the mid-morning darkness of your mourning,
O Israel again your candles,
your canticles
for the young dead!

Sequins
at the corners of your eyes
falling
like two
amens.

Sisyphus

It's no good Sisyphus,
it won't balance.
All it takes is a little extra shove
and you make the plateau, but no,
you live with what you've got and
if that small failure of strength is
what you've got--turn around
and lumber down after the rock,
Y'know, the grass on either side
of the furrow you've made going up
and down
has grown higher than your head and
if only you could see it, the sky
is a mad blue and light
as air.

The bullet was safer
left
in the temple.
The eye was dead
anyway
and the lead
wouldn't rust in its groove
in the bone.
Leave it alone.

The danger to his body
past
he could live on.
The hurting nerve cut
at last
at his end,
the cauterised world
could recede.
He'd planted his seed.

The kernel of death at
rest
will root by proxy,
the father's bequest
flower
in his son.
The ice-blue bud
of death-in-life.
Surer than bullet, than knife.

Flower Garden

Denis Diamond

I have a small garden in Jerusalem
where things will start growing soon
and eventually, flowers will bloom,
to rival all the parks of the earth:
      bright blooms,
      light in the heat,
      sheets spread
      over the stones
      to silence thunder,
      melt snows;
and clay pots from Bethlehem
filled with ferns,
geraniums
and a palm from Tel Aviv.

I have a small garden in Jerusalem,
small as a map
of all the parks of the world.

Letter To The Ruler Of The Zulus

1.
Africa whispers since the blood.

But you have heard jackals prowl
long shafts under the city.

    In Johannesburg, it's easy to forget
    the aloes;
    platforms for kraals on valley slopes;
    fruit smells of dung fires;
    old desires in wattle plantations
    and pine forests--
    so easy in Johannesburg,
    whe re the sun
    filters through
    alien cycads
    in our seasonal gardens,
    to forget what was never really known
    and all there really was to know.

You have heard of millions,
lost in the mines.

2.
Your mad subject, Madugu,
comes back lately
in these after-blood months,
cloaked in her dust
to haunt my twisted dreams
in which the shrouds of European beadles,
harbingers of gaseous death
and crematoria,
are exchanged for a khaki patch skirt
in which she probably also stitched
bits of my father's shirts
and grains of Egyptian sand
from the turn-ups of his military trousers.

3.
All kings understand
their mad subjects' laughter,
full of tomorrow's ghosts,
of the dead to come,
of still-born infants and murdered children.
Laughter in the king's hall
chills the lingerers on the paths to his court.

Some who came away from the railway stations in Poland
said it sounded over the marshes there
from a hundred thousand or so children
screaming themselves to sleep
before they died.

Something like that worries me again.

From the steps of my father's shop
where your people came to buy
gum boots and vaseline
and strings of beads,
where we hollowed out half loaves of white bread
and filled the cavities with red cold drinks,
one day, we watched
the whirlwind column dust
across the village
and move beyond the hospital
near Eloff's dam.
Everyone had fled.

Only Madugu moved about,
collecting rags and bottles for her bag:
        tall
        laughing
        mad.

She must have told you about it,
one way or another,
but I wonder if she mentioned
two white children
standing on the steps with their gaping mouths,
stained and red.

4.
Your court
has probably fully discussed the matter of your death,
or at least, the succession,
and some may even have conspired about these things.

I am perturbed
about your life
and your career:

Particularly so,
I want you to know,
when I drink
a sip or two
of my children's raspberry cordial.

You will have heard of us,
children, remaindered here
after the European calamity,
whom Madugu saw,
raspberry-stained,
gaping children.
You will have heard of us,
reflecting the whirlwind in our eyes.

That day she kindly showed me
leopards and snakes and herds of elephants.
But it is terrible to see these things
in Johannesburg,
to be a white poet in Johannesburg.

In this place a poet needs a king.

Section 1V

Armageddon,

and Other Problems

Another Final Battle on the Stage of History

Jillian Becker

Abstract   Taking its point of departure in remarks made by Ulrike Meinhof during the 1972 trial in West Germany of Horst Mahler, this paper goes on to examine some of the ideas and assumptions of the members of the terrorist group to which he belonged. Meinhof's as well as Mahler's views of the Jews in Germany and their fate, including their charge of a conspiracy on the part of the malevolent powers, are quoted and make it clear that as terrorists they conformed to a grandiose millenarian tradition. This millenarian tradition has had a long history in Germany, comprising anarchic, egalitarian, and communistic elements. Examples are the followers of John Hus and Thomas Müntzer. The need for group identification is also strong in the millenarians of the present day who believe in and act unquestioningly upon tenets such as those of terrorist groups like the Red Army Faction which, fortunately, has not gained the following of such predecessors as Hitler's Third Reich.

In December 1972, Horst Mahler, a lawyer who had organized a terrorist group in West Germany in 1969 and was arrested in October 1970, was brought to trial in Berlin. He was charged with conspiracy to commit crimes and with armed robbery. One of the witnesses called at the trial was Mahler's erstwhile accomplice, Ulrike Meinhof, who had been arrested some five months earlier, in June 1972, and was awaiting trial on charges of armed robbery, conspiracy, murder, and attempted murder.

She appeared in court on the 27th day of Mahler's trial.[1] She refused to sit in the place reserved for witnesses. The Presiding Judge warned her that if she would not cooperate, she would be seated in a special plate-glass box which had been installed for another witness, Karl-Heinz Ruhland, who needed protection because he had agreed to give evidence against the group to which he had himself once belonged.

Meinhof replied: "You threaten me with your Eichmann box, you fascist, you pig. You want to lock anti-fascists into that box in which Genscher [Federal Minister of the Interior] belongs."

The court informed her of her rights and duties as a witness. Her only response was, "Blah! Blah!"

She was threatened with a fine.

"All right," she said. "Just get on with it."

Asked her profession she replied, "Anti-fascist."

She was reminded that she must tell the truth.

Meinhof: "We always tell the truth. We are here because we can no longer endure your lying."

In giving her evidence, she said, "I am related to Horst Mahler. We were both born in the 30s; we had the same family background; we both grew up during the Second World War."

The Judge asked whether they were blood relations.

Meinhof: "Oh, of course, blood, that is what you want."

The trial proceeded, and suddenly Meinhof screamed out, "There you are waffling about bank robbery, while experiments on human beings are being conducted in Cologne-Ossendorf!" Hysterically she complained about the "inhuman conditions of detention" to which Astrid Proll, she said, was being subjected at Ossendorf, "a penal institution, whose symbol is a smokestack." She said, "You pigs obviously want a prominent suicide."

The Presiding Judge: "Frau Meinhof is obviously very agitated."

Meinhof: "I have been agitated for thirty-eight years now, over the state of affairs in Germany."

Mahler was given permission to question Meinhof. He told her that he "had to play this shit game" but he was concerned with "making it difficult for them to suppress certain things." And he began to read aloud from an underground publication. The court had rejected his application to read it out loud, so now he wanted to use it to question her.

Amicably, the Presiding Judge suggested that he could hand it to the journalists if he wanted it made public, upon which Mahler suggested that the Judge himself read it aloud. The Judge declined, and Mahler proceeded to read the document.

The polemical declaration which Mahler read was being circulated in 1973 as an "RAF" (Red Army Faction) underground publication under the title *The Action of the Black September in Munich—on the strategy of the anti-imperialist struggle*. It was almost certainly written by Mahler himself. It argued a point of view of which the following is a representative extract:

> With their action in the Olympic village, they [the Arab terrorists who killed the Israeli athletes] have carried the apparently only local conflict between the imperialist metropolis Israel and the Palestinians from the periphery of the system to the center—they have forced the character-masks of the Federal Republic law-and-order-state to take off the makeup and appear as what all character-masks of imperialism objectively are: warring parties against the freedom movements of the Thirld World—in the final analysis: extermination strategists and fascists.

The action, Mahler asserted, was "anti-fascist . . . because it was in memory of the 1936 Olympics." And he proceeded: "Israel weeps crocodile tears. It has burned up its sportsmen like the Nazis did the Jews—incendiary material for the imperialist extermination policy."

Ulrike Meinhof did not entirely agree with all that Mahler said. She interrupted his reading several times with comments such as, "That is not a perfect theory, though it does go something along those lines." And eventually she put what she believed was the right theory, concerning the Jews—at present, and in Nazi Germany—in her own words: "Without pronouncing the German people 'not guilty' of fascism—for the people truly did not know what went on in the concentration camps—we cannot mobilize them for our revolutionary struggle."

After the war, she said, the Left had reacted to fascism in a "careless, stupid, and brazen manner." Personalities were pushed into the foreground, but no deeper view was taken. "How was Auschwitz possible, what was anti-Semitism?" That should have been cleared up then [by "the Left"] instead of its concurring in the view that Auschwitz was the expression of evil.

"That's the worst of it," she said, "that we all agreed on that, Communists along with the others."

But now, she asserted, she herself had recognized that anti-Semitism in its essence is anti-capitalism. It used the hatred of the people of their dependence on money as a medium of exchange, their longing for communism.

"Auschwitz," she said, "means that six million Jews were murdered and carted on to the rubbish dumps of Europe for being that which was maintained of them—Money-Jews."

What had happened, she said, was that "finance capital" and banks, "the hard core of the system of imperialism and capitalism," had diverted the people's hatred of money and exploitation away from themselves and on to the Jews. Not to have made these connections clear was the failure of the Left, of the Communists. The Germans were anti-Semitic, and therefore they were supporters of the RAF. Only they did not know it, because they had not been pronounced "not guilty" of fascism, of murdering Jews, and had not been told that anti-Semitism was actually hatred of capitalism.

Because they had not been told that hatred of the Jews was actually hatred of capitalism, the German people had failed to support the Red Army Faction. But now she was making it clear, and it was on these grounds that the action of the Black September in Munich was to be praised.

However, she went on to claim a "historical identity" with the Jews of the Warsaw ghetto, who had "tried without arms to start a rebellion and then let themselves be butchered." "And with that," she said, "we have broken through the whole 'blah-blah.' "

Mahler wanted to continue reading from his document, but Meinhof said she had had enough. "I'm fed up now. I want to go now." And she pretended to faint. She was asked whether she wanted something to drink but she said no, she only wanted to leave, and with the permission of the court she embraced Mahler and was led out.

Ulrike Meinhof was clearly in no state to put forward a reasoned argument at the Mahler trial, and she made no great effort to do so. She declaimed histrionically rather than explained her views: she was "acting to the gallery." But at the best of times she was not a clear thinker; and her confusion in court was symptomatic, not merely of temporary emotional disturbance, but of character; and what she revealed were certain characteristic assumptions which are, for that very reason, particularly interesting.

The ideology which Meinhof and her associates had embraced, "world communist revolution," condemned Israel as an arm of American "imperialism," and Zionism as racism.[2] But the making of a case against the Israelis presented them with peculiar difficulties; for they were the self-appointed champions and leaders of the German "people" in an armed revolution which they hoped to have launched with their acts of terrorism.[3] And in order to justify morally the violent crimes with which they were charged, Meinhof and her fellow terrorists represented themselves as righteous fighters against the same sort of regime as had prevailed in Germany during the Third Reich; and insisted they were being subjected to the same treatment at the hands of the authorities of the Federal Republic as the Jews at the hands of the Nazis ("experiments are being conducted on human beings"; "a penal institution whose symbol is a smokestack"; Genscher "belongs" in the "Eichmann box").[4]

Not to condemn the treatment of the Jews by their German persecutors would be to deprive themselves of their most cherished propaganda weapon. And the simple expedient, popular with the extreme Left, of making a distinction between the Israelis and the Jews would not quite adequately serve. For unless the German "people" were "pronounced 'not guilty' " of racial persecution of the Jews, they might find the words condemning anyone for "racism" sticking in their throats.

Fortunately for the Red Army Faction, the very ideology which created the difficulty provided them with a solution if only they could apply it. What was necessary for them to do was to reinterpret the history of the Third Reich in such a way as to exonerate the working class of Germany from culpability by putting the blame for the racial persecution and genocide on to other—that is to say the "capitalist" or "exploiting"—classes.

To achieve this, Meinhof's first and obvious recourse was to say that "the people did not know." This she says; but does not after all believe it herself. She goes on to try another explanation: "The people" had indeed hated the Jews. But not *as* Jews. It was rather because "finance capital" had diverted their hatred, which was really a "hatred of their dependence on money as a medium of exchange," away from itself on to the Jews. So when the masses participated in, or connived at, or did not prevent the killing of the six million (assuming now that they did know about it), it was because they had been persuaded that the Jews were representative of economic exploitation and therefore received their just deserts in the extermination camps.

But did Meinhof herself believe that the identification of the Jews with what she regards as economic exploitation was without moral justification or factual foundation? Did she believe that "the people" had been entirely misled, and that they therefore in turn had made a mistake, albeit an honest one? It seems not. What she says is this:

"Auschwitz heisst, das sechs Millionen Juden ermordet und auf die Müllkippen Europas gekarrt wurden als das, als was man sie ausgab— als Geldjuden." (Literal translation: "Auschwitz means that six million Jews were murdered and carted on to the rubbish dumps of Europe as that which was maintained of them—as Money Jews.")

If it is not absolutely clear from this that she herself believed they *were* "Money-Jews," what is by now perfectly clear is that their murder *as "Money-Jews"* is not to her wrong, as it just might have been if they had been murdered *as Jews*. So, if the people did know, and were responsible at all for mass murder, it was not murder purely for reasons of race hatred, which would have been wrong according to the ideology of the Left in the 1970s, but more for reasons of class hatred, which is not wrong: and therefore the people can be "pronounced 'not guilty' " of genocide.[5]

But Meinhof did use the word *"Geldjuden,"* intending it to convey the loathing and contempt it had long carried, and as a sign of race hatred, anti-Semitism, but with an excuse tacked on which reflected both a traditional and a contemporary Communist rationale.

If we can conclude that to Meinhof they *were* "Money-Jews," *were* "finance capital," in the logic which Meinhof did not see or attempt to see, they "diverted" the people's hatred *away from themselves* as "capitalist exploiters" *on to themselves* as Jews! Even Meinhof seems to have been aware that something was wrong with all this. Uneasily she felt—so it appears—that there was still something she ought to say about Jews, about the victims with whom she was, after all, claiming equality of victimization. There was still the very important requirement not to appear as a racist herself. Some Jews must be exempted from condemnation. So with the Jews of the Warsaw ghetto, she claims "fellow feeling."

But it seems that she still felt dissatisfaction with her own argument. And it was probably out of a sense of frustration that obdurate facts continued to give her the lie, and that her own repeated claims to extraordinary humanitarianism were now betrayed and made her want to do violence to all opposing arguments, with words, since she now lacked other weapons: ". . . broken through the whole blah-blah!" she says.

The idea of conspiracy on the part of malevolent powers who use economic means to oppress the people was implied by Ulrike Meinhof in her speech to the court at Horst Mahler's trial, and she also trotted out that old canard of anti-Semitism that the Jews are such economic oppressors. More explicitly, Mahler himself expressed belief in conspiracy in the declaration he made in his own defense.

He declared:

You charge me with conspiracy. . . . But you yourself, the gang of General Motors, Ford, Armco, General Electric, ITT, Siemens, AEG, Flick, Quandt, BASF, Springer, Unilever, United Fruit, and certain others—the transnational consortia of capital, all together the imperialistic Monopoly Capital—are the most monstrous criminal association in history. To destroy this with all necessary and obtainable means is a necessity of life for more than 3 billion people.[6] . . . The imperialist system, which presents hell on earth to ever-increasing portions of humanity, may only be defeated by the action of the armed people and not by incantations, moral appeals, and parliamentary trifling. The Red Army Faction has taken up the idea of arming the people. . . .

So he himself desires an international movement for world revolution:[7]

The imperialist system forms a worldwide unit which transcends national boundaries. . . . Exploitation and repression are globally organized. . . . It is essential to recognize the global configuration of imperialism as the determining condition of the proletarian revolution; only in that way will it become a world revolution.

And Mahler makes it perfectly plain that he and his group are driven by grandiose millenarian ambitions:

Not with cheap words, but with deeds, have we come to stand on the side of the overwhelming majority of the people, who today all over the world are taking up arms to free themselves from imperialist suppression and any kind of exploitation. . . . This . . . is a world war—it will be the last and at the same time the longest and bloodiest war of history, because the exploiters do not hesitate to use the most horrendous torture actions to retain their dominance. It is not a war among nations but a war of classes, which will sweep all national, social, cultural, and religious boundaries and barriers forever from the stage of history.

The New Left movement whose massive demonstrations of protest came to a rather abrupt end about 1969 in Europe, a year or so later in America, and catapulted a few excited and violent people, reluctant to give up the movement's revolutionary aims, into terrorism, was itself a millenarian movement.[8] In his important and admirable book, *The Pursuit of the Millennium*, Norman Cohn writes:

> It is characteristic of this kind of movement that its aims and premises are boundless. A social struggle is seen not as a struggle for specific, limited objectives, but as an event of unique importance, different in kind from all other struggles known to history, a cataclysm from which the world is to emerge totally transformed and redeemed. This is the essence of the recurrent phenomenon or . . . persistent tradition—that we have called "revolutionary millenarianism."[9]

The New Left was of this kind, and so were—or are—its offshoots: the Red Army Faction, the Movement Second June (Germany); the Red Brigades, the Armed Proletarian Cells (Italy); the Angry Brigade[10] (England); the Japanese Red Army; the Weathermen (U.S.A.); and numerous similar groups in South America.[11]

It seems to me that there are three ways in which traditional millenarian ideas could have reemerged into public life in the 1960s and 1970s so little changed from their earlier manifestations. First, by direct learning. Second, as a result of the tradition having soaked, as it were, the culture of Europe, influencing connotations even of individual words, the vocabulary of values. Third, by the same sort of fanatical personalities, driven by the same sort of inner needs, conceiving the same vague visions and pursuing them in the same way, not imitating, but innately resembling their millenarian antecedents.

Certainly some of the founders and leaders of the Red Army Faction—Ulrike Meinhof, Horst Mahler, Gudrun Ensslin, Andreas Baader—all resembled, in various ways and to differing degrees, millenarian fanatics of the past.[12]

As for the tradition, it permeated the cultural air which these gently reared, carefully taught, affluent young persons breathed. In Europe as a whole, and Germany in particular, there had been a long history of religious dissent for centuries before the Reformation, often erupting in militant revolt, with leaders proclaiming their battle to be the last on the stage of history, ushering in the Kingdom of Christ, which would last for a thousand years, after which the world would end. They were, they claimed, fighting a righteous battle, fulfilling apocalyptic prophecies (such as the Book of Revelations), and their enemy was Antichrist. Supremely self-righteous, they dreamed of a better world after their victory, usually anarchic, egalitarian, communistic. Many held an ideal of a "return" to a golden age, a simple life, a natural state, Eden: a nostalgia for a condition of innocence, as before the Fall. Antichrist, the enemy, had many legions. Of these the Jews were a part. Avaritia, Luxuria, Dives were working the misery and destruction of suffering humanity, taking the form of clergy, rich townsfolk, some (but not all) lay rulers, and the Jews. In pursuit of peace, love, holy poverty, mercy, happiness, innocence, plenty effortlessly provided, equality and justice, they took up arms, tortured, burned, destroyed, massacred, and used the most extreme forms of terrorism. Oppression, want, tyranny, despair were their actual accomplishments.

The example I choose is that of the Hussites, both because it is typical, and because it seems highly likely that if any of the founders and leaders of the Red Army Faction knew anything directly of an idealistic millenarian movement of the past, Ulrike Meinhof knew of the Hussites; for her foster-mother, Professor Renate Riemeck, wrote an authoritative work on John Hus, the Bohemian religious reformer.

John Hus was burned as a heretic in 1414. But he himself was not an extremist. He taught that the Church should be disobeyed if its decrees contradicted or distorted the law of Christ as revealed in the Scriptures. It was only after his death, and because of it, that he became the figurehead of a rebellious movement. Multitudes of the discontented found a uniting cause in his martyrdom. The most extreme of the Hussites were the Taborites, apocalyptic phantasists, who idealized apostolic poverty and moral purity and believed that they were fighting the hosts of Antichrist and had a divine mission to purify the earth by destroying sinners. Anyone, they held, who was not with them was against them, and must be ruthlessly destroyed. When they had thus cleansed the earth, the millennium would come, and the surviving saints would live together in a community of love, peace, and equality, free from all law, all compulsion, all rents, taxes and dues, with all goods held in common. Thus they had the outline of a new social order, but no program, no defined method of bringing it into being. As anarcho-communist rebels, in pursuit of their classless society, they waged their war against the wealthy town dwellers. And they had ambitions to carry their crusade beyond Bohemia once their communist paradise had been created there, by going out and conquering the rest of the world. ''Unfortunately for their social experiment, the Taborite revolutionaries were so preoccupied with common ownership that they altogether ignored the need to produce.''[13] Where they did conquer, these thirsters after justice exercised tyrannical power over the common people, harassed and oppressed them and ruthlessly extorted rents, dues, and taxes.

Except that the communist and anarcho-communist groups of recent years, such as the Red Army Faction, failed to gain the great following that earlier movements did, the resemblances are so numerous and clear that it is hardly necessary to list them. The one similarity which might have been disputed by those who are aware of, but have not looked closely into, the proclaimed ideals of the RAF, is that of anti-Semitism. Their claims to being anti-materialistic—thoroughly contradicted by their manifest cupidity[14]—is well known; but their identification of economic oppression, or what they called *Konsumterror,* with ''the Jews'' was not revealed except, half-involuntarily, by Ulrike Meinhof at Mahler's trial, as I have shown. For the rest: communism or anarcho-communism, anti-capitalism, egalitarianism; vague beliefs in a revolution which will transform everything forever; pacifism, ideals of moral purity; the sort of people they hoped to gather to their cause; lack of a program; world revolution ambitions, the final and most important battle, to be led by them; their own carefully planned martyrdoms; cruel revenge vented on ''deviants,'' as well as merciless cruelty to their declared enemies; their use of terror—all are traditional. Furthermore, such movements usually began in the higher social strata, among the better educated and well-off, so in this too there was a close resemblance between the middle and upper-class terrorists of Europe, America, and Japan in recent years, and earlier millenarians.

The nature of the religious beliefs was not quite the same, though some of our latter-day terrorists had a religious upbringing, and were themselves religious in the common meaning of the word. Gudrun Ensslin, co-leader and founder of the RAF had a rigidly puritan Protestant upbringing, with a pastor father and a Pietist mother. Daily searching of the conscience was prescribed, a perpetual striving for moral perfection, with its necessarily accompanying despair of ever achieving it, and its frequently accompanying intolerance of those who seem happy without even trying to be good. And Ulrike Meinhof not only had parents who were believing Protestants, but had herself, as a student, sought the spiritual refuge of a devout sect. But both Meinhof and Ensslin were religious personalities in a wider meaning of the word. For both, the moral fervor they brought to bear on what they preferred to call political issues was of the religious crusading kind. They and their fellow terrorists in their own and similar movements held the same kind of belief in absolute standards of good, a self-righteous certainty that they were on the side of good, and that they were fighting a vast conspiracy of evil; a simplistic dualism which again puts them in line with many a millenarian crusader of the past.

Millenarian movements were "in no way typical of the efforts which the poor made to improve their lot. *Prophetae* would construct their apocalyptic lore. . . . That lore would be purveyed to the poor—and the result would be something that was at once a revolutionary movement and an outburst of quasi-religious salvationism."[15] Indeed, it could happen that such a *propheta* would step into a genuinely political conflict and turn it into a millenarian disaster. The German Peasants' Revolt was in the first instance a political and not a millenarian revolt.[16] When Thomas Müntzer and Niklas Storch stepped in to encourage the peasants to overthrow the princes of Saxony—incidentally two exceptionally tolerant princes,[17] the Elector Frederick and Duke John—with a doctrine of social revolution, complaining that the princes were "too rich," they gained them nothing, but only nudged them to their own destruction. When Philip of Hesse went, contemptuously, to do battle with them, Müntzer told the peasants that God was on their side, a miracle would happen, he would "catch the cannonballs in the sleeves of his cloak."[18] But the cannonballs found their mark, the revolt collapsed, and Müntzer fled and hid, but was found, tortured, and beheaded.

From Engels down to the Communist historians of today—Russian as well as

German—Marxists have inflated Müntzer into a giant symbol, a prodigious hero in the history of the "class war." This is a naive view, and one which non-Marxist historians have countered easily enough by pointing to the essentially mystical nature of Müntzer's preoccupations, his general indifference to the material welfare of the poor. Yet it may be suggested that this point too can be over-emphasized. Müntzer was a *propheta* obsessed by eschatological phantasies which he attempted to translate into reality by exploiting social discontent. Perhaps after all it is a sound instinct that has led Marxists to claim him for their own.[19]

Müntzer was venerated by the Anabaptists, whose movement spread in the years following the Peasants' Revolt. It too was an egalitarian and communist millenarian movement. Its "King" and "Messiah of the Last Days," John Leyden, ruled tyrannically over his terrorized flock in the town of Münster. A handsome, swaggering man, who liked to arrange real life as if it were being presented in a theater, and who had been unable to hold an ordinary job, he had more than a little in common with Andreas Baader. When he and his two closest henchmen were at last defeated by the armies of the Bishop of Münster besieging the town, they were tortured to death, and put in cages hung from the church steeple. They hang there to this day, and were hanging there when Ulrike Meinhof went to Münster to study at the University, and edited a short-lived periodical in support of the Peace Movement in the late 1950s.

If the Communists have Müntzer as one of their favorite German chiliast *prophetae,* the Nazis had theirs too. An unknown revolutionary of the early sixteenth century wrote *The Book of a Hundred Chapters.* In it we find that "the route to the Millennium leads through massacre and terror."[20] He wanted to lead a crusade against the rich, after which equality and communal ownership would come into being as the new justice. He combined this belief with fervent nationalism. "The Germans once held the whole world in their hands and will do so again, and with more power than ever."

Cohn writes:

In these phantasies the crude nationalism of a half-educated intellectual erupted into the tradition of popular eschatology. The result is almost uncannily similar to the phantasies which were the core of National Socialist "ideology". . . . There is the same belief in a primitive German culture in

217

which the divine will was once realized and which throughout history had been the source of all good—which was later undermined by a conspiracy of capitalists, inferior, non-German people and the Church of Rome—which must now be restored by a new aristocracy, of humble birth but truly German in soul, under a God-sent saviour who is at once a political leader and a new Christ. It is all there—and so were the offensives in West and East—the terror wielded both as an instrument of policy for its own sake—the biggest massacres in history—in fact everything except the final consummation of the world-empire, which, in Hitler's words, was to last a thousand years.[21]

It may seem that nationalism was one element of the German millenarian tradition that had disappeared by the time the RAF came along, if by "nationalism" one means exaggerated patriotism. German nationalist fervor had, understandably, abated after the Second World War. But the need for group identification was nevertheless strong in these latter-day millenarians. They were people who needed to be part of a gang, who shirked individual responsibility. (Notice Meinhof's need to claim relationship with Mahler. And Gudrun Ensslin told her sister that her "real" siblings were Petra Schelm and Thomas Weissbecker, two of her dead comrades.) They all believed ardently that the collective was of much greater importance than the individual:[22] devotees of international rather than national socialism.

One final example of millenarianism in the past is worth mentioning, for it had a bearing in our century on both Nazi and Marxist ideology.

In the thirteenth century, Joachim of Fiore "elaborated an interpretation of history as an ascent through three successive ages"[23]—the Third Age, a kind of heaven on earth, enduring until the Last Judgment. He added ideas of communism, apocalypse, and the return of a golden age.

"The long-term, indirect influence of Joachim's speculations can be traced right down to the present day, and most clearly in certain 'philosophies of history,' " writes Cohn. He instances the theories of historical evolution of Hegel and others among the German Idealists, and the Marxian dialectic of the three stages of primitive communism, class society, and communism regained. "And," he writes, "it is no less true . . . that the phrase 'the Third Reich'. . . would have had but little emotional significance if the phantasy of the third and most glorious dispensation had not, over the centuries, entered into the common stock of European social mythologies."[24]

218

The Third Reich was to last a thousand years in the prophecy of Hitler. It lasted only a dozen, but its millenarian leader did gain a large following. Fortunately, the crusades of the RAF and its resemblers of recent years gained no following at all, and can have very little significance even in the history of such movements.

Notes

1. This account of the proceedings is taken largely from the *Frankfurter Allgemeine Zeitung* of December 15, 1972. Other newspaper accounts are briefer, but serve to confirm the facts sufficiently.

2. *In The Economic War Against the Jews,* (Corgi, London, 1979), Terence Prittie and Walter Henry Nelson write: "Anti-Zionism has been a convenience for bigots, for it permits the anti-semites to pose as anti-Israeli, while denying any anti-Jewish bias." (p. 172.) They substantiate this very fully, and also supply ample proof that the Arab enmity toward the Jews does not date merely from the inception of the modern state of Israel, but is centuries old. "If there had been no other reason for Zionism," they say, "it would have had to be invented in order to bring the centuries-long oppression of the Jews of the Arab world to an end." (p. 169.)

3. There is much evidence in their own underground publications that they saw themselves as leaders of an armed revolution of the masses. It is apparent in Mahler's declaration in court, referred to in the article. Much more evidence can be found in *Über den bewaffneten Kampf in Westeuropa,* which was republished as *Rotbuch 29,* Verlag Klaus Wagenbach, Berlin, 1971, especially on pages 17, 19, 23, 46; *Das Konzept Stadtguerilla,* which was republished in *Stadtguerilla* by Alex Schubert, Verlag Klaus Wagenbach, Berlin, 1971, especially on pp. 109–16, 125; and *Dem Volk Dienen,* issued as an underground publication only. It will also be noticed in their own writings that they explicitly advocate the use of 'terror': see e.g. *Über den bewaffneten Kampf in Westeuropa,* section 6, *Terror gegen den Herrschaftsapparat—ein notwendiges Element der Massenkämpfe* (Terror against the Rulership Apparatus—a necessary element of the mass struggle), pp. 33–40. The last two sentences of the section read: "The rulers use fear, which they produce through terror, to keep the proletariat compliant. So what can be said against the use of fear by the suppressed which they induce in their enemies through terror, so as to set themselves free at last?"

4. I have pointed out and discussed elsewhere the envy of victims and fascination with suffering in general (I call it *Leidensneid;* it is manifested, for instance, by the imitation of the appearance of poverty) among affluent young

radicals of the 1960s and 1970s. See Jillian Becker, *Hitler's Children,* Panther, Granada Publishing, London, 1977, 1978, pp. 69–71.

5. Ulrike Meinhof did not give an opinion as to whether the people were not guilty of the killing, enslavement, and persecution of any other races, Gypsies or Slavs for instance, to exonerate them from the charge of ''racism'' in general, only this ambiguous argument to clear them of ''anti-Semitism.'' For a concise account of racism in the history of socialism, see George Watson, ''Race and the Socialists,'' in *Encounter,* November 1976, in which he writes, for instance (pp. 20, 21): ''Marx and Engels were not socialists who also happened to be racialists, or racialists who also happened to be socialists. They openly believed that the one conviction requires the other. . . . Equality (according to Marx and Engels) may be pursued—may have to be pursued—by killing those who are genetically unequal.'' The author also refers in his article to Ulrike Meinhof's statements at the trial of Horst Mahler, and asks, ''How much was socialism, and how much national-socialism in her passionate self-defence?'' (p. 23.)

6. Mahler's insistence that the developed countries are responsible for the poverty of the less developed, is widely held in the developed world. For a clear and impressive argument against it, backed by convincing facts, see Professor P.T. Bauer's ''Western Guilt and Third World Poverty'' in *Commentary,* New York, January 1976 Professor Bauer writes, for instance, ''. . . allegations that the West is responsible for the poverty of the so-called Third World . . . have come to be widely accepted, often as axiomatic, yet they are not only untrue, but more nearly the opposite of the truth.'' (p. 31.). And again, ''So far from the West having caused the poverty of the Third World, contact with the West has been the principal agent of material progress there.'' (p. 32.) He explains in the course of the article how Marxist-Leninist ideology reinforced mistaken notions which gave rise to the wide acceptance of the view that the West caused the poverty of the Third World. He further points out that, ''. . . people in the West who are sufficiently disillusioned with their own society to have become disaffected from or even hostile to it . . . see the Third World as a useful instrument for promoting their cause in what is in essence a civil conflict in the West.'' (p. 38.)

7. It should be noted that during his years in prison, Horst Mahler has changed his mind about many of the views he held in the 1960s and early 1970s, and in particular has declared himself to be no longer in favor of terrorism.

8. Tom Wolfe in ''The Me Decade and the Third Great Awakening,'' on p. 131 of *Mauve Gloves and Madmen, Clutter and Vine,* Bantam, London, 1977, writes: ''It is entirely possible that in the long run historians will regard the entire New Left experience as not so much a political as a religious episode wrapped in semi-military gear and guerrilla talk.''

9. Norman Cohn, *The Pursuit of the Millennium,* Paladin, London, 1970, p. 281.

10. The Angry Brigade was influenced by the French "Situationists." For the millenarian flavor of their political views, see e.g., Raoul Vaneigem, *The Revolution of Everyday Life,* Practical Paradise Publications, London, 1972.

11. But not all the millenarian groups which arose out of the New Left were "urban guerrilla" movements. There were—and still are—numerous cults, religions, and quasi-religions, of which many erstwhile supporters of the New Left became adherents. Some of these seem lunatic, exhibiting characteristics of such groups in an exaggerated form. One example was the Charles Manson "family," a drug-taking, murdering, orgiastic group, with weird but distinctly millenarian beliefs: a final war, between blacks and whites, which the blacks would win, though Manson ("Man's son," both "God and Satan," as he called himself) would then emerge from hiding in the desert of California, wrest victory from the blacks because they would find themselves simply unable to govern, and so establish his own blessed reign, a lasting peace on earth.

12. For details of their lives and characters, see Jillian Becker, op. cit., especially Parts One, Two, and Three.

13. Norman Cohn, op. cit., p. 217.

14. For instances of this, and their preference for high living standards and luxury goods, see Jillian Becker, op. cit., especially e.g., pp. 230, 245–46.

15. Norman Cohn, op. cit., p. 281. And on p. 282: "Revolutionary millenarianism drew its strength from a population living on the margins of society—peasants without land . . . beggars and vagabonds—in fact from the amorphous mass of people who were not simply poor but who could find no assured and recognised place in society at all." Cf. Herbert Marcuse, one of the Marxist philosophers most favored by the New Left, who writes in *One Dimensional Man,* Sphere Books, London, 1972, pp. 199–200, that the true revolutionaries now were not the working classes but "the substratum of the outcasts and outsiders . . . the unemployed and the unemployable." The Red Army Faction did not despair of leading the working classes too, but in fact they led neither the proletariat nor the *lumpenproletariat.*

16. Norman Cohn, op. cit., p. 245.

17. Ibid., p. 244.

18. Ibid., p. 255.

19. Ibid., p. 251.

20. Ibid., p. 120.

21. Ibid., p. 125.

22. I have said (in *Hitler's Children*) that the chief real motivation for these terrorists was ego gratification. Following the usage that Karl Popper prefers (see *The Open Society and Its Enemies,* Routledge and Kegan Paul, London,

1969, fifth edition, p. 101), I distinguish between "individualism" and "egoism." The individualist is *opposed* to collectivism. The egoist, by contrast, often seeks emotional satisfaction in membership of a group or tribe, as Popper explains. Furthermore, the Red Army Faction and similar terrorist groups selected individuals for attack and killing on the grounds that they were to be regarded primarily as representatives of groups—capitalists, managers, bankers, industrialists; judges, public prosecutors; shoppers in department stores; etc. As this is precisely equivalent to persecuting individuals on the grounds that they "represent" this or that national or racial group, one might hear the moral indignation they like to express over "nationalism" or "racism" (even without remarking Ulrike Meinhof's view of Auschwitz as the just deserts of *"Geldjuden"*) as having a hollow ring.

23. Norman Cohn, op. cit., p. 108.
24. Ibid., p. 109.

The Shopping Trip

Rose Moss

On the last sunny day before the world came to an end, Leah
and Jonathan debated what to buy Uncle Chaim for his birthday.
They were, of course, unaware of the full significance of the occasion and saw the problem rather as a matter of choosing for a
relative they did not know very well, in fact, hardly at all, than
as a commemoration of a life as near eclipse as their own. In
the end, because they hardly knew more of Chaim than that he had
chosen to live in France because France was the mother and flower of civilization, they could think of nothing more apt than a
bottle of Grand Marnier, a French version of Scotch. It wasn't
very witty, but they hoped that by being French their gift would
transcend the insult of a choice otherwise too commonplace for
respect.

Even if they had known Chaim better they wouldn't have bought
anything really expensive. They were as bourgeois as he, although he sometimes conceived of them as "American" and
therefore rich (they thought him "French"). They were bound to
choose something on a modest scale. Not for them the gift offered on the first day of the apocalypse by Neiman-Marcus as
suitable for "a pessimist," an updated Noah's Ark with enough
room for 8 passengers, 4 crew members, 92 mammals, 10 rep-
tiles, 26 birds, 14 fresh water fish, 38 insects, one veterinarian
(in case God didn't intend anyone to survive this Deluge it seemed
best to rely on human resources), one French chef, one Swedish
masseur, one German hair stylist, one English valet, one French
maid, one Italian couturier, one English curator librarian. Neiman-Marcus offered nothing but the best, and being in Babylon,
like Cambridge Mass 02138, whence the Americans had come to
France on vacation, found no difficulty in culling that best from
all over the world with the aid of those merchants who, now that
they wept and mourned, for no man bought their merchandise
any more, were only too eager to extend themselves, go a little

further, and offer their service with a smile--contingent on receipt of some of the take, $588,247.00 catalog price for the ark.

Had the Americans wanted an ark (which they did not--they weren't even sure they wanted one when, as Prof. Z.Brzezinski complained "everyone else is running around, beating their chests, becoming apocalyptic, without any sustained effort to understand what is going on") they would have turned to Neiman-Marcus for it. For one thing, their past experience did nothing to indicate that the essentials of post-diluvian life would include a Swedish masseur. As mentioned before, they were bourgeois, indeed as petit bourgeois as the uncle they had come to visit. (They would, however, have been tempted by the French chef). For another, Neiman-Marcus projected a delivery date four years after receipt of the order for an ark. It was not a reassuring schedule for days in which a pessimist might find good reason to wonder whether the world could last that long. Furthermore, an ark was a primitive device and not perhaps appropriate to the means now to be employed by a weary Jehovah to deal with the world. They couldn't take the offer seriously, it must have been a joke, for Edward Marcus, chairman of the board, was reported to have said in those days "basically we felt that an ostentatious spreading around of money was not particularly appropriate at this time." Nevertheless, the offer was not "without meaning" (Trotsky's phrase--about the Cossacks who winked at the crowds they were supposed to quell during the bread riots of February 24, 1917).

The morning of Chaim's birthday, however, opened without a cloud in the sky. When Jonathan pushed the shutters of their French hotel room open and looked down to the sunny courtyard where he could see the maid who did their room--she was rinsing dishcloths--he felt a relaxed, expectant happiness. The future was good. Its immediate imminence was croissants and cafe au lait. The child Michael refused croissants. Leah tried to tempt him with bread and butter and jam, but he wasn't eating in France, he was upset. Because, so far as he could see, the world he knew had disappeared. It was no use that his parents told him it was still there and would come back. His appetite was down, and even warm chocolate was not going to console him.

What's more, he didn't want to be pushed, touched, carried, fed, pulled limb by limb out of his clothes, washed, wiped, turned over, wrapped, dressed, combed, and stuffed. He showed as much by hollering, twisting, kicking, rolling, stiffening, and, when Leah turned away for a moment to find a pin, by sliding off the bed and crawling toward the sink--an interesting area enriched by a waste basket, plumbing, bidet, screen, and two suitcases that had been, though he hadn't understood it at the time, the first portents in the old world of its disappearance.

His mother didn't like him to play among the plumbing, but found it difficult to reach him. It was fun. She exasperated quickly, visibly. He was as quick as a fish in water, a David, a pickpocket, a guerrilla. She called for aid. Instead Jonathan gave advice. "Let him play a bit. He won't get much chance later."

"It's not very hygienic."

Jonathan did not answer, having learned long ago from his mother before his wife, that the best defense is no defense.

Leah recognized defeat, and prepared for the long day ahead by packing a large canvas bag. Its capacious and versatile utility had attracted her in Cambridge Mass 02138 where she had bought it for the trip to France and for the promise that it would carry them (an ark surrogate) through just such days as this sunny birthday which they would spend with Uncle Chaim away from the hotel. She provided it for emergencies of an everyday kind: for hunger, raisins and milk; for boredom, books and toys; for ignorance, maps and guidebooks; for changes of sky, jackets; for grief, tissues and Linus blanket; and for elimination, European disposable diapers (less satisfactory than their American equivalents. The Europeans didn't quite have the hang of disposability. They clung to the old.)

To say that the bag would carry them through misleads, of course. They would carry it. Its weight, which could not be pared down beyond a certain point if one wanted to survive, would grow heavier every hour (though they shared the burden, the child in a back pack borne by one parent, the bag lugged by the other) until the bearer felt like St. Christopher carrying the whole weight of the world in small compass. Since the Americans were not mythical saints their exhaustion contributed to the acerbity of family relations;the visit to Uncle Chaim was not all pleasure. By the next day, however, they looked back with nostalgia to the bag whose effectiveness against emergencies epitomized the predictability, stability, resourcefulness, sanity, familiarity, and simplicity of that time so unlike the time of the

apocalypse, in which it was hard to conceive--even after making
a "sustained attempt to understand what is going on"--what to do
about it. Especially when the seven trumpets of the seven angels
sounded and there followed:

1) hail and fire mixed with blood, and they were cast upon the
earth and the third part of the trees was burned up and all green
grass was burned up;

2) a great mountain burning with fire was cast into the sea
and the third part of the sea became blood, and the third part of
the creatures which were in the sea and all life had died, and
the third part of the ships were destroyed.

3) there fell a great star from heaven, burning as if it were a
lamp, and it fell upon the third part of the rivers, and upon the
foundations of waters, and many men died of the waters because
they were made bitter;

4 a) the third part of the sun was smitten, and the third part
of the moon and the third of the stars, and

b) an angel flew around saying with a loud voice "Woe, woe,
woe to the inhabiters of the earth. "

Which seems the least one could say under the circumstances,
though of course men were not satisfied with that and appointed
Senate, Blue Ribbon, and Royal Commissions to investigate what
was happening. The International Red Cross was totally ineffec-
tive, refugees streamed everywhere. The newly founded Disaster
Committee of the United Nations which had been planned to deal
with contingencies like tidal waves, cyclones, earthquakes, and
genocidal war (disasters more or less to be expected, like those
of the Americans setting out for a day away from the hotel,
though of course on a different scale) had not been able to pro-
vide for outlandish calamities like God's judgment.

The bag packed, the child dressed, the father shaved, the
mother made up, they set off. They enjoyed the sequence of
morning chores that had by now, the second week of their visit,
assumed a ritual time through which they deployed the concierge,
the blanchisseuse, the post office, the bank, the corner store
where they bought milk for the child, and the fruiterie--where
the child demanded bananas, for, an American child, he ate
imperially. It was not so much that he disdained to live off the
land as that, fruits of empire being staple fare in Cambridge

Mass 02138, bananas tasted familiar and assuaged his anxiety
about the world's capability to disappear. He could eat and feel
less homesick. The same with imperial armies everywhere--
thus Hershey bars in Saigon, canned asparagus in Algeria, plum
pudding at midsummer Christmas in Australia. And for exiles
of wars, colonies, and remnants of empires, for Romanoffs in
Manhattan, von Braun in Houston, Patels in Durban, Rosselinis
in Addis Ababa, Hartunians in Watertown, there were piroshki
to eat in New York, sauerkraut in Texas, curry in Natal, ravioli
in Ethiopia,lamejuhns in New England, all integrated somehow
into the local diet. (Conversely, there were no yak steaks in New
York for the ambassador to the United Nations from Bhutan, a
country of few imperial pretensions.) Thus, also, Duke Ellington,
on tour in Minsk, USSR, although he admitted to a fancy for
broiled sturgeon, still said, "I'm a cheeseburger man. There's
nothing like a cheeseburger. " Their exiled palates were homesick for the taste of childhood and the time of that first paradise
inhabited by known neighbors, tradesmen, aunts, parents and
siblings; homesick for the time before birthdays brought intimations of mortality, for the time when time moved slowly, syrupy,
when its gravest impediments were the interminable intervals
between today and tomorrow, now and next week, when aeons intervene before Christmas, or Chanukah, or Divali, light years
before Easter.
   Which must have been the time of some of the children of
Nice bearing their longing through the same streets as the Americans, childhood and adult times flowing like two currents in one
river. Its banks this sunny day were adorned with signs of the
imminent morning when the shirts and dresses in the store-
keepers' windows would arise and stand, and by virtue of the
life in them (not yet incorruptible, for the day would furnish
evidence--dirt, blood, and chocolate smears--that as yet moth
and rust could raven up this world's freshness) would praise
the Lord at the Mass of the Resurrection. Then, Lent and its
abnegations being over, the children of Nice would go forth to a
heavenly vision of chocolate eggs, rabbits, nests, marzipan
and glace fruits (specialities of the region), cakes shaped like
lambs and the Lamb, hard candies as bright as jewels, nougats,
cookies, tarts, napoleons, Japanese ladies, and secret centers
wrapped in chocolate and in silver, gold and colored foils that
stood ready at the time of their revelation to give a taste as

sweet as honey and the honey comb, a vision appropriate to a
child's age of a bliss traditionally set forth, as to St. John, by
a city illuminated in a light as of a stone most precious, even
like a jasper stone, clear as crystal, which illuminated the
foundations adorned with: the first a jasper, the second sapphire,
third chalcedony, fourth emerald, and continuing in this order,
sardonyx, sardius, chrysolite, beryl, topaz, chrysoprase,
jacinth, to the twelfth, an amethyst--ornaments probably not,
in that city, indebted to the style of the same Sun King whose
touch in the confections of Nice assured the Americans, plea-
surably, that they were in France.

Since Michael demanded bananas, Jonathan, who shared a
taste for the fruit, stopped at the fruiterie. He was an indulgent
father, and was not deceived by the child's recent refusal of
croissants. He granted his son the desire of his heart.

Leah was not enthusiastic about her husband's decision to give
the child bananas then and there. She retained a curious mixture
of inhibitions about eating in public, part school rules (her school
had adopted a British style), part a prickle of consciousness
about being watched. She felt the eyes of the hungry, the poor
she had always with her, ready to look with big eyes behind barbed
wire, to run after her like children running along train tracks who
stretch out their hands for pennies, bread, bruised fruit, anything
the passengers will throw out. She gave donations to Biafra, Ap-
palachia, Mississippi, and Bangladesh. It was not least to quell
these images and their iterations (accumulating, of course towards
the end) that she sympathized with revolutionary hopes when
these became the fashion in Cambridge Mass 02138. Before the
withering away of oppression, however, the child had to be fed,
in spite of her discomfort about eating in public. She accepted
the banana peel that Jonathan gave her.

"Our first piece of trash for the day, " she noted.

They had both commented on the relative absence of trash in
France: the cleanliness of the streets, the frail tissue of paper
that served to intervene between a baguette and sweating palm
rather than the double waxed paper and polyethylene bag that
saved American loaves from humanity and other unhygienic contacts, the reusable bottle of wine that could be filled again at the
market, the expectation in stores that purchases need not be

bagged, the absence of the accumulation of cardboard, paper,
cellophane, and plastic that in Amerika protected each purchase
with as much recklessness as evinced also in defense strategies
that wrapped conventional defense in nuclear, old generation
missiles in new, and the State in power to kill all enemies, past,
present, and to come, more than once merely (which might have
been considered satisfactory in countries like France that did not
stand in the first rank of terror, or where reason might have suggested multiple annihilation to be a supererogation of virtue) but
twice, thrice, quadruply--indeed, considering the possibilities
of toxins, nerve gases, bacteria, viruses, hormones, herbicides,
blights aimed at the food supply, and other ingenuities forbidden
by the Geneva Convention, power to kill to the nth power, an awe-
some thought (though of course the Lord God of Hosts was not to
be mocked by these toys). Jonathan and Leah couldn't see the
sense of it, and disapproved of French economy except in the
matter of diapers. They felt conspicuously American when they
made trash (although it was not yet the day when waste threatened to waste all, and it would seem that the angel of God would
by way of trash fulfill the curse on Babylon, "Reward her even as
she rewarded you, and double unto her double according to her
works: in the cup which she hath filled, fill to her double. How
much she hath glorified herself and lived deliciously, so much
torment and sorrow give her.")

"We'll get rid of it soon," Jonathan consoled her. Consolation
was his matrimonial wont for problems of no immediate, radical
solution. He was a meliorist, and did not despise palliatives. He
did not share his wife's preference for surgical solutions (and
problems) and had developed a certain talent for the medicinal
word.

Furthermore, he was gifted with an eye for practical, though
not necessarily final, solutions, and when, almost immediately,
they passed a small shop where they saw a florist preparing the
day's stock, he suggested that they ask the hospitality of his
waste disposal system now receiving discarded blooms and broken stems.

"Let's buy some flowers too," she assented, "for Chaim's
birthday."

It wasn't necessary, they had a gift. But Jonathan also liked
flowers, and was willing to indulge her eagerness to celebrate
escape from the sclerotic streets of Cambridge Mass 02138

where, at the time of their vacation in Nice, the ice age still
preserved, in lieu of mammoths and sabre-toothed tigers,
particulate emissions, fly ash, frozen dog urine, Xmas tinsel,
squashed Pepsi-Cola cans, commercial sand which had been
intermittently sown with salt on the streets and highways of
frozen America by the decree of innumerable city fathers not
versed in Vergil, trampled gloves without their mates, metal
washers, advertisements designed to suit all potential recipients
but not cared for and in spite of their fulsome promises, dropped
dead letters, candy wrappers, and drained ball points. The
tels of snow that obstructed movement had not melted yet, nor had
their ruined artifacts been swept into the city dump, but the Americans were in a new world now, and the husband was prepared to
condone a slight extravagance in honor of their spring freedom.

     Not having any notion of Chaim's taste in flowers, Leah chose
to satisfy her own taste within the limits of petit bourgeois extravagance, and opted for anemones, in the contemplation of
whose red and purple globes she was happy enough to wait while
the florist received a consignment of iris and tulips which he
counted in German--for he was another who kept the past in his
mouth. He was an immigrant from Alsace, he told her when he
engaged in conversation over their piece of trash and small purchase. And when they took up their gift and wished him good day,
he smiled at them with what she took to be unfeigned friendliness
(she wanted to enjoy the spring in France) such as they had often
encountered, in spite of warnings from previous tourists, in
their daily and pedestrian dealings with French tradesmen, the
blanchisseuse, the baker, the aged concierge at the hotel (who,
however, maintained an air of having seen it all before in his
dealings with the Americans), and particularly with the family
who owned the trattoria.
     Where of an evening they would stop for elements of a supper
to be eaten in the hotel room where the child's impatience of
decorum would be of no concern to others. Their experience of
French restaurants in his company was an excruciating example
of how blood relations cramped together against their will, but
retaining their different purposes, understandings, and tolerance
of compromise, could cause greater misery--because there was
no escape, the child was theirs until death did them part--than

strangers, friends, or spouses; from these there could be some
divorce. Even strangers, they had been told often enough, were
part of the one family of man. It was a truth to appall if one
thought about it in certain situations. As, for example, when
French strangers in their family stared because Michael would
not be reverent during the service of the meal. They identified
his ancestors by the child's pagan behavior. In the context of
his wanton energy and noise Leah and Jonathan were as undeni-
ably American as in their own trash. Hoping to maintain friendly international relations and avoid incidents, they are in their hotel
room.

And established friendly relations with the family who owned
the trattoria, whose daughter, seeing them emerge from the
florist's, waved and smiled, as they did too. So they cemented
ties established by their inadequate French (and other misunder-
standings) which this daughter sometimes corrected in a genial
way when they discussed the merits of boiled eggs, applesauce,
and other bland fare internationally recommended for children.
It was not yet the day, the eve of their departure, when this
same daughter saying au revoir would give them a colored post-
card (la Baie des Anges) on which she had written the family's
name and address as an invitation for the Americans to write
and maintain their ties until the happy time when they would come
again to Nice to visit their relatives.

It was a revelation to the Americans. Their world was not her
world nor their times hers. She lived still among gemeinschaft
relations, they in flux and gesellschaft that required of them
modular civility, and dispensed with entangling bonds. Holding
on would strangle them in a world where everyone progressed
and regressed at different rates, going in different directions;
where everyone traveled or took other trips that forced farewells;
wives,   analysts, lovers, and colleagues accepted grants and
positions that, destroying propinquity, destroyed familiarity and
old friends, past spouses, neighbors, and parents fell by the
wayside (profuse with other discards).

But for the moment the Americans, not wholly socialized to
the pace of disintegration in Cambridge Mass 02138, were a
little frightened at the way things fell apart. They preferred the
balms of Nice, and friendliness that did not seem to be the product of marketing techniques that had supermarket girls in Amerika wear yellow buttons reading SMILE (soon to be superseded

by a glyph smile that on buttons, shirts, cushions, cookies,
shopping bags, balloons, plastic book covers, and decals, vied
with the symbol of peace, a dying fad, to become the emblem of
the people who covered themselves with peace and joy, but as
wolves with sheeps clothing. They would have preferred to lie
down with the lamb, but they were cursed to be such men of whom
it has been written, homo homini lupus).

Basking in French friendliness, they idled among other pleasant stores whose wares they admired--a bakery that housed good
bread; an epicerie where they knew an irascible woman going
bald who, of an evening, did not sympathize with their ignorant
inquiries about the local cheeses stored in the same refrigerator
as the milk; a restaurant closed at this hour; and a fishmonger's
on whose marble slab they saw Mediterranean fish of legend and
epic, and the rascasse and loup that received special mention in
the guidebooks.

They enjoyed the sunshine and pedestrian scale of their route.
They did not think that they were come into the middle way, in a
dark wood, in a bramble, on the edge of a grimpen, where there
is no secure foothold. Nevertheless, they were drawing towards
it, coming to the maturity that in their youth had been adver-
tised as the prime of life, but reaching it too late. The fashion
had changed, and in spite of Ringo Starr they had lost at both
ends. ("When I was nineteen, I thought thirty would be the end
of the world...but it's nothing. It's okay.") There was no going
back to youth now from their thirty-two years and six weeks,
thirty years and eight months, husband and wife in the relation
approved by the mores of their past, soon to be called into question, like everything else, by the changed relations between the
sexes, between the generations, between imperium and colony,
artist and buyer, parent and child, everywhere the powerful and
the wretched of the earth reversing roles in a transvaluation of
values, a peripeteia and anagnorisis, a fanshen that put the first
last and the last first. (Fanshen, literally, means "to turn the
body," or "to turn over." "To China's hundreds of millions of
landless and land-poor peasants it meant to stand up, to throw
off the landlord yoke, to gain land, stock, implements and
houses. But it meant much more than this. It meant to throw
off superstition and study science, to abolish 'word blindness'
and learn to read, to cease considering women as chattel and
establish equality between the sexes, to do away with appointed

village magistrates and replace them with elected councils. It
meant to enter a new world." William Hinton, <u>Fanshen.</u>)

Though they knew it couldn't last. They would go back to
Cambridge Mass 01238 after their vacation in France, and even
now their shopping expedition must come to an end. They were
expected at Uncle Chaim's. Not being like Dante in this pass of
middle age offered an alternative route, they made their way to
the bus stop with only one more digression, to a small liquor
store where they bought their gift of Gran Marnier. For how
were they to know the pessimistic interpretation Chaim would put
on a gift that, though no ark, suggested by its inexpensive and
ephemeral nature that they would not buy anything that might
outlast his stay on earth? Although they were over thirty, they
were too young to guess how this late birthday must be fraught
with warnings of mortality, as is always the case with birthdays
after a certain age.

Of course they did not guess that not Chaim alone but the whole
world was drawing to its end. They were on vacation, and not
reading the newspapers. Even if they had heard the news they
might not have thought anything imminent. The four horsemen
had been galloping about so long that the sound of their hooves
seemed as natural as cars, nothing particular this last sunny day
before the day the world came to an end, when there was hardly
a cloud in the sky.

Lionel Abrahams

THE MOMENT

Felix was twenty-seven, and nothing had happened yet. Ten years before he had imagined he could stop waiting, and had asked Marjory Cane, who was fifteen, as one would ask for the loan of a cup of sugar, to lie with him. Adolescents ask questions and receive answers of each other by their lips and finger tips. He had taken none of this instruction and his naked words were ruder than any touch. Her repulse left him with too much shame and fear for him to feel the thwarting of his desire.

It was the first of many fiascos. Their eruptions each threw a crust of shame over his desires. Later these had settled down into the strata of his feelings, eventually to compound a suspicion that the woman's love which alone would let him begin to be himself would never come to him, that sex, after all that was said, written, felt about it, did not really exist but was a fiction, a hoax — the suspicion, even, that he himself did not exist. These doubts and the tension of his unrequited hunger were growing to a point of obsession and unbearableness.

In the fifth year after he had abandoned university in mid-course he decided to return and take his degree. The university setting — with so many lovely bodies in the still-fresh bloom of their responsiveness to each other — brought his frustration to an edge. Each brightly sensuous day that passed seemed overlaid on a flatter and emptier darkness. He was twenty-seven and nothing had happened to him. If another year passed in this way, he felt, he would slide into some kind of madness or even die.

He knew Evelyn Heiner slightly from a series of cultural meetings he and Becky had been attending the year before. She was dumpy-bodied and wore her hair in an Eton crop and had not attracted his desiring eye. Now, after having worked for some years, she had become a student — like him, older than most of the others. During his canteen hours he often found himself in her vicinity because they had a number of friends in common. She was a comfortable person, banteringly voluble, sometimes even uproarious.

He was surprised when, with the year well advanced, she sought him out alone one day and asked if she might visit him at home to get his help with one of her assignments. The visit turned out to be brief — a friend with a car brought and fetched her — and its given reason proved to be a pretext. They spent a few minutes discussing the topic of her essay, and then she produced a piece of verse in which she declared her love for him.

Whatever her offer might mean, the moment dizzied him because it promised a possible end to the waiting that was so exhausting him, and he responded immediately by begging for the permanent rescue: 'Will you marry me?'

The request froze her with embarrassment, almost produced one more fiasco. But she had years and ease behind her and laughter to mask the flaw of the situation. She said, 'That's a bit sudden. Let's not talk about marriage. Yet, anyway . . .' She reddened and her voice went low as she spoke the incredible words, 'I want us to make love . . .'

There was time then for an exchange of urgent kisses to seal a promise, then she left him gyrating in a new universe.

The examination season had begun and they were chained to their books, so in the following weeks she managed only one more brief visit. At first his anticipation filled him with a pleasant tingling relish. It both excited and relaxed him. But as days and weeks mounted so did his tension. His body, hot and swollen with appetite, his knowledge that now his lust did not lock him into aloneness and shame but was to be shared, increasingly distracted him. Yet his desire was not steady and simple. At different times when he looked at Evelyn, the woman who was promised to him, his desires flared or wavered. One rain-threatened day she appeared at university enveloped in a rumpled dun raincoat and in a raucous mood

that had her gracelessly prancing and bellowing as she walked
with some friends. He watched her: his girl, bound to him by a
poem, a promise and his own desperation. He could feel
nothing but reluctance and dismay.

But the desperation was there — reasserting and sharpening
itself in this suspended time. He found himself demanding of
her on the telephone, 'When?' — and the day for the event she
wanted but seemed to have grown afraid of was fixed.

It was the morning of the last day of November. Behind the
closed door of his bedroom, where, he could assure Evelyn, his
mother (whatever she might be thinking about the nature of the
visit) would not interrupt them, the thing, the thing itself, the
actual ultimate event, unromantically but incredibly, even
gloriously, took place. While they stripped, before she had
removed her dress, she crouched down to the floor and
embarrassedly asked him not to watch as she made some
necessary intimate preparation. But then she was naked to him.
The sight and touchability of her naked body, drugged him.
Half outside of his own believable reality he exchanged
voracious kisses and caresses with her. His urgency seemed
partly to amuse her. Other details also contrived against
romance in the final conjunction. He should lie flat, she
decided, and she would mount him, to make things easier for
him. And during the entry she gasped and moaned with pain,
blaming a long spell of celibacy for the inelastic, shrunken
condition of her flesh.

But as she came over him and he felt his deepening
containment in her body, waves of feeling flushed from his
centre to the extremities of his limbs, the top of his head. It was
a feeling that was the palpable meaning of romance. The scent
of roses, the pleasure he took in the keenest lyrical poetry, came
to his mind. He laughed, his whole body, mirthlessly but
joyfully, uncontrollably, laughed when his orgasm came. He
tried to suppress the convulsions, the silly giggling, snorting,
hooting that came from the nets and knots of his nerves and not
from his will. But his embarrassment was small against the
knowledge that he was saved. Evelyn Heiner had saved him.

During the remaining days of the university term, and
through the vacation, she came to give herself to him once or

twice a week. Watching her leave him after they had made love, as she crossed to the tram stop, he marvelled that within so short a time of being with him in nakedness and passion she would be sitting indistinguishable among other passengers in the commonplaceness of a tram.

For a long time he remained drunk as much on the thought of at last being a lover as on the passional release. To his parents so much of what he felt and did went untold, but he did let them know — sure they would be happy with him — what Evelyn was to him. The first evening that she stayed for dinner was a Saturday when they, by custom, went to the local cinema. They asked Evelyn and Felix to come as well, but the invitation was awkwardly refused, and the house was left to them. They were quite alone in it for the first time, and were for the first time making total love at night (as distinguished from the feverish exchanges of hampered caresses in dim corners at parties or in motor cars). There was a good freshness, a near beauty, to the full nakedness of her body as she moved through lit and darkened rooms using the freedom of the house to accommodate their love-making.

He was to be again with her by night several times, and for whole nights, moreover. But the snatched two hours of that Saturday evening, at the end of which his father drove her to her boarding house, had an irrecoverable quality of sensual sweetness.

It was her dissatisfaction with her boarding house that led to the beginning of a strain. They had been together several times at an old house in Hillbrow where a friend of his was living in rented rooms. This friend, Joel, had made it clear to Felix that he found Evelyn uncongenial. So when she asked him to recruit Joel's help in getting her a room in the same house, he could not hide his reluctance, and her good nature seemed to evaporate as she sourly reproached, lashed and pressed him. He ended up unhappily yielding a promise to try.

Despite Joel's feelings he complied with the request, and recommended Evelyn to the landlady as one more lodger, and shortly afterwards she did move into the house. It was in that bohemian setting that she became accessible to Felix for night-long visits.

But it was after the first of these visits that Felix was shaken by a surprise flank attack in his emotions. He could not see where to lay the blame: on the fact that now the last detail in the form of romantic possession had been complied with (he had shared the night with his love, had slept with her); or on the possibility that Evelyn had displayed some reserve in her responsivness, some new lack of passion in the new situation (she had slept in a long flannel night-dress; had been reluctant to renew lovemaking when they awoke in the morning). But the cause hardly seemed to matter in the face of the feeling itself. The shock was that he was capable of such an emotion. Capable? Incapable was a more appropriate word, for the emotion was emotionlessness. A pervasive feeling of flatness, as though all the solidity, the colour, the juice, had been sucked out of the world. Now that, at last, he had had the whole of his desire, now that fulfilment was at his call, desire had snuffed itself out in him.

Why had no one told him of this possibility? Why had he never read about this experience? It must be because this numbing was some sickness of his own. Everything at last being granted, he, like a spoiled, bored baby, no longer wanted it. But this was no toy. This was sex, love, the fruition of his manhood. This cold repulsive ash was life. He had expected that the experience of intercourse would transform him by freeing him from the rigidities of his stale virgin state and from the obsessiveness of his desire: the locks would fall off his manhood and he would become easy and winning with women, and patience would let his energies and imagination out of the strict channel of sexual straining to flow over and open the neglected fields of his creativeness. But his knowledge of the long-guarded core-secret had freed him into a sick slackness and unsluiced his imagination into sand. After all, after all, for him at least — being perhaps in his secret heart afraid of what he had always thought he longed for — there was nothing to want, and nothing to say.

Inhabiting some other world, Joel had blazoned among the grafitti on the walls of the kitchen in that house: 'Cunt is king!' To Felix through all the years it had been the kingdom of heaven, but now that he was admitted he found a desert of new shame — he was a hypocrite, a hollow dreamer, some curious kind of coward — and all-embracing dismay. He stood in a Hillbrow street in the morning sunlight waiting for a bus to take him to town on the first stage home. It was not tremendously long since bus riding and access to the city had been beyond his independent power. He could remember being unable to walk . . . All these things had been reached by him, their mysteries opened to him. Now, staring at the peopled street, he almost resented whatever had been granted to him, whatever he knew: the conclusion they forced on him was, 'So, this is all!'

This new sense of himself persisted but its strength was intermittent. It was not strong enough to immunise him against a jolt of jealousy when he accidentally learned that on a camping jaunt with other students, Evelyn had been escorted by an older man, not a student.

'Evelyn and Samuel Merkle!' he involuntarily interrupted the girl who was describing the expedition. 'But Evelyn's supposed to be *my* girl . . .' The three friends present seemed embarrassed, and so did he immediately feel, at this indiscreet protest. But he had reacted with a pang, without control.

All the same, when Evelyn confirmed to him that she had become deeply involved with Samuel Merkle, that she was lost to Felix in circumstance as well as in the inadmissable cabinet of his own feelings, the bruise to his pride was salved by his relief at the ending of their affair.

Still, this was too dull and petty a freedom to be relished, and he felt some self-reproach at even thinking of it as a freedom. In any case, the overwhelming relic of all that had happened was his flat desirelessness. Even the knowledge that it was the turning-off of Evelyn's passion that had desiccated their love-making did not free him from the feeling that the great bluff of his ordinary male aliveness had been called. As the knowing bluffer he might have been cleansed and increased by this hard thrust into truthfulness. But he was the one who had been bluffed — into believing that in himself and in the world he was planted in, there was so much, potential, substantial and sweet, whereas all there was was as tasteless and thin as paper — and he could acknowledge only impoverishment.

And so, on a day not long after the new university year had begun, Felix came to the strangest of moments. A girl walked past him, her lithe legs cupped by the inverted spreading corolla of her skirt. When she had gone, he found his breathing perturbed by what she heralded. A hopeless pang told him that he was re-entering desire, the prison in which he had lain, and certainly would again, an incorrigible fool of a detainee, at the mercy of unreachable girl after girl. The knowledge was painful, but he could only welcome it with joy.

Lionel Abrahams

INVISIBLE WORM

'I want to give you joy.'

The bones of her face were almost naked. Yet the transparency gave not onto the skeleton but onto spirit, making a paradox of her presence among ordinary people, in ordinary lounges and motorcars, in Johannesburg. Once she had presented herself to Felix, the rest of whatever had been reality was displaced. She was the familiar, unrecognised reality under everything, making all the meaning of his life draw to one sharp focus and filling him with a religion as much as with love.

Dr Peter Williams had spoken to him about Lucilla Maxwell, a 'tormented' girl whom he and his wife were trying to help, and had shown Felix a drawing from her hand, a portrait of finespun pencil lines that breathed onto the paper more than a face, a life. It was not art of the 1960s, but by its supercession of fashion as much as by its poignance, it affirmed art itself.

The first time Felix met her at the Williamses' house, she spoke little, but with an intensity that involved her body in a considering agitation, as though she hunted through her being for the phrases precise and vibrant enough for her meaning, which she brought out with a prayerful pressing together of her hands. She seemed begging indulgence, apologising for the strength of her feelings, the intelligence of her discriminations.

Felix was talkative, being encouraged by Peter to repeat for the other guests his anecdotes of several recent adventures. But hardly a direct word passed between himself and Lucilla Maxwell. This was the party season and within days he saw Peter again. Lucilla had mentioned to him that Felix had been in her thoughts since that evening. Flippant to mask his surprise and pleasure, Felix responded, 'Well, I haven't exactly forgotten her, either . . .'

At Peter's New Year party, as before, the room threw up some strange barrier between them for though they communicated much with their eyes, they were hardly allowed the opportunity for the exchange of a few words, and none tête-a-tête, during all the hours of the party. Either of them seemed at every moment to be detained in talk with someone else. She had come with two young men from her university who were up in Johannesburg for the vacation. For almost an hour, as the party tapered toward its end with a lingering handful of guests, one of these escorts held the floor with a strange, sophisticated yet confused harangue against Robert Graves's deification of the female. Felix, concerning himself with logic, was one of those who occasionally offered a counter-argument, qualification or question. Meanwhile Lucilla sat at the opposite side of the room, silent, but intently listening.

At last the party broke up. Peter had promised to drive Felix home, but now Lucilla urged him to accept a lift with her instead. She had a two-door car, and one of her escorts was driving. Felix was given the seat beside the driver. He chattered and gave directions as they wove through the suburbs. He was being anecdotal again, resigned to tempering the otherwise blocked night by this minimal communication with the girl.

She was seated behind the driver, and it was as though she breached a wall when, with no more prelude than a cry — 'Oh, Felix!' —, she thrust herself between the heads of her two friends, threw her arms around Felix's neck and, suddenly in the wrench of sobs, laid her head on his shoulder. He was struck into a silence, out of which he could only fetch, once or twice, her name, as he stroked her head. Was it simply sorrow that had so unexpectedly overwhelmed her? He felt that it was something else. The evening had destined a communion betwen them, and now, in the last minutes, but still the first hours of the new year, it was coming to fruit.

The two young men seemed spellbound and oblivious of what was happening. Felix gave his last few directions in a chastened voice. When they reached his house, the girl sprang from the car and stood while he moved toward his gate. He turned and said to her, 'We must see each other.'

She pressed her hands urgently together and brought them

twice up toward her face and down in emphasis, as she responded: 'Soon! Soon!'

Having got her telephone number from Peter, he spoke to her next day. And soon she was with him — at his house, at hers, at the nearby resort lake, at the bird sanctuary. She told him how long she had known of him and wished to meet him; she wanted to draw his portrait, to read his writings, to show him things she had written, to know and be known to him. There had been turmoil in her life and unsuccessful loves. She had been engaged last year to the scholar who had been discussing his thesis on Graves, but things had gone wrong. She had been briefly, extraordinarily involved with another of Peter Williams' friends, but had felt stifled and distorted by the formal religious demands he had made of her. She leaned on Peter and his wife, who were solicitous, generous, understanding. But (something other than words said it) it was for him, for Felix, that she had been looking, waiting.

The religion of her was hardly emergent in him yet when he spoke about her once more with Peter, who seemed to be committing her to his care. There was something he felt Felix might be able to do for her. Felix argued his own possible unworthiness. His blocked sexuality had driven him to childishly lurid manoeuvres in the past: he had forced a twisted intimacy out of situations in which girls had turned to him for some kind of support, respite, illumination. Whatever wholesome intentions he might start with, his urgencies might overwhelm him and he might put Lucilla into a difficult, if not hurtful situation. But it seemed that by his ingenuousness he transformed his warning, in Peter's eyes, into a reassurance.

Yet his frankness was pressed from him by an exhausting weight of history. At thirty-seven, all the strung-out years of silly, obstinate desire, and the few punctuating episodes of gratification that soon went sour or were cut short, had, he thought, worked a boyish romancefulness out of him, set him to oscillate between cynicism about his chances and a hard-boiled greed. He was neither optimistic nor clean. An enduring hopefulness had fallen away lately, as his cleanliness had done long ago. So he was small and dry, gravelly against himself and his circumstances when Peter brought Lucilla to him, but it was

243

as if her coming was the very medicine his condition needed.

The third time they were together at his house, she put into words her gift of herself to him: 'I want to give you joy.' If he wished he might take her in bodily love now; she would give him this if he required it. But there would be an imperfection. They had a need to grow a little more in their closeness. She was disposed to his desires, but if he could wait . . .

She wanted to give him joy. The words almost were enough. It was a joy to be making with her toward the ripeness of a belonging together that would be perfect — joyful and spiritual at once. Yes, he would wait. Not, certainly, because Lucilla apart from the wonder of her face, was almost bodiless, emaciated to an emanation of feminine grace draping stark bones. He acquiesced in the postponement because it was in favour of perfection. That was what their embrace would manifest. His sense was, for both of them, of finality and arrival. After long wanderings, confusions, torments (she had slash-scars on her wrists), they had arrived in each other. In him, he felt, in his recognition, she could rest in consummate peace.

They were in a state in which the word 'forever' had no need to be spoken. 'We'll have a little house,' she murmured one day as they lay together, each stroking the other's face, 'where you'll write and I'll paint . . .' And her words absorbed the whole of future time. And then, after ten days so, it came out that there were circumstantial priorities. She had to return almost immediately to her university and attend to certain matters before she could begin the last year of her course in painting. In not having prepared him for this disruption she was, in a manner, diminishing its importance: it concerned no more than time and space. Moreover, she imbued her departure from him now with an aspect of peril for herself — in leaving him she was going from a protective nest naked into a storm of forces that oppressed, abraded and cut at her. He, whom she had found during this vacation, was all in all — but there were matters which must be completed before she was free simply to be with him. She was driving down with one of her two escorts of New Year's night. The other, her ex-fiancé, had left earlier.

The intensity of happiness in the ten days he had had with her lifted Felix beyond commonplace judgements of commonplace facts. More than her electing and centering upon him, more than the womanly promise she embodied, more than her beauty (though each of these was an expression of the central thing), it was the style of her thinking that spiritualized all values for him.

Yet it was only after she had left that the religion of Lucilla asserted its full force on his faith. In his letters to her he penned its gospel. Hers to him were rarer, but they were many paged missives, accumulated piece by piece over weeks, writings in pencil, ink and typescript that made him party to intimate flares of emotion and perception. They were gifts of herself by which he was ever more bound to her, and the gift-like aspect was emphasised in her always sending the thick-packed envelopes by Express so that they arrived at unpredictable times, even, once, on a Sunday morning. They were the prophesies and revelations of the religion — always marvellous in their poetry and in their proof of her continuing bond with him. More than once she telephoned him across the hundreds of miles, to disburden herself of some unease and hear the comfort of his voice. The comfort of his voice!

When she had been explaining why she must go, she had suggested that he might come to visit her. Her letters intimated that she bent desperately under barely definable burdens and demands. Now the opportunity of a lift to her town and back after three days presented itself. He telephoned her, explained the circumstances, asked, 'Do you want me to come?'

'Ah, Felix, do you want to come?'

'Of course! You know I do. But what I want to be sure of is, is it right for you? Now?'

'If it's right for *you*, then it's right . . . and you must come.'

'Well, then I'm coming . . . where can I stay?'

'Shall I book a room for you in an hotel? . . . It'll be wonderful to see you.'

He loaded himself with gifts: marrons glacês, a favourite volume of prints from his bookshelf . . . And he prepared his heart for more than a renewal of the magic of those ten days at the start of the year: he was coming to her now as her lover.

In the event he was and was not. He entered the quite foreign country of her student life. A welcoming note from her was waiting at his hotel, and soon after his arrival she was there, running to him in the lobby, naked-footed and in flowing white, and giving him a kiss which sanctified his coming.

She had a flat in the house of Mrs Young, one of her lecturers, which she shared with a classmate nicknamed Dozer who was the subject of the first portrait Felix had seen from her hand. Dozer was big-boned, strong, earthy and full of slangy playfulness. When it came to words that moved toward abstractness, she was slow, absorbent, passive. Felix saw quickly that the two girls complemented (but Lucilla was complete!) and needed each other. And they were hardly separable. This was one thing that disappointed him. Dozer was easy to be with, responsive to all that was anecdotal and playful in him, while an occasional remark, gesture or anecdote of her own, not to speak of Lucilla's tender respect for her, intimated a richness of resource below her unpretentious surfaces. But for so many hours of his little time her presence was between him and his angel.

All the same, it was clear that she knew of the intensity between them — perhaps she knew more about the intricacies of Lucilla's feelings than he did himself, and she was, in all things it seemed, subservient to Lucilla's wishes. And so there were intervals when Felix was alone with Lucilla. But neither then did simplicity come. Late on his second evening, when their happy leisurely supper was over, Dozer went out. Lucilla let Felix draw her into her room where they lay on her bed feeding intimacy with murmurs and caresses. He became, as every reason, hope and circumstance had been leading him to become, urgent for her body. But she held his hand and gazed with sorrow, though still tenderly, into his face as she said, 'No. No. Please, Felix, forgive me. I can't now. It wouldn't be right for me now.'

'Why not?'

'Please understand, dearest Felix — please don't be angry. It's because of George . . .' George Wright was the young music lecturer who had accompanied her back on her drive from Johannesburg. 'George loves me so much. He has wept because I won't go to bed with him. And I'm sore at having hurt him so. I'd be thinking about him. I wouldn't be happily with you. I would feel wrong.'

Felix was silent. His clearest thought was, I shouldn't have let you go away — I should have taken you when you offered me joy. He could put up no fight, make no assault on her decision, not even question the cogency of her reason for it, not only because the reason expressed her character, but because this refusal, cutting through the nerve of his expectancy, caught up an old pattern of his experience and paralysed him. To have the old rejection of his bodily reality re-enacted by her, was to suffer a small death, a wrenching apart of matter and spirit.

He somehow contained it. The thought that she was in crisis over George Wright, and that the sexual proscription was bound to this phase, helped him. And moreover, the physical expression was a marginal part of the apocalypse she represented to him. He was willing to suffer for its sake. He had to recognise in her, despite all mere events and obstacles, some profounder completing of himself. He felt it, and she spoke of a matching recognition of inner completeness for herself in him. They had more to live for together than sex.

So he contained the shock. But as one contains an internal haemhorrage. During hours when they were with Dozer and other people, while he was sitting to Lucilla for his portrait in the big communal studio at the university, when he was alone in his hotel room, he was assailed by questions: Why was he here? What had he come for?

In the end it was the portrait that justified his visit. One of Lucilla's torments during the preceding weeks had been a creative block — and painting was a lifeline to being and meaning for her.She committed each stroke with the contortions of torment and her composition seemed a structure built out of flames. It was no wonder that she would involuntarily, against desire and faith, hold back for weeks or months at a time from the immolation her art involved her in. Watching her at work — besmeared with solvents and pigments, entangled with recalcitrant paraphernalia, oscillating between the easel and the distant viewing points from which she turned her eyes like blowtorches on the strokes she had so far dealt to the canvas — he felt he was witnessing more than a process, an agony of incarnation which, by paradox, freed the spirit through the very act of its imprisonment in material limits.

After his second day of posing, when the existence of the portrait was assured, they were visited after supper in the flat by Mrs Young, whom Felix had already met more than once. The progress at the studio was unknown to her, since this was the week-end and Lucilla and Dozer had been exercising their privilege, as senior students, of access at any time. Lucilla was sitting beside Felix when Dozer asked playfully, 'Should we tell your secret?'

Lucillia responded with a shy nod, but before Dozer could speak Mrs Young scanned their expressions and said, 'I can guess. You're going to be married . . .'

Amid embarrassed laughter, Dozer said, 'Oh, no! She's got painting again . . . A portrait of Felix.'

The appropriate congratulations were given, and afterwards the faux pas was not referred to, but for Felix the air rang with its reverberations. It demonstrated how outwardly visible was Lucilla's bond with him, and it expressed also the social acceptability of a consummation that might have belonged only to the realm of his fantasies.

Another incident hit even more strongly at his doubts about Lucilla's happiness or peace in his presence. On the last evening of his stay, Dozer, who had made her affection for him very plain, said to him in Lucilla's presence, 'Why don't you come and live with us?' Lucilla was silent, but unprotesting, unsurprised. He felt that she and Dozer must have discussed the suggestion before. All the same, perhaps because indeed Lucilla herself had not given the invitation, he could only treat it as a kind of joke, to be countered, at least provisionally, with arguments of its impracticability and his commitment to tasks at home.

But there it was, a gesture made, a value acknowledged, a possibility opened. It salved the sore of his disappointment, so that not many days later he was telling Moh and Dad that he might marry Lucilla. And something in his air made them receive the news with solemn pleasure and no protest about her being gentile or question about the problem of his earning a living. Within two months he visited Lucilla again, making the

journey by train. This time there were no shocks, no climaxes
of disappointment, but neither were there, until almost the last
minutes before his departure, episodes to relieve his pain at her
remoteness, his bewilderment over the question why she had
permitted him to come: her manner, whenever intimacy might
have been possible, expressed tolerance for his presence, a
desire to be good and gentle toward him, but an unreadiness,
an incapacity to make their deep bond manifest.

She was painting a large self-portrait, in which the whiteness
of her skin was described by the interwrithing of strokes of a
range of different colours. From some viewpoints it took on the
aspect of a thing most cruelly flayed. From other, when all
blended into the fragile oval of the head, it was the face of a
child who had walked through Hell. She gave him, had drawn
for him a pencilled self-portrait that was an unequivocal expression of grief. Why did he not read it as a message to
himself? Because she was tender enough to give him the
drawing. Because she was his religion. 'Let me be your monk,'
he begged her. Her grief was parcel of her holiness, her martyr's
passion. If she would accept him he would have no need of
manhood. But this plea of his only disturbed her.

She had painted a mysterious crucifixion. He studied it for
hours as he sat in the studio in which she and Dozer worked
and a tide of fellowstudents and friends flowed around them.
Toward the end of his stay he wrote down some lines, a
dialogue that symbolised his interpretation of the painting.

Hesitantly, he showed it to Dozer, who insisted that Lucilla
see it. When she had read it she was breathless with gratitude.
'Thank you, thank you! You've shown me the truth of my
painting. This was what I was trying to express without really
knowing in my head. Please, oh please, may I show it with the
painting when I exhibit?'

'It would be an honour,' he said. 'But are you sure you want
to do that?'

'Yes, yes! I must do that.'

A few hours later, as they were driving through the rainy
evening to the station for his train back to Johannesburg, she
began to glow with the full celebratory responsiveness toward
him that had been missing. Her pressed hands dipping to him,

she said, 'It's a little miracle the way your poem has helped me to understand what I was trying to do in the crucifixion.'

'Well, it's hardly a poem . . .'

'Yes, yes! It's a beautiful poem — and it also speaks about us.'

'About us? Oh! I didn't think of it that way.'

'But it does, it does! The truth came out. It's a confirmation, about you and me.'

As last time her portrait of him had been the revealed purpose of his visit, so this time it was his poem.

The mid-year vacation brought Lucilla to Johannesburg, with George Wright, who stayed with her at her parents' home. Her complex relation with him and with her parents, her inability to maintain her painting even though she had a room to use as a studio, each laid its own stress on her feelings. There were Peter Williams and his wife, and there were other friends, old worshippers, would-be suitors. Yet in the absence of Dozer, who was spending the holiday month with her parents on their farm, she was strangely alone and naked in the world. And she turned to Felix, relying on his full acceptance, for some sort of shelter. The month was broken into, broken up, by socialities and chores, by her illnesses, and the daily hours of her efforts to paint. Yet they were frequently, for hours on end, simply alone with each other, when she manifested a need of him, just him, and in this she re-created him as only gods create. This was what had to be, what, for some arcane reason, was being postponed, but only postponed. This year of separation had to be done with: it was involved with art, which was part of the same spiritual fruition that included their love. But he was waiting for her final return to him. It was essential and inevitable.

Peter was a sensitive amateur photographer, and one afternoon came to Felix's house with Lucilla and used a spool or two of film in an attempt to fix for the eye something of her quality and of the way in which she and Felix conjoined. Felix was passive in the operation: the world of cameras and Lucilla's world were different in his mind, and he responded protectively to her faint uneasiness over the whole exercise, though he knew she had many photographs of herself. Yet they bowed to

Peter's artist's authority when, dissatisfied with the long-sleeved blouse she was wearing, he had Lucilla strip to her brassiere and put on a sleeveless pullover of Felix's instead. And they bowed further. After a few studies of Lucilla alone, Peter had Felix sit with her and began photographing them as lovers, and Lucilla permitted this commitment to what would be a sort of public record — for what Peter was reaching toward in the course of his score or more of shots was not a note for the personal memory but an artist's crystallization of their relationship.

This became clearer after the contacts came and Felix was invited to choose the pictures he wanted for enlargement. (Lucilla had by now returned to university.) Peter added his own preferences as well, and after the prints were delivered it was with pride of achievement that he showed them to many friends. They were an achievement. Lucilla with the slender nakedness of her arms, the flying ends of her pony-tailed hair about the egg-fragile head, the subtlety of her expression, was an archetype of love, flight and the need for protection. Felix's image expressed his need and fulfilment, his weakness and strength, above all his bliss. A notion about privacy fluttered in his conscience as he let mere acquaintances see the pictures, but he received their comments and compliments with gratification. He framed and hung one of the studies of Lucilla — in which her eyes and mouth spoke as they had cherishingly spoken to him during their best moments together — and stowed the others as treasure. With her letters, when they came, they sustained him through his rite of passage to the year's end.

The July vacation had also given him a deepened impression of Dozer. Lucilla had read him a letter she'd received from her. Its eloquence startled Felix. It was, in fact, a love letter, and an inspired passion of adoration and commitment was the only way to explain such an outpouring from one to whom words always seemed a recalcitrant element.

But if Dozer was partly Lucilla's involuntary creation, Lucilla's being was seen to lie in Dozer's debt after a crisis that threatened it a few weeks later. A turmoil of apprehension in Lucilla had gathered into a maelstrom that dragged her from the studio, the flat, Dozer's presence, spun her, in her little car, out along the open road toward nothing, in a renewed pursuit of death. Dozer had found another car, chased and overtaken her, and won her back from suicide by the only power she had, her caring, which seemed the only power of all that could have saved her.

They learnt later that Lucilla's crisis coincided with the moment of the Prime Minister's assassination. The source of the desperation, her premonition of the social wound that would be felt as such even by many of the politician's enemies because the scene of his murder was parliament, lifted Lucilla's suicidal relapse above simple personal significance. It was not that, in this year when she had found Felix, her bond with him had proved futile against the force that repeatedly before had threatened her life. She had been swept up by an eruption of her prophetic sensibility. He grieved that she had courted death again in 'his' year. He blessed the protective love of Dozer that had saved her. But he absorbed the incident into the canons of proof of her spirituality.

Nearly three decades past his childhood flirtation with Christianity, Felix, to whom till now Christian affirmations like 'Murder in the Cathedral' and 'The Wreck of "The Deutschland"' had been bewildering and repellent, found that his love had led him into strange territory. He could understand suddenly how intensity opened the soul to overarching truth that dwarfed humanistic hopes, health, happiness — how even life was only a phase in the divine progress. He read Kierkegaard, he read 'The Varieties of Religious Experience'. He did obeisance to the idea of suffering, not only because Lucilla did the same, but because she, the artist, the child within the archetypal woman, like Jesus whom she painted and pondered on, suffered and by suffering was characterised and shaped — as though by its means alone she could have come into earthly being and could sustain her destiny.

When in one of his letters he asked her (the question remained unanswered), 'Am I to think of you in connection with my bodily love?' it did not mean that his earlier plea, 'Let me be your monk,' had been hollow: by her wish and acceptance, her continuing reassurance that thus she needed him, he would have been empowered to fill this role. But he

needed to know what forms of expression he must prepare for
their love when they came together at this year's end. His
energy lay dormant for the direction of his imagination. Lucilla
was his saint (in another letter he wrote, 'I'm afraid I've become
a spiritual snob. I look at the women I know, at women in
buses, on the streets, everywhere, and in no face do I see
anything that approaches your soul-beauty'). But he needed to
know how they were to be together, what he must make of
himself for her.

As the months passed without the definitive signal, the
passion he was holding in abeyance for her, at rare intervals
flickered and flared in the sexual form. Then, in the desiccating
climate of his ignorance his urges began to split him apart.
Pending the permission to spring toward her, or the command
to sublimate, his sexuality began to rear and roar, baffled and
directionless. Keeping himself for her, he allowed an imper-
sonal autonomy to a lustful self inside himself, and in its
assertive hours it raved for intimacies. Let only one of the
women on buses, whose skirt-secrets he filched with his eyes,
know and signal that she knew what he was doing and collude
with him, and that would have been substantial. But as things
were, this self that wanted secrets starved in its own secrecy.
And its noise became the silence of half-forgotten guilt when he
wrote to Lucilla, or read her letters.

He had other letters to write and read besides hers. There
were old friendships that had flowered or been kept alive in
letters. And there was the endlessly trickling correspondence of
his literary business. He prided himself on the explicitness and
helpfulness of what he wrote to aspirant writers. It was one of
these who suddenly held out to him the possibility of another
satisfaction. Among the pieces sent for his comments by a
young woman in Kimberley was a story containing a des-
cription of female masturbation. It was written with no sign of
the nonchalance that was characteristic of the new liberations,
and nor did Felix read the sentences with nonchalance. He was
fevered by the sense of a wild possibility. 'Dear Mrs Steen,' he
wrote to the author, 'You may be surprised by the tone of this
letter. I have been in a state of excitement since reading your
last lot of work. The three poems are much more controlled

and substantial than any you have shown me before . . . But it is
the story that has particularly stirred me up, and perhaps not
for strictly literary reasons... Your frankness suggests a
person with whom extraordinary things are possible... will
you let me write to you with a total openness?'

Veronica Steen's reply expressed'... a burning curiosity
about the *extraordinary* possibilities you speak of ... I'd like
very much to have a really close communication with you.'

Encouraged but still hesitant, he wrote warning her. 'You
may be shocked and repelled by what I have in mind ...'

'Nothing can shock me ...' she replied.

He still hesitated. Veronica Steen was marginal to his life.
She held out fires of unreality for him to play with. His real self
wanted Lucilla, and the year whose end would bring her to him
was rounding out. She would come in late November. It was a
question of weeks.

Early in November a telephone call from Peter Williams,
who had been told by Lucilla's father, brought the news that
she had collapsed with a burst appendix and was critically ill.
Felix telephoned Dozer. Lucilla had ignored her pains during
the time of winding up toward the exams. She'd nearly died
during the emergency operation and was terribly weak now,
but the doctors thought she would be all right. No, there was no
point in his coming down — no-one except her mother and
Dozer was allowed to see her ...

A week later a post card from Dozer assured him that Lucilla
had pulled through. She was very frail but they thought she
would be able to take her exams, sitting in a wheel-chair. They
didn't know when she would be well enough to come up to
Joeys — probably a few weeks later than had been planned.
Dozer would be coming up too, early in the new year.

Felix telephoned again to find out if he should come. For the
time being, Dozer explained, they could think about nothing
except getting Lucilla strong enough for the exams. They
would let him know when it was right for him to come.

The year was whirling apart in a confusion of passions. Felix
telegraphed flowers to Lucilla in hospital, wrote her a letter full
of thanksgiving for her survival, grieved for her and waited for
her. At the same time he hovered for weeks over Veronica

Steen's latitude. At last he put it to her beyond the reach of any ambiguity: 'What I'm angling for is an exchange of sexual intimacies — and I don't want to pretend it will be innocent or natural. If you can't reciprocate at least say you'll bear with my outpourings.'

In the second week of December Lucilla came. She had been home for four days before telephoning him. She wasn't driving. She agreed to take a bus and meet him at a city tea room. In her enhanced fragility, her new paleness, she was like a thing unborn but exposed. Something agitated and remote in her manner, once she had kissed him in greeting, made his reaching toward her tense and tentative. She had been very near to death.

'Do you still have pain? Are you over it all now?' he asked.

'I'm tired.'

'Yes, I understand that. You shouldn't have come out today. You should have let me come to your house, told me which bus stop to get off at . . .'

She shook her head with a firmness born of desperation. 'I'm tired of relationships.'

When he had taken it in he protested: 'But we haven't found our relationship yet!'

She nodded and nodded. 'But I'm tired, so tired . . .' She would say nothing better that day.

This wasn't the end of things. As, since their first ten days, he had felt that she had been in his life from its beginning, so, now that she was pronouncing this negation, she was not closing him out of her life, nor herself out of his. She was freeing herself from a particular net of his expectations (she knew how deep but not how undefined his expectations were), and once this had been thrust off, she was free to stay within his reach.

A few days later on the telephone he said to her, 'The thing is, there *is* something that binds us together. You are like . . . you are my sister.'

'Oh, yes, yes!' Her agreement was urgent. 'But it's something even closer than that . . .'

For a moment he absorbed the words in silence. 'Oh, God! Lucilla . . .' he said at last, 'when can I come and be with you?'

'Soon, Felix. Dozer's coming up next week, and soon's I can

I'll have the Williamses over to dinner so that they can meet her, and I want you to come too.'

He left it. He settled for her acknowledgement of that 'Something even closer'. In fact he had no cause to struggle for: nothing he might do could make Lucilla to him what she was not — and nor could any accident undo what she was and remained to him after all. Only his own actions and time . . .

On the second of January he wrote to Veronica Steen, 'Thank you for accepting me. Now I'll open to you, my woman, my intimate, my secret love, my joy . . .'

THE BIRDS

BARNEY SIMON

IT SEEMS more like winter now than autumn. The cold came
quickly, before a show of red, and the leaves in the park are
dead and brown. There is only the grass left now and the
birds that feed upon it.

I try to work at least six hours a day, but the paraffin heat
in my bed-sittingroom is heavy, and it is becoming increasingly difficult to concentrate. I decided for the sake of
discipline as much as anything else that I would sit at my
desk that long, even if only to scribble noughts and crosses.
Just a half-hour food break. But I find that in this weather I
also need fresh air. I work like this, with a biro on paper—I
hate to type—so there are no busy sounds from my room even
if I am working. I can see by the way my landlady looks at me
that she listens and worries. I must remember to explain. It
might seem an easy alternative to noughts and crosses,
putting it down like this, but I swear that it is not. Not for me,
that is, so please don't take it lightly.

Yesterday the paraffin made me dizzy, quite nauseous, and
so I went out to the park. I told you how it is, how dead how
sad. There were very few people about, some parents with
heavily muffled children, some old men and women, some
dogs. I wanted to go back inside, I felt so cheated about the
autumn. I walked over the grass to the menagerie. It is only a
simple one in a corner of the park with animals like deer and
chickens and rabbits that the smallest child can identify.

There was no-one there. It consists of three small wire enclosures with the birds separate, the rabbits together with the guinea-pigs and the largest for three deer. The rabbits and guinea-pigs were sheltering in their coops and the chickens were pecking at the ground, the deer were quite close to me. I leaned forward with some grass in my hand and whistled and called but they stayed out of reach. I moved on to the birds and rested my face against the cold rusty mesh. They were rushing about pecking madly, compulsively, at the earth; I could see no worms or seed, they seemed just to be swallowing dirt. I stood watching them for a long time, the pigeons with their dark eyes and their glossy ruffled necks, the chickens high-stepping and frozen-faced with their lewd scarlet combs, and the brown little sparrows, pecking, pecking up and down...

I do not know when the man arrived, but suddenly he was beside me. I was leaning against the wire feeling its movement with my sway, when it jolted and pressed into my cheek. I turned and bumped against someone. He was standing ridiculously close to me. There were yards of mesh to lean against and no-one else about. He was a small pale man, unshaven and dressed in a soiled khaki rain-coat. His face was sharply drawn, almost monochromatic, with lines like incisions across his forehead and down either side of his mouth. He coughed suddenly, showing his dim stained teeth. I moved a few paces along the fence.

I had better tell you about myself. I am tall, not ugly and have a sense of humour. I like people but something always seems to go wrong. I don't know. I thought at University that it was the course and that I just didn't fit in with intellectuals, but it wasn't better in the advertising agency or the gents' outfitters or the bookstall or even Lyons' Cornerhouse. God knows. I mean I'm prepared to talk, to give things, and what I say seems easy and inoffensive, but there must be something about me that I can't assess. Conversations go taut and last a very short time. People never sit beside me in buses. It's crazy. It was so difficult for me to say those things. I try not to put significance to them—I know I shouldn't—but I have no choice. It's always more difficult to admit to unhappy things about myself that I have no control of, than those that I *can* accept blame for. Underneath, I think, I feel that I'm an ill-fated, doomed being, and I'm terrified of dropping any clue of this. There, in a feeble, crude kind of way I've done it. But I must try to put down what happened yesterday, Saturday afternoon, because—well, to me it's important...

The little man stood at his part of the fence, completely ignoring me. He stared trance-like at the birds, his arms crossed at his chest, his hands hidden in his coat. I noticed that his coat was without buttons. Suddenly he stepped forward to the fence and uncrossed his arms, his coat falling open. He was holding a bird in each hand. He reached over the fence and let them loose. They fluttered queerly to the ground on the other side. They were in so filthy and ruffled a condition that it was impossible to distinguish what type of birds they were. It was surprising to see that they could fly. But there was something special about them, a certain grace in the quick glimpse they allowed of their wings—or perhaps in the set of their heads and their dark bright eyes. They settled and began immediately to peck at the earth.

The little man clung to the wire, his amber-stained hands above his head. I could not help turning to him. "Excuse me," I said softly, afraid of frightening him, for at no time had he shown any awareness of me, "but what kind of birds are they?"

He wasn't even surprised. He watched the enclosure. "Oh," he said, "they do look a bit mucked up, don't they? But they'll clean off in time." He spoke in a soft, high voice, in a dialect I could not identify. He paused, and it seemed that he would ignore my question.

"But—" I began—

"They're doves," he said, not looking at me or changing his posture, "wild doves."

He turned suddenly and faced me, his hands in his pockets holding his coat closed, his shoulder resting against the wire. "We've had them since they was babies." He took his hands out of his pockets and his coat fell open to reveal the dirty tartan lining and a worn black suit. "Since they was little balls of fluff." He illustrated their size with his hands. "Two others died," he said, "but these was strong 'uns. We had to feed them with an eye-dropper. We kept them in the basement months. But.they just got bigger and bigger—you can't stop time you know." He smiled, and I nodded, terrified that anything I might say would stop him. "And they smelt up the place something awful. We've got a spare-room we could've used, but you know, they need more than that—you can see their wings. Anyway, today, while the boy was out, I thought I'd just let them go..." He turned back to the enclosure, resting his head in a relaxed, child-like posture on the fence.

Still afraid of losing him, I said nothing, and was careful not to look in his direction. It was not as cold as it had been, but there seemed to be even fewer people about than before. Away on the far side of the wide green lawn were the trees, skeletal and intricate, black against the white sky and a rich sepia against the grass. Everything, the people dotted about the park, the small kiosk, the dogs, even the animals close by were in a monochrome of sepia, white and black. It was unreal to see them move.

I watched the birds again. I could hear the distant sounds of trains being shunted on a railway and for a moment they seemed to me the calls of young people laughing and teasing. I looked up startled, but the little man had not changed his posture. The doves were pathetic, pecking and moving in a tight clumsy manner, their original colour lost in the mess of excrement, dust and loose feathers that covered them. A white hen approached, pecking at the ground. Suddenly as it reached the birds it stopped, its head thrusting threateningly back and forward. It turned on its springy yellow feet and moved away, its eyes glazed, holding its head high. The encounter was almost comic. I looked up, ready to laugh with the man. "You didn't think," I was about to say, "that the smell might be too much for them too." But he had not changed his expression. His body was in fact slightly tenser. Perhaps through the threat the hen had at first seemed to imply.

I watched his face, and found myself visualizing the basement. The dark stairs which marked the end of the papered ground floor walls, bare and crudely plastered, lit by a single light-bulb. The table of damp-softened wood on which the coop lay made from boxes by the man and his boy in their small concrete back-yard, and filled with straw. I thought of the eye-dropper carefully filled and re-filled with water until it was clean, and the special foods which they bought or read about and prepared. I thought of the dimness of the basement, cold and concrete, of the electric light that was perhaps perpetually on, and the dusty fan-light, showing whitely as a rectangle in the grey. I thought of their watch together, of the fragile transculent creatures held gently in his yellow horny hand. I thought of their growing, and I became terrified. The sound of their wings in that dark enclosure beneath the earth. Floating feathers. A bird silhouetted against the fan-light. The man and his boy standing there ducking as they transferred from perch to perch. And all the time there would be the excrement—unnaturally ignorant of earth and air, slum-bound and sick, everywhere a diarrhoea. I thought of the birds, young and grey and alert, touching here and there into the stench until all was smothered and lost. I looked at the doves, feeble and unrecognizable, rocking as they moved. There was no joke in it.

I looked up quickly at the man. He had not moved. He turned to me blinking slowly and then looked at the birds again. *Why* did you do it? I wanted to ask him, but then I realised that I need not ask. *How* did you do it? might have been closer, said in envy. He and his boy had had a relationship with the birds. All doomed perhaps, sick, but God's creatures together. They had attempted it kindly—with the deepest Christian kindness—taken the responsibility of these lives unto themselves to have and to touch and to give their home and living time to. Without compromise or affection they had let them join their lives. *"Where* did you get them?" I asked.

The man did not answer me. He remained in profile. Two children ran past dressed identically in red knitted caps and blue coats. I noticed for the first time that several white birds like gulls had settled on the grass beyond.

"I'm sorry," he said suddenly, "I never told you it all. You see—" I looked up at him. "... then—you see," he began again, looking directly at me, "it's my boy. He's mad on shooting. Every spare day he gets he goes on his motor-bike to Epping. Just shooting birds. He bought the gun himself—his first wages. Sometimes he just shoots them and leaves them and sometimes he brings them home to eat. Not me—d'you know what I mean?" He stepped toward me, his hands deep in his pockets, shaking his head. "D'you know what I mean—I just don't like it—not just the meat I mean—all of it. But *he* likes it—he goes—he just wants to—well you know—I always had to leave him alone—he's a good boy, quiet like—"

He stopped and turned for the first time right away from the enclosure. He looked up and down the path, and then abruptly he started again. "One day he went out, a Saturday afternoon like today, but summer, and he stayed out till late, till dark. He came back long after supper. Well he comes in—he's a big strapping boy you see with a mop of black hair on him and he comes in with his hair all over his face and leaves and twigs in it and on his pullover and he puts his gun behind the door and some dead birds in the pantry and he sits down at the table and stretches himself out like and he says something like 'Dad didn't I half have a day—' something like that."

Suddenly the man squatted and stared down at the ground but he continued again immediately. "And then he tells me what happened. He shot a few sparrows and things and gave them to kiddies that was playing there and they followed him around. Well anyway it was getting late, and when he was on his way home he saw two wild doves flying above him and he shot at them and one fell. 'Flying Dad!' he said to me, 'and I hardly aimed.' The other one flew around where the dead one was and then landed on a tree high up. He got it too, first shot. He heard the plop he said and he heard it flapping about, but it never fell, so he walked around like and saw it caught there in the branches. So no trouble to him he just climbed up after it. When he gets up near the top he sees that it was right next to its nest like and there were these four little things peeping away there with egg-shell still lying around. He felt real sorry, he said, —no he didn't—no—'You would've felt real sad, Dad,' he says to me so he climbs down again with the dead bird, no trouble to him, and he picks up the other one from the ground and he comes home. So I says to him, 'Where they?' and he leans back in his chair like a bloody king and he says, 'In the pantry,' so I go there and there're just these two dead birds with bloody heads, so I says 'Where're the little ones?' and he says 'Oh I left them in the nest'—so I shout at him—'You dirty bastard!' I shouts, 'You dirty bastard, leaving them out there to die—you go and find them or don't come back no more—you dirty bastard,' I said..."

He smiled at me and climbed to his feet. "So then, maybe an hour or more and he's back with this little nest in his hands, and he puts it down on the kitchen table. Little balls of fluff they were, but two of them was dead. So we put the rest in a shoe-box and we get special instructions from the zoo and feed them and we keep them in the kitchen until they start moving around and then we moved them into the basement. You know what I mean? I mean who can look after them when the boy and me's at work? You know there's lots of cats in the neighbourhood and jealous types and that sort of thing and kiddies—"

"And your son?" I interrupted.

"Oh," he laughed, "he loves 'em—treats them like gold. He fixed up the basement really beautiful he did—mesh on the fan-light, bits of tree, you know—sawdust and gravel for the floor—he even painted beautiful palm-trees on the wall with some yellow doves on them and all... Oh," he laughed again, "the birds, they became nearly his whole life you could say—apart from his daily work I mean. He's not like other boys—no cinema, no Palais—we haven't even got no telly—he just never wanted it. That's his whole life now—down in the basement hours with the birds or else he's off with his gun to Epping. Still with the birds." He paused. "He's there now." He crossed his arms, his coat wrapped about him like a kimono. It seemed as decisive a departing gesture as a buttoning-up.

"But what'll he say?" I asked desperately.

He ignored my question. "Well, you see, there was this

smell—there wasn't nothing you could do about it. That didn't bother the boy nothing, but I mean you know—it wasn't a *right* smell. And there was their wings—you watch them, they're a bit mucked up, but you watch them when they flap—they've both got beautiful sets of wings—beautiful. Well and they just kept opening them and opening and with that smell and all that wind from their flapping I couldn't stand to go down no more—and I told the boy—'It's not natural,' I said, 'it's cruel,' but he wouldn't listen to me, he said they was happy and I shouted look how they was full of shit and we had a real jaw-up and for four days now we haven't been talking. We even cook our own food. If it wasn't for the birds he would've left home I'm sure." He suddenly laughed. "But if it wasn't for the birds we wouldn't of had an argument, would we?" I tried to laugh.

"Anyway, last night I comes home from the local, y'know eleven-like—after closing—and I decide what the hell with the bloody birds, if he wants the bloody birds let him keep them. So I get upstairs and I knock on his door and I say to the boy, 'It's your home—you do what you like.' And then suddenly I hear his voice from across the landing, from the small store-room and he says, 'Don't worry Dad, I've fixed it all right.' And I say 'What d'you mean?' but he just says 'Good night Dad, don't worry.' So I open the door to his bedroom and switch on the light and I see he's taken his bed out and his wardrobe—everything—and there's wire mesh on the window and there's palm trees painted on the walls and a real bit of tree tied up with string and these birds are flapping about the light with those poor mad wings of theirs. Oh so this morning when I got up he was already gone to work and my breakfast was waiting for me all out on the table. I knew he was going to stop off at Epping on his way back from his work, so when I finished the chores I brought them here..."

The sky was dimming and the wind had come up again, icy. "...I forgot about the cold." We both turned to the fence. All the birds had moved to shelter. I could not see his doves. I was suddenly aware that we were the last people left in the park. There was not a living creature in sight. "Hey," he said,

"it's turned real cold hasn't it?" I nodded, closing my collar.
"Well," he said, "I've been at it quite a time, eh." He turned
about with a quick gesture, "I must go and see the boy." He
began to move away. I watched him for a moment, and then
unable to stand still in the cold, I turned and walked in the
opposite direction, toward my room. I did not keep to the
path, but cut across the wide green field. As I walked, the cold
seemed to abate. Or to matter less. In the centre of the field I
sat down on a bench facing a plane tree. It was bare except
for a leaf, triangular and solitary, at the top. Suddenly, as I
watched, the leaf was torn loose and lifted by the wind. I
watched it rise twisting and lifeless far into the sky. Below,
beyond the trees, I noticed the white birds again, almost
silver in the gloom, pecking slowly, carefully, at the rich
green grass of the football fields...

from The Keep

Jillian Becker

When she wasn't reading or writing, or studying Uncle Fred's
theories on history and botany and zoology and anthropology (until proper arrangements could be made for the the poor child with
her face), Josephine could look through the albums at leisure, but
found that she preferred the window, from where she could see
not only that representative piece of continent, but other, distant
parts as well. She did not choose where to look. But she drew
no blinds. Once she saw right into the huts on the karroo. There
was yellow newspaper, and the kind of transparent paper that
Frances used to wrap food in, stuffed between the tin walls and
the tin roof. And she felt the cold that crept along the ground
where the children slept, pressing against one another. Africa.
It too would be a tale, for her to tell to a child, perhaps.
    And though the picture was too big for her to see much of it
yet, perhaps in time it could be constructed, deserts from a
square of red earth, plains from a clump of uncut grass, even
cliffs of granite from a garden stone: a country added to the
little space, the few and partial ranges, the sand and water, the
plants and beasts she knew already: a wide world extending before Simon, who was out in it, free in it, and oh, as dangerous
in it as fang and horn and flame.
    She saw him, once, riding down a green valley, beside a river,
through long grass. Small wild pink lilies were crushed under
his horse's hooves. The horse's mane was blowing the same way
as the grass. Over the nek towards which he rode was a waterfall, whose sound was composed of drums and shouting voices.
She let him ride out of sight, but before she looked away he had
reached the nek, and his horse was stepping high, legs on legs,
through the bands of reflecting heat stretched between the mountains. He seemed a skeleton rider on a skeleton horse. Or were
they the legs of many horses? An army of skeletons, shouting
and drumming? Uncle Fred, with a bush-hat and a telescope,

266

waved to her from under an acacia tree. Whatever had he been looking at? In which direction? Ahead was only that unused wilderness, the miniature of Africa, which was now, from his present standpoint, a barrier to any forward view.

For some undiscoverable reason--unless it were the Kronowsky custom of sequestering the chattels of the dead--the pouffe was brought from the other house and put in the room with Josephine.

Although Freda was spoken of, usually in the present tense, her death was never mentioned. Nor any other death; not even the most remote in space or time. For the old people reached an agreement that the child must be sheltered from any reminder of death.

As though dying would never happen again.

As though Africa were indeed a heaven such as the one Nanny Binney thought highly of; or mortality nothing but a fable, once told by the spirit to the bone.

CONTRIBUTORS

<u>Lionel Abrahams</u>: born in Johannesburg in 1928, he has been very much part of the South African literary scene as a writer, editor and critic. He ran the <u>Purple Renoster</u> from 1957-1972, founded Renoster Books, and Bateleur Press with Patrick Cullinan, and edited the works of Herman Charles Bosman. In 1977, he was awarded half the Pringle Prize for his writing.

<u>Jillian Becker</u> was born in Johannesburg in 1932; father: a surgeon, historian and member of Parliament; mother: a satirist and translator of poetry from French, Russian, German, Hebrew, and Zulu. In addition to three novels set in South Africa, she has written a study of German terrorism in the 1970s, <u>Hitler's Children</u> (Lippincott, 1977), writes for literary journals and many national dailies and weeklies in England, where she now lives, and has worked for radio and television.

<u>Denis Diamond</u> was born in Vryheid, South Africa in 1945, and reared in a small village in Zululand. He went to the university in Cape Town, and was Executive Director of South African Jewish Board of Deputies from 1974-1979, when he emigrated to Israel. He has written in both English and Afrikaans, and co-authored <u>Six Million Did Die</u> with Arthur Suzman (1977).

<u>Shirley Eskapa</u> graduated from the University of Witwatersrand in 1963, and now lives in London with her husband and three children. Her recently published novel, <u>Blood Fugue</u>, deals with white Johannesburg society and the racial problem.

<u>Nadine Gordimer</u> was born in a small town in the gold-mining area of South Africa. She has been called "South Africa's unchallenged First Lady of Letters." With more than a dozen volumes of fiction, she has achieved an international reputation as a literary voice for South Africa, and has won innumerable literary awards. She was married to Reinhold Cassirer in 1954, and has a son and a daughter.

<u>Dan Jacobson</u> was born in Johannesburg in 1929. He attended Boys' High School in Kimberly and the University of Witwatersrand. After a career in business and journalism in South Africa, he settled in

England in 1955, and has won several distinguished literary awards.

Joan Jacoby makes her home in Johannesburg, where her work
has been published in The Bloody Horse and Poetry South.

Bernard Levinson was born in Johannesburg of an Argentinian
father and a Russian mother. After a childhood in Chicago during
the Depression, he served on a hospital ship in the Middle East
during World War 11, and returned to South Africa to become a
psychiatrist.

Ross Moss, born and educated in South Africa, now makes her
home in Massachusetts. Her writing interests are varied and include a play, Prometheus (ATKV-Hall, Johannesburg, 1953),
"Songs," set to music by Tod Machover, scholarly studies and
two novels set in South Africa.

Riva Rubin born in South Africa, has been living in Israel since
1963. Recipient of a PEN short story award in South Africa in
1962, she wrote the narrative for a bronze medal winner at the
New York Documentary Film Festival, and was recently awarded
the Dulzin Prize for Literature.

Helen Segal is "alternately" a teacher and legal typist, as well
as the author of two books of poetry and the mother of three sons.

Barney Simon is well known for his progressive work in South African theater. Co-founder and Artistic Director of the Market Theatre Complex in Johannesburg, he also conducts theater workshops
to teach health education in Zululand and the Transkei, and has been
active in the creation of texts with actors, as well as in the script-
ing of films. In the United States, he directed two plays by Athol
Fugard, was on the editorial panel of The New American Review,
and commissioned to write the film for Enemies--A Love Story,
by Isaac Bashevis Singer.

Rose Zwi was born in Oaxaca, Mexico, of parents who had come
from Lithuania, and then had moved to Johannesburg when she
was two years old. She received an Honours Degree from the
University of Witwatersrand, after which she began her writing
career.